The Goede Vrouw of Mana-ha-ta

The
Goede Vrouw of Mana-ha-ta

At Home and in Society

1609–1760

BY

Mrs. John King Van Rensselaer

New York
Charles Scribner's Sons
1898

Windham Press is committed to bringing the lost cultural heritage of ages past into the 21st century through high-quality reproductions of original, classic printed works at affordable prices.

This book has been carefully crafted to utilize the original images of antique books rather than error-prone OCR text. This also preserves the work of the original typesetters of these classics, unknown craftsmen who laid out the text, often by hand, of each and every page you will read. Their subtle art involving judgment and interaction with the text is in many ways superior and more human than the mechanical methods utilized today, and gave each book a unique, hand-crafted feel in its text that connected the reader organically to the art of bindery and book-making.

We think these benefits are worth the occasional imperfection resulting from the age of these books at the time of scanning, and their vintage feel provides a connection to the past that goes beyond the mere words of the text.

As bibliophiles, we are always seeking perfection in our work, and so please notify us of any errors in this book by emailing us at corrections@windhampress.com. Our team is motivated to correct errors quickly so future customers are better served. Our mission is to raise the bar of quality for reprinted works by a focus on detail and quality over mass production.

To peruse our catalog of carefully curated classic works, please visit our online store at www.windhampress.com.

Preface

It has been well said in the preface to the Lives of the Lindsays that " Every family should have a record of its own. Each has its peculiar spirit running through the whole line, and in more or less development, perceptible in every generation. We do not love our kindred for their glory or their genius, but for their domestic affections and private virtues. An affectionate regard to their memory is natural to the heart; it is an emotion totally distinct from pride—an ideal love. Our ancestors, it is true, are denied to our personal acquaintance, but the light they shed during their lives survives within their tombs, and will reward our search if we explore them."

Encouraged by these wise words, I am emboldened to lay before the public the results of my researches into the lives of the women who, by their industry, their courage, and their piety, helped to create a colony in the New World, and I have followed out the history (as far as was possible) to their descendants of the third and fourth generation. The information contained in this volume was culled from various sources, many of them not open to the public, such as private family papers to which I have fortunately had access, and some of which

Preface

I had inherited, they having been lain aside by an older member of the family with the view of compiling a family history, which was never accomplished. Family traditions have been used which have always been given for what they are worth and always noted, histories were consulted that have been long out of print, and are now to be found only on the back shelves of some old-fashioned library, as well as those that are commonly known and often consulted by the public. All of these I have woven into a web. If the pattern is not clear, or the colors are not properly assorted, it must be excused, as being the work of a woman, done in a womanly way, from a woman's point of view.

History is generally written by men, who dwell on politics, wars, and the exploits of their sex. Household affairs, women's influence, social customs and manners, are seldom chronicled, and are only to be discovered underlying what are deemed the important events of life, more by inference than from anything that is actually written about them.

This conglomerate history of the lives of the dames of Mana-ha-ta has been compiled with infinite difficulty, owing to the scanty data that have been preserved concerning them. It was customary to destroy all letters that dealt with family life, particularly anything concerning the women of the family, as if in their lives and daily occupations there was something to be ashamed of.

Preface

Volumes of letters and trunks full of bundles of old papers have been preserved in many families, but in all those that I have laboriously studied, I have not found more than about a dozen written by women; but those were filled with interesting details, and were far more valuable to the historian than those of the men of the day, which were on dry business affairs that might have been of importance at the time, but are of no value now, and make one wonder why they were preserved. Among them are sometimes provoking references to family affairs that excite the curiosity without gratifying it, although there must have been as much to say of the women of the past as there is of the women of the present or of the future. The life of the "Goede Vrouw of Mana-ha-ta" was written between the lines of contemporaneous history; I have merely taken the liberty of placing her in the foreground, with the men of the day in shadow as her background, thereby throwing her into strong relief, instead of (as is usually done) reversing the process.

The books that I have consulted are: Puritans in England, Holland, and America; Macaulay's Essays, Walpole's Letters to Sir Horace Mann, Documents Relating to the Colonial History of the State of New York, Life of Bishop Berkeley, Diary of William Pynchon, Settlement of the Jews in North America, Early Maryland, Queens of American Society, Old New England Town, Impressions of America, Memoir of an

Preface

American Lady, Historic Tale of Olden Times, Klam's Travels, Voyages of de Vries, Five Indian Nations, Letters on Smith's History of New York, Calendar of Dutch Manuscript, Calendar of Wills, New York, Old New York, Old New York and Trinity Church, New York Genealogical Record, Manual of the Common Council of New York, the histories of New York, viz.: Valentine's, Dunlop's, Brodhead's, Booth's, Lamb's, Hunt's, Francis's, Denton's, Watson's, Knight's, local histories of Putnam County, Dutchess County, Westchester County, Norwalk, Fairfield, Pennsylvania, Rhinebeck, Long Island, Newtown, Flushing, Flatbush, Staten Island, Albany; Documents of Colonial History, Records of North America, Family Records and Events, Huguenot Family, Biography of the Lewis Family, The Van Rensselaers of the Manor of Rensselaerswyck, Annals of the Family of the Van Rensselaers, Historical Gleanings, Lion Gardiner and His Descendants, Winthrop's History of His Time, The Family of Bolton, Registers of the Old Dutch Church at Kingston, Records of the Old Dutch Church, New York; Records of the French Church, New York; Original Lists, McKean Family; Cutt's Genealogy, Todd Family, History of Harlem, New Jersey Archives, Newspaper Extracts, New York as It Was, Journal of a Voyage to New York, 1679; Memoir of Sir William Alexander, Life of Lord Stirling, Life of Major-General William Alexander, Sixth Earl of Stirling, etc.

Contents

I

Two Dutch Colonies in America

Hendrick Hudson and the Wilde Menschen—The First Traders at Mana-ha-ta—Indian Castle of Laap-haw-ach-king—Giovani da Verrazzano—Fort Orange—Der Heer Van Rensselaer—College of XIX.—The Patroons—The Laws Regulating Purchase—The Colonization of Mana-ha-ta in 1624—Purchase of the Island—Erection of a Fort—Derivation of the Name—Dr. Denton, the English Author, and Diedrich Knickerbocker—Provision for the Comforts of the Settlers—The Midwife and the Kranck-besoeckers . *Page 1*

II

Women of the Seventeenth Century

Education of the Dutch Women—Queen Elizabeth and the Hollanders—Industries of the Housewife—New Flowers in America—Pioneer Women—The Servants of the West India Company—Serving-maids—Mesdames Van der Donck and Varleth . *Page 10*

III

Prominent Pioneer Women

Peculiarities of the Names—Marriage of Annekje Jans—"Annekje Jans's Land"—Dominie Bogartus—Tryntje Jans—Dr. Kierstede—The First Market—The Wilden's Gift—The Old Dutch Bible—The Nickname of Stone Street—A Slaap-bauck—The Kraeg—Labbadist Missionaries—The Phillipse Manor—Cornelia Lubbetse—The Two Governors . . . . *Page 18*

Contents

IV
The First Settlement on Mana-ha-ta

The Wilden's Castle—Canoe Place—Kloch-Hoeck—Indian Industries—Wampum and Sewant—Oyster-shells and Lime—The First Tide-mill—The Catiemuts Windmill—Negro Cemetery—Earthen-ware—Windmill Sails as Signals—Flax and Its Preparation—Der Halle—Weather Predictions—Iphetonga—The Great Dock—The First Exchange—Imported Cattle—The "Teawater Pump" . . . . *Page 39*

V
Homes of the Settlers

Birth and Christening Customs—Caudle-parties—Christening-gifts—Izer-cookies—Folk-lore—Lullabies and Fireside Tales—The Aanspreecker—Pall-bearers and Their Presents—Funeral and Marriage Ceremonies—Brides and Their Quaint Costumes—Dress . . . . *Page 54*

VI
Habits, Amusements, and Laws

The Dutch Learn from the Wilden—Samp-Mortar Rock—The Wilden's Industries—Houses and Furniture—Education of Children—Strange Laws and Punishments—The Kermiss—The First Clubs—Games—The First Hospital and Orphan Asylum—The Rattle-watch—Brant—The Fire Brigade—Light in the City . . . . *Page 72*

VII
Rensselaers of the Manor

The First Patroon—Prince Maurice in Amsterdam—Governor Wouter Van Twiller—The First Gold Thimble—Arent Van Corlear—Colonization of Rensselaerswyck—The Dorp of Beverswyck—Size of the Manor—Signatures of Sachems—Jealousy of English,

Contents

French, and Dutch—Piety of the Patroon—Map of the Manor—Death and Will of the First Patroon—Successors to the Title—Der Groot Director—Charles Stuart and the Dominie . *Page 85*

VIII
Der Colonie Nieu Nederlands

The Second Governor—Nutten Island—The Murder of Brinckerhoff—Arrival of Governor Stuyvesant—The Accomplished Mrs. Bayard—Wreck of Dominie Bogartus and Governor Kieft—The White Hall—The Wilden—Swedes, French, and English—Encroachments of the Massachusetts Colony—Governor Stuyvesant and His Council—Lady Moody—The Quakers—Imprisonment of Director Van Slechtenhorst—Jeremias Van Rensselaer Assumes the Directorship . . . . *Page 100*

IX
New York vs. New Amsterdam

Alarming News—Visit of Governor Stuyvesant to Rensselaerswyck—Indian Outbreak—The Brave Governor—The English Fleet—The Earls of Stirling and Their Property in America—The Birth of New York—Feast Days and Holidays—The Predicament of Governor Nicoll—Colonel Lovelace's Reception at Rensselaerswyck—Refinement of the Dutch Families—Anecdote of the Ambassador of the Court of St. James—Recapture of Mana-ha-ta—Sunday Observances—New York and Its Cosmopolitan Inhabitants—The First Assemblies . . . . *Page 113*

X
Passing of the Pioneers

Death of Governor Stuyvesant, and His Epitaph—Death of Mr. and Mrs. Van Cortlandt—Their Children—Purchase of the Van Cortlandt Manor—The Marriage and Home of Dominie Selyns—Death of Annekje Jans—The Varleth Family—Madame de Peyster and Her Children—Marriage of Maria de Peyster and Death of Her

Contents

Bridegroom—The Second Marriage—The Spratts and the "White Ladye of Baldoon"—The Food of the Early Colonists—Introduction of Vegetables into the Colony—The Wilden's Names for Fish, etc.—Patriotic Crabs—Manufactory of "Sout"—Poems on Fish . . . . *Page 143*

XI

The Dutch and Their Neighbors

Boers and Yankees—Threatened Amalgamation of the Colonies—The Naming of New England—Its Delegate to the King—Revolt of New England—Confusion in New York—Train Bands—Jacob Leisler—Colonel Bayard's Arrest—Judith Varleth's Romantic History—John Spratt, the Speaker of the Assembly—Persecution of the Van Cortlandts . . . . . *Page 163*

XII

New York in Infancy

Robert Livingston, First Lord of the Manor—His Scotch Ancestors—The "Queen's Mary"—The Rev. John Livingston—His Retreat to Holland—His Marriage to Mary Fleming—Her Piety and Benevolence—Plans for Emigration—Robert Livingston Arrives in 1674—The Patent of the Manor—The Price Paid to the Indians—The Marriage of Robert Livingston—His Eldest Son—Mrs. Philip Livingston's Wedding-gifts—The Marriage-chest—Guysbert Livingston—Robert "Second" and Clermont—John Spratt—Mary Leisler's Marriage—Arrival of Governor Slaughter—Leisler and Milborn Hanged—De Smit's Vlye and the New City Hall—The First Dutch Church and Its Bell . . *Page 176*

XIII

The Pirate and His Escapades

Governor Bellomont and "My Lady"—Captain Kidd—Money Pond on Montock—The Quidder Merchant—The Isle of "Wight"

Contents

—Captain Lion Gardiner—Kidd's Visit to the Lord of the Isle—
The Treasure Unearthed—Kidd Hung in Chains—Lord Bellomont's Coffin-plate . . . . *Page 200*

XIV

Society Under the English Rule

Death of John Spratt—Marriage of His Widow—Colonel Provoost Made Mayor of the City—Death of Mrs. Spratt-Provoost—Colonel Provoost's Troubles—Madame Knight's Journey to New York—Lord and Lady Cornbury—The Court of Their Excellencies—Miss Van Cortlandt as Maid of Honor—Escapades of the Governor—Mr. Bedlow and His Island . . . . *Page 213*

XV

Wedding-bells and Caudle-cups

Neltje and Polly Spratt—The Weddings in the de Peyster Family—The Children's "Companies"—The Marriage of Miss Spratt to Samuel Provoost—His Death—Mrs. Provoost Lays the First Sidewalk in New York—Lord Cornbury and His Visit to Jamaica—A New Way of Erecting a Church—Weddings in the Van Dam Family—Recall of Lord Cornbury—Lord Lovelace and His Sudden Death—Governor Hunter—Change in the Government at Rensselaerswyck—Kiliaen, the Fourth Patroon, and "Quidder"—The Governor's Visit to the Manor of Livingston—He Stands Sponsor to Robert Hunter Morris—The Indian's Summary of Governor Hunter's Character . . . . *Page 228*

XVI

James Alexander

Alexander's Family in Scotland—His Mathematical Instruments and Library—The Official Position Occupied by James Alexander—Governor Burnet—His Godfather Prince William of Orange and the Christening-gift—Tastes and Occupations of the New Governor

Contents

—His Silver-gilt Tea Equipage—The Marriage of the Governor to an American—Dr. Colden and His Family *Page 246*

XVII
My Lady of "Petticoat Lane"

The Assemblies—Prominent Families—James Alexander Weds the Widow Provoost—Petes and Gossips—Emigration of Mr. Alexander's Nephew—Petticoat Lane—Tea-parties—Supper-parties—Bogart's Biscuits—Death of David Provoost—Death of Madame de Peyster, and Her Will—Birth of William Alexander—Death of Governor and Mrs. Burnet—Colonel Montgomerie—The First Public Library—Trinity Church and St. Paul's Chapel *Page 260*

XVIII
Petticoats and Politics

James Alexander Made "Freeman of the City"—Van Dam, Governor—His Successor, Colonel Cosby—His Bad Character Precedes Him—He Insults Colonel Morris—Disputes with Van Dam—Mrs. Cosby—The Governor's Ball—Lawsuit Against Van Dam—Miss Euphemia Morris—The Family Coach—Miss Cosby's Elopement—Colonel Morris Leaves for England . *Page 276*

XIX
New York in 1732

Trouble Between the Governor and His Council—The Anonymous Letter—The Prosecution of Zenger—"The Ladies, God Bless Them"—The "Weekly Journal" Ordered Burned—The Attorneys Disbarred—Mrs. Alexander's Common-sense—Her Trip to Philadelphia—The Zenger Trial—Andrew Hamilton—Balls and Dinners—Death of Cosby—The Successor—The Attorneys Restored to the Bar—The Servant Question—Horace Walpole on the Slave Trade . . . . *Page 290*

Contents

XX
Matches, Batches, and Despatches

Perth Amboy—The Hamlet of Greenwich—Death of the Fifth Earl of Stirling—William Alexander now Successor to the Title—Mary Alexander's Engagement to Peter Van Brugh Livingston—The Children's "Companies" Again—Birth of "Gentleman Phil"—Captain David Provoost—John Provoost's Marriage—The Negroes—"Major Drum"—Fires and Robberies—Father Ury—The GRAND Grand Jury—Cuffie and His Kind-hearted Mistress

Page 321

XXI
New York "in the Forties"

The Gout and Its Remedies—Bishop Berkeley—The Wilden Visit the Town—Their Wares, their Manners, and Pursuits—The Kindness of Mrs. Alexander—Different Methods of Spinning—Evening Amusements—Newspaper Advertisements—The Jersey Boundaries—Iron Furnaces—Earthquakes—Death of Dr. William Alexander—Marriages of William, Betsey, and Kitty Alexander—Troubles with Army and Navy—Lady Carteret—Her Granddaughter—Captain Digby Fires on Colonel Ricketts's Yacht—Marriage of "the Widow Parker"—Sir Danvers Osborne—His Reception and Suicide . . . . . . *Page 347*

XXII
The Last of the Dutch Matrons

Chief-Justice de Lancey as Governor—Social Evening Amusements—Society Library—King's College—Braddock's Expedition—Governor Shirley—William Alexander Appointed Major and Private Secretary to the Governor—The Acadians—The Young Partners—Sir Charles Hardy—The Earthquake—Death of Mrs. Livingston—Death of James Alexander—Major Alexander Sails for England—Lord Stirling—Death of Mrs. Alexander, the Last of the Dutch Matrons . . . . . . *Page 380*

THE PIONEER WOMEN OF MANA-HA-TA

THE CHILDREN AND GRANDCHILDREN OF

CORNELIA LUBBETSE
ANNEKJE LOCKERMANS
ANNEKJE JANS
ARIENTJE JANS
MARGARET HARDENBROECK
CATRINA VAN DE BOURGH

Johannes de Peyster, m. Cornelia Lubbtse.

Der Heer Abraham de Peyster, b. 1657; m., April 5, 1687, Catharine de Peyster, dau. of Isaac de Peyster and Maria Ranlenac.

- Johannes de Peyster.
- Catharine de Peyster, m., 1710, Philip Van Cortlandt, son of Stephanus Van Cortlandt.
  - Stephen Van Cortlandt, m. Mary W. Ricketts.
  - Pierre Van Cortlandt, m. Joanna Livingston.
  - Catharine Van Cortlandt, 0.
- Elizabeth de Peyster, 0, m., November 8, 1759, John Hamilton, Governor of New Jersey.
- Abraham de Peyster, m., July 1, 1772, Margaret Van Cortlandt, dau. of Jacobus Van Cortlandt.
  - Abraham de Peyster, 0.
  - Catharine de Peyster, m., 1745, John Livingston.
  - Frederic de Peyster (called "the Marquis").
  - James A. de Peyster, m., February 6, 1747, Sarah Reade, dau. of Joseph Reade.
- Mary de Peyster, 0.
- Joanna de Peyster, 0, m. Isaac de Peyster.
- Pierre G. de Peyster, m., December 19, 1733, Catharine Schuyler, dau. of Arent Schuyler.
  - Frederick de Peyster.
  - Arent Schuyler de Peyster.
  - Swanthia de Peyster.
  - Pierre G. de Peyster, m., May 29, 1771, Berthick Hall.

Maria de Peyster, m., 1680, Paulus Shrick, 0.; ———, m. John Spratt, ———, m., August 26, 1687, David Provoost, 0.

- Cornelia Spratt, 0.
- John Spratt, 0.
- Mary Spratt, m., October 15, 1711, Samuel Provoost.
  - Maria Provoost, 0.
  - John Provoost, m., 1741, Eva Rutgers.
  - David Provoost, 0.
- ———, m., 1721, James Alexander.
  - Mary Alexander, m., November 8, 1739, P. Van Brugh Livingston.
  - James Alexander, 0.
  - William Alexander, m., 1748, Sarah Livingston.
  - Elizabeth Alexander, m., 1748, John Stevens.
  - Catharine Alexander, m., 1748, Elisha Parker, m., December 21, 1758, Walter Rutherfurd.
  - Ann Alexander, 0.
  - Susanna Alexander, m., 1762, John Reid.

NOTE.—A zero (0) indicates that the person left no descendants.

Johannes de Peyster, m. Cornelia Lubbtse—Continued.

- Isaac de Peyster, m., December 27, 1687, 0, Maria Van Balen.
- Jacobus de Peyster, 0.
- Johannes de Peyster, m., October 10, 1688, Anna Bancker.
  - Elizabeth de Peyster, m., 1715, Jacobus Beekman.
    - Annetje Beekman.
    - Gerardus Beekman.
    - John Beekman.
    - Jacobus Beekman.
  - ———, m. Abraham Boler.
    - ———, Boler.
    - ———, Boler.
  - Johannes de Peyster, m., November 24, 1715, Anna Schuyler.
    - Anna de Peyster, m. Volkert Peterse Douw.
    - Rachel de Peyster, m. Tobias Ten Eyck; m. Myndert de Peyster.
  - Cornelia de Peyster, m. Matthew Clarkson; m. Gilbert Tennant.
  - Gerard de Peyster, m. Mary Octabe. m. M. Oates.
    - John de Peyster.
    - Anna de Peyster.
  - Maria de Peyster, m., October 31, 1731, Gerardus Bancker. m. Joseph Ogdon, 0.
    - Anna Bancker.
    - Evert Bancker.
    - Elizabeth Bancker.
    - Johannes Bancker.
  - William de Peyster, m., 1730, Maria Kennock.
    - John de Peyster.
    - William de Peyster.
    - Gerard de Peyster.
    - Nicholas de Peyster.
    - Abraham de Peyster.
    - James de Peyster.
    - Anna de Peyster.
    - Margaret de Peyster.
  - Catherine de Peyster, m., 1730, Hendrick Rutgers.
    - Catharine Rutgers.
    - Anna Rutgers.
    - Elizabeth Rutgers.
    - Henry Rutgers.
    - Mary Rutgers.
- Cornelius de Peyster, 0, m., September 20, 1694, Maria Bancker.
- Cornelia de Peyster, 0.

NOTE.—A zero (0) indicates that the person left no descendants.

Ann Lockermans, m., February 26, 1642, Oloff Van Cortlandt.
- Stephanus Van Cortlandt, obtained Patent of Manor from Governor Dongan, 1685, m., September 10, 1671, Gertrude Schuyler.
  - John Van Cortlandt, m. Ann Sophia Van Schaick.
  - Ann Van Cortlandt, m. Stephen de Lancey.
  - Margaret Van Cortlandt, m., March 12, 1692, Samuel Bayard.
  - Oliver Van Cortlandt, 0.
  - Maria Van Cortlandt, m., October 15, 1702, Kiliaen Van Rensselaer, fourth Patroon of the Manor of Rensselaerswyck.
  - Gertrude Van Cortlandt, 0.
  - Philip Van Cortlandt, m. Catharine de Peyster.
  - Stephanus Van Cortlandt, m. Catharine Staats.
  - Gertrude Van Cortlandt, 0, m. Col. Henry Beekman.
  - Guysbert Van Cortlandt, 0.
  - Elizabeth Van Cortlandt, 0.
  - Elizabeth Van Cortlandt, m. Rev. William Shimer.
  - Catharine Van Cortlandt, m. Andrew Johnson.
  - Cornelia Van Cortlandt, m. Col. John Schuyler.
- Maria Van Cortlandt, m., 1662, Jeremias Van Rensselaer, "der Groot Director," Patroon of the Manor of Rensselaerswyck.
  - Kiliaen Van Rensselaer, fourth Patroon, m. Maria Van Cortlandt.
  - Johannes Van Rensselaer, 0.
  - Anna Van Rensselaer, m. Kiliaen Van Rensselaer; m. William Nicoll.
  - Hendrick Van Rensselaer, m., May, 1689, Catharine Van Bruggen.
  - Maria Van Rensselaer, m. Peter Schuyler.
- John Van Cortlandt, 0.
- Sophia Van Cortlandt, m. Andrew Teller.
- Catharine Van Cortlandt, m. John Duval; m. Frederick Phillipse.
- Cornelia Van Cortlandt, m., July 12, 1682, Brant Schuyler.
  - Philip Schuyler, m., August 28, 1713, Ann Elizabeth Staats.
- Jacobus Van Cortlandt, m. Eva Phillipse.
  - Margaret Van Cortlandt, m. Abraham de Peyster, Jr.
  - Anne Van Cortlandt, m. John Chambers.
  - Mary Van Cortlandt, m. Peter Jay.
  - Frederick Van Cortlandt, m. Frances Jay.

NOTE.—A zero (0) indicates that the person left no descendants.

Annekje Jans, m. Roelof Jansen van Maesterlandt.
m., 1638, Rev. Everardus Bogardus.

- **Sara Jansen,** m., June 29, Dr. Hans Kierstede; m., September 1, 1669, Cornelius Van Borsen; m., July 18, 1683, Elbert Elbertsen.
  - Hans Kierstede, m. Janetje Lockermans.
  - Roelof Kierstede, m., 1670, Eike Alberts Roosa.
  - Blandina Kierstede, m. Petrus Bayard.
  - Lucas Kierstede, m. Rachel Kip.
  - Catharine Kierstede, m. Johannes Kip.
  - Rachel Kierstede, m. William Teller.
  - Jacobus Kierstede, m. Rachel ———.

- **Tryntje Jansen,** m. Lucas Rodenburg; m., March 29, 1658, Johannes Van Brugh.
  - Helena Van Brugh, m., May 26, 1680, Tunis de Kay.
  - Anna Van Brugh, m. Andreas Grevenraet.
  - Catharine Van Brugh, m. Hendrick Van Rensselaer.
  - Johannes Van Brugh, 0.
  - Peter Van Brugh, m. Sara Cuyler.
    - Catharine Van Brugh, m. Philip Livingston ("the Signer").
  - Maria Van Brugh, m. Stephen Richard.

- **Tytje Jansen,** m. Peter Van Wen.
- **Jan Jansen.**
- **Annekje Jansen.**

- **William Bogart,** m., August 29, 1689, Wyntie Sybrant, m. Waeburgde Sille, widow of Francis Creiger.
  - Blandina Bogart.
  - Everardus Bogart.
  - Tytje Bogart.
  - Cornelia Bogart.
  - Anna Bogart, m. Jacob Brown.
  - Maria Bogart.
  - Lucretia Bogart.

- **Cornelius Bogart,** m. Helena Teller.
  - Cornelius Bogart, m. Rachel de Wint.

- **Jonas Bogart,** 0.

- **Peter Bogart,** m. Wyntia Bosch.
  - Anthony Bogart, m. A. Knickerbocker.

NOTE.—A zero (0) indicates that the person left no descendants.

Govert Lockermans, m., February, 1641, Ariaentie Jans; m., July, 1641, Maryje Jans, 0, widow successively of Tymen Jansen and Dirck Cornelisen van Wenveen.	Maria Lockermans, m., 1664, Balthazar Bayard.		Samuel Bayard, 0.
			Annekje Bayard, m. Samuel Verplanck.
			Anna Maria Bayard, m., October 28, 1697, Augustus Jay.
			Jacobus Bayard, m. Hildegonda de Kay; m. Helena Van Brugh.
			Judith Bayard, m. Gerardus Stuyvesant.
	Janetje Lockermans, m., February 12, 1667, Dr. Hans Kierstede, Jr.		
Margaret Hardenbroeck, m. Peter Rudolphus de Vries.	Eva de Vries, m., May 7, 1691, Jacobus Van Cortlandt.		Margaret Van Cortlandt, m. Abraham de Peyster, Jr.
			Anne Van Cortlandt, m. John Chambers.
			Mary Van Cortlandt, m. Peter Jay.
			Frederick Van Cortlandt, m. Frances Jay.
———. m., 1662, Frederick Phillipse.	Philip Phillipse, m. Maria Sparks, dau. of Governor Sparks of Barbadoes.		Frederick Phillipse, m., 1726, Joanna Brockholst.
	Annekje Phillipse, m. Philip French.		Anna French, m. David Van Horne.
	Adolphus Phillipse, 0.		
	Rombout Phillipse, 0.		
William Beekman, m. Catharine Van de Bourgh.	Henry Beekman, m. Jane de Loper.	Col. Henry Beekman, m. Janet Livingston; m. Gertrude Van Cortlandt.	Margaret Beekman, m. Robert Livingston, Jr.
	Gerard Beekman m. Magdalena Abeel.	William Beekman, m., October 11, 1707, Catharine Peters de la Noy.	Cornelia Beekman, m. William Walton.
			Gerard Beekman, m., 1751, Mary Duyckinck.
			James Beekman, m., October, 1752, Jane Keteltas.
	Johannes Beekman, m. Abje Lawrence.		

NOTE.—A zero (0) indicates that the person left no descendants.

I

Two Dutch Colonies in America

Hendrick Hudson and the Wilde Menschen—The First Traders at Mana-ha-ta—Indian Castle of Laap-haw-ach-king—Giovani da Verrazzano—Fort Orange—Der Heer Van Rensselaer—College of XIX.—The Patroons—The Laws Regulating Purchase—The Colonization of Mana-ha-ta in 1624—Purchase of the Island—Erection of a Fort—Derivation of the Name—Dr. Denton, the English Author, and Diedrich Knickerbocker—Provision for the Comforts of the Settlers—The Midwife and the Kranck-besoeckers.

EARLY in the seventeenth century two Dutch colonies were planted in America that were destined to become the corner-stones of a great, free, and independent country. One of them was founded with but little encouragement or support from any established government, notwithstanding which a rich and extensive plantation was created, that was soon self-supporting, and owed its birth and prosperity to the bounty of a gentleman of Holland; the other plantation was founded by a rich corporation, and the two were bound by ties of common interests. These two settlements were the colony of Rensselaerswyck, at the head-waters of the Hudson River, and that of the West India Company, on the island of Mana-ha-ta. The sun that rose on January 1, 1609, and peeped over the island of Sewan-ha-ka at that of Mana-ha-ta, and sank behind the "Great Rocks of Wiehocken," beamed on a peaceful scene of forests, river, and streams, in strong contrast to the piles of stone and brick that now entomb those once lovely islands.

When Hendrick Hudson, an adventurous captain in the employment of the Dutch East India Company of Holland, sailed into the beautiful bay into which emptied the waters of three great rivers that were afterward named the Hudson, Hackensack, and Passaic, he found tribes of red men, quietly pursuing their vocations of hunting and fishing. The "Wilde Menschen" (as the voyagers called the inhabitants) welcomed the new-comers, while regarding them with awe, as they believed them to be gods from another world, and, eager to be rid of their unwelcome visitors, hastened to point out the channels of the Mohicanehuck River to the adventurous navigator of de Halve Maen, who explored the great stream as far as tide-water, and satisfied himself that it was not the passage to Asia, of which he was in search. He therefore returned to Holland, with a cargo of skins received in barter with the Wilden, and reported to his employers his discovery of a mighty land, inhabited by red men, where the rivers teemed with fish and the forests with beasts covered with furs of uncommon beauty and richness.

These peltries were valuable commodities in the eyes of the directors of the great East India Company of Holland, and although not as highly prized as the spices, teas, and coffees of Asia, where their store-houses or trading-posts were already firmly established, they were by no means loath to extend their possessions to the new-found world, if by so doing they could enrich the coffers of the company. Under their auspices a handful of hardy traders were soon settled on the pile of rocks that terminated the island of Mana-ha-ta. Rude huts were hastily built on a point of land that the adventurous settlers believed was protected from surprises from the savages, as it was nearly surrounded by water; and that also was convenient for the vessels of the company to ride at anchor, and load or discharge their cargoes close to the little settlement.

The value and quantity of the furs obtained on the first venture of the company encouraged a further expenditure on its part, and in 1621 it was determined to push farther into the interior, directly into the heart of the country, where the natives had already established for themselves a convenient trading-post, and erected a "castle" named Laap-haw-ach-king, or "Place of exchanging wampum." The Dutch threw up a rude fortification of wood and stone on the site of an ancient pile of earth, that they found in a convenient situation for defence. This most antique pile is stated by some writers to have been built in 1524 by Giovani da Verrazzano, who, it is claimed, discovered the river, and sailed to its head-waters on La Dauphine and there planted the flag of France, and claimed the territory for his master, the French king. The Dutch were quite unconscious of this fact, and established themselves quietly on the site of the present city of Albany and called their tiny embankment Fort Orange.

This post was established at the instance of one of the principal directors of the Dutch East India Company, der Heer Kiliaen Van Rensselaer, who also advocated the formation of a new "College," as a branch of the original company, that should be charged with the control of affairs in the western continent. The East India Company therefore instituted the College of XIX., and Kiliaen Van Rensselaer became a member of it and by the college was appointed one of nine commissioners to manage the corporation. These councillors were members of the original company, assumed the title of the West India Company, and were clothed with full authority to undertake the plantation of colonies on the western continent, not only by the East India society, but also by the government of the States General of Holland, as had already been done by their association in the East.

Only men of wealth and of the highest known integrity and burghers in their own right were eligible for this trust, which carried the grave responsibility of creating a government in the New World, and it is to them that we owe the original of all the best and wisest laws of this country that, after the Dutch colonies were annexed by the English, were permitted to survive. These laws were culled from those of Holland, at that time the most enlightened and cultivated country of Europe.

The College of XIX. provided for a landed and baronial aristocracy in the New World, thereby following the custom of the day, when a title was borne by all persons owning important estates, the proprietors of which took their surname from the land they owned. Under this provision all purchasers of large tracts of land were granted the title of patroon, a title which was analogous to that of the old feudal barons; but the patroons of America were, in fact, to be reigning monarchs, with full power over the lives of their subjects, with armies under their command, fighting under their banner, and bearing their arms, colors, and insignia. Courts of justice were to be held in the name of the patroon, from whose dictates there was no appeal.

It was decreed by the College of XIX. that, as the patroon was bound by the terms of purchase to colonize in America at his own expense, the people sent across the ocean, under these terms, should acknowledge themselves as his subjects, and they were to be required to take an oath of fealty and allegiance to him; while the patroon was called on to acknowledge fealty to none but the States General of Holland.

The college also determined to colonize on their own account and place a plantation at the most advantageous spot they could select, and their choice fell on the island of Mana-ha-ta, for which a code of laws was also framed similar to those governing the patroonships.

The Goede Vrouw of Mana-ha-ta

As soon as these measures were complete, manors were offered for sale, but only to members of their own society.

A number of their manors were sold, but only two members of the confederacy fulfilled the conditions of the purchase, and the rights of governing the property therefore reverted to the company, and only one of the original patroons, der Heer Kiliaen Van Rensselaer, founded a family in the New World, and was created Patroon of the Manor of Rensselaerswyck by patent dated June 7, 1629.

The first shipload of settlers came to America in 1624, commanded by Captain May. Eight men and one woman, named Catelina de Trico, landed on Mana-ha-ta, while the rest of the voyagers proceeded to Fort Orange. Two years afterward, on May 6, 1626, Peter Minuit, the governor sent by the West India Company to take charge of the colony, purchased the island from the tribe of Mana-ha-ta, and at once proceeded to erect a block-house, surrounded by red cedar palisadoes, close to the traders' huts, and on the point of the island called by the Wilden "Capsey," or "The place of safe-landing." These rocks have long since disappeared under what is now known as the Battery Park of New York, and the Whitehall, Bowling Green, Bridge, and State Streets pass over the site. The ground occupied by the fort is now covered by a row of houses facing north and overlooking the Bowling Green.

There has been a strange misapprehension on the

part of historians, who have blindly followed a mistake made by an English writer of little authority, who declared that the word Mana-ha-ta signified an orgie, and that it had been given by the savage inhabitants to the island to commemorate a grand revel held there by the sailors of de Halve Maen, overlooking the fact that the tribe which lived on the island was known to its neighbors by that title long before de Halve Maen sailed into the harbor.

As early as 1670 a native of the colony, a student and minister of the Gospel, by the name of Daniel Denton, wrote "A Brief Relation of New York," and pointed out the mistake into which his brother historian had fallen. Dr. Denton had lived among the wild men from childhood, and was well acquainted with the Algonquin dialect, and he scoffs at the statement made by the superficial foreigner, that Mana-ha-ta or Manhattoes or Manhattan, as the word was variously spelled, bore the interpretation given to it, and states, "in that language drunkenness or orgie is termed kee-wash-kwa-bee," and points out the impossibility of deriving Mana-ha-ta from that word. Dr. Denton also declares that there was no evidence to support the assertion that the name was intended to refer to any feast or drunken revel, and no historical proof that the aborigines and the sailors held a feast together on the island. There is more than a shrewd suspicion that the scribbling traveller was deceived by a jocose remark made by a townsman to mislead him, and that he recorded impressions without taking the trouble to verify them. This is the more to be regretted, as other historians have blindly copied the tale which has given the name of Mana-ha-ta an unworthy signification. They might have followed, with as much reason, the statements of Diedrich Knickerbocker, who was convinced that the name originated in a custom among the squaws, of wearing their husbands' hats, and "hence arose the appellation of Man-hat-on, first given to the Indians and afterward to the island;" and this odd derivation for the name is rather more pleasing than the interpretation other writers have given it, and quite as authentic.

Immediately after the erection of the fort, a line of palisadoes was thrown across the island from the East to the Hudson River, a horse-mill was located on what is now South William Street, near Pearl, and its loft was arranged as a place of worship. Brick-kilns and lime-kilns were established, saw-mills erected, and the company made every provision in its power for the well-being of its subjects. A midwife by the name of Maryje Jans (or Jonas) was sent to the colony, and also two men, by name Sebastian Jansen Crol and Jan Huyck, the "Kranck-besoeckers," or "Sick Men's Comforters," who were ordered to nurse and doctor the injured, and also conduct prayer-meetings, read the Bible, and look after the welfare and morals of the community.

Under these wise provisions the lands inside the stockades were soon occupied by sturdy Dutchmen and their vrouwen, and thus the nucleus of a thriving settlement was planted on one of the most beautiful spots in the world, and which went by the name of the Colonie of the New Netherlands.

II

Women of the Seventeenth Century

Education of the Dutch Women—Queen Elizabeth and the Hollanders—Industries of the Housewife — New Flowers in America — Pioneer Women — The Servants of the West India Company — Serving-maids—Mesdames Van der Donck and Varleth.

HISTORIANS chronicle the valor and hardihood of the settlers of a new country, and dwell on the exploits of the male sex, but they seldom refer to the stoical endurance and capability of the female emigrants, although, without the gentle sex, the life of a pioneer would be almost unendurable.

To the heroism and thrift of the Dutch women who ventured to America, the wealth and prosperity of the colony were largely due. It has often been said that the position occupied by the wife and mother throws the most light on the civilization of a people, and it is a well-authenticated fact that the women of the Dutch Netherlands of the sixteenth and seventeenth centuries were more highly educated, better protected by the laws of the country, and held a more prominent position, than any of their contemporaries.

Holland was the only country in which girls received

the same education as boys, and shared their studies; until the latter were old enough to select a trade or profession for themselves, when the former were withdrawn from school and carefully trained in household duties. While England, France, Spain, Germany, and Italy restrained their girls and treated them as toys; denied them education and prevented their independence, the men of the Dutch Republic of two centuries and a half ago recognized the equality of their women, educated them to fill responsible positions, and encouraged them to cultivate a love for literature, painting, and music, a course which made the women of that day quite equal in intelligence and refinement to those of the nineteenth century.

The comforts and adornments of the homes in Holland far exceeded those of any other country. They were filled with handsome furniture and pictures. The burghers and their wives wore rich silks, satins, and other stuffs, trimmed with fur and lace. They loved books and knew their value, and had them handsomely bound in wood and leather, clasped with silver and gold.

Queen Elizabeth despised the sturdy Dutch burghers, and called them "base mechanicals," and would not credit the reports that reached her ears of the luxuries and refinements of their homes, which far exceeded her own surroundings. It was not until the accession of Charles II. to the throne of England that the palaces of the king wore a comfortable, home-like air, and this was due to his having lived the greater part of his life in Holland, whence he imported the luxuries that he had been accustomed to have when residing in that country.

The housewife was the manufacturer of the day, and under her own roof produced all the necessaries for family use, such as clothing and food.

Placed on a desert island, a Dutch woman of the seventeenth century was capable of making for herself everything needful to support life. All ordinary cooking was done under her immediate superintendence, but it was her hand alone that prepared delicious dainties of pastry, preserves, and pickles. She drew perfumes from the flowers of her garden by aid of her still; she saw the hops planted, gathered, dried, and brewed. She culled herbs and simples, and concocted medicaments, and was always prepared to act as an amateur doctor to her household. She instructed her maids in carding and weaving the woollen goods for her own and her good-man's clothes, and herself spun the fine thread of flax that had been grown in her private garden, for linen shirts, towels, etc., or knit the stockings of the family.

This concentration of industries rendered a Dutch woman self-dependent, industrious, and thrifty. On her judgment, prudence, and foresight everything hinged, and the men of the family were entirely dependent on their wives for clothes, drink, medicine, and food. Even in mercantile pursuits the women had a voice, and their opinions were sought and valued.

Women of the Seventeenth Century

The sensible education bestowed on the women of Holland quickened their judgment, and the enlightened laws that permitted her to hold real estate, or carry on business in her own name, whether single, married, or widowed, gave her confidence and independence, and it was no uncommon thing to find women venturing their own savings in mercantile pursuits, quite independent of the men of the family, who never questioned the right and propriety of such proceedings.

The pioneers of Mana-ha-ta were a few hardy traders who emigrated under the auspices of the West India Company of Holland, but they did not come alone. They were accompanied by their wives, who bravely undertook to create homes in the New World. These courageous women were wisely encouraged to emigrate by the company, who looked after the interests of their colony in a truly patriarchal way.

The pioneers of Mana-ha-ta were never called upon to struggle with want and privation, as was the case in the rest of the American colonies, the first plantations of which were failures, the colonists generally being swept away by starvation. The Dutch were accustomed to colonize, and already had plantations on the eastern hemisphere when they turned their attention to America; so that the "India" companies understood how to organize and establish settlements, considered the welfare and prosperity of their servants, and arranged for their comfort and health with particular care.

The officers of the society selected competent persons to govern the colonies, and under their superintendence country people and farmers were chosen as emigrants and induced to cross the ocean; and one of the first shiploads included six families, numbering forty-five persons, who brought ploughs and other agricultural tools with them, bricks for building chimneys, and mechanics' tools, and two skilled workmen, one a carpenter and the other a bricklayer. They provided mill-hoppers, grindstones, wheels, and sails, and also several houses, which were shipped in sections all ready to be put together. The company selected workmen and craftsmen, sailors and soldiers; everything was wisely planned for, and done with method, and in consequence the colony of the New Netherlands that was planted at the mouth of the Hudson River was a model of its kind.

The houses of the emigrants were not bare log huts, but were at once brightened by the touch of facile feminine fingers, and converted into pleasant homes. The goede vrouw hung her neat lattice of leaden-sashed windows, with snowy curtains, made by her own hands, stuck a beau-pot of flowers on the ledge, set her spinning-wheel or distaff by the hearth-stone and her huge loom under the sloping roof of the "bock stoep." She also planted before her house a garden of flowers and herbs, the seeds of which had probably been brought from Holland in one of her own capacious pockets; and these soon made a material change and improvement in the flora of North America, as the garden strays wandered over the country; and the women even changed the landscape by planting rows of Lombardy poplars in front of every stoep, which stand like sentinels to point out the houses of the first Dutch settlers, and these stamped the character of the inhabitants and betrayed their love of Patria.

The English vessels began to visit the colony of the New Netherlands, and their owners were surprised and dismayed to find it so independent and prosperous. They hoped to find a people who would be large importers of English goods, and after the English occupation Governor Moore wrote, as late as 1767, an official letter to the Lords of Trade on the subject, in which he states that "every family makes a coarse cloth called lindsey-woolsey, the warp being of linen and the woof of wool. The custom prevails through the whole province, and a sufficient quantity is manufactured for the use of the family. Every house swarms with children, who are set to work as soon as they are able to spin and card, and as every family is furnished with a loom, the itinerant weavers who travel about the country put a finishing-hand to the work."

Needless to say this independence was discouraged and the English government endeavored to prevent the manufacture of American goods by taxing them, a course of proceeding that was successfully resisted by the local legislatures.

The families that emigrated to America under the auspices of the West India Company were of different stations of life. While farmers were necessary to till the soil, overseers were required to superintend these laborers. Soldiers required officers, and trading-houses needed properly educated merchants, and as the heads of each department were generally relations or friends of the rich Amsterdam merchants who composed the West India Company, they naturally were cultivated persons of good standing in their own country.

The wives who accompanied their husbands to the New World were always attended by their maids, who were bound to render service for a given term of years in return for their free passage to the New World. But buxom females were at a premium in the colony, not only as servants but as wives; for it was not every man who had emigrated with a helpmate, and one of the chief trials of the colonists' wives was the loss of their carefully trained maids, who were enticed from their service before the term contracted for had expired.

This circumstance is amusingly shown in the official documents of the colony. In a record dated Monday, September 15, 1653, Hans Fromer demanded that "Mme. Anna Van der Donck shall give lawful reason why she forbid the bond of matrimony between him and Maeyken Huybertsen." The defendant's son, Guysbert Van der Donck, appeared before the burgomasters and schepen in the place of his mother, and exhibited the contracts between mistress and maid, which provided for a free passage to the New World, in return for service for a stated term of years.

Women of the Seventeenth Century

The authorities released the maid from her service and permitted her to marry, which encouraged all the other maid-servants in the province to rebel; and in consequence the next victim was Madame Judith Varleth, who was compelled by the council to release her maid from the bond, and required to pay her many "belts of wampum" and several "ells of linen," and permit her to set up house-keeping on her own account. These rulings of the councillors, who seem to have been carried away by sentiment for the love-lorn damsels, caused dismay in their own households, and their wives rose in rebellion at their governmental decrees; and the storm that broke over their devoted heads was not allayed until they made arrangements for importing shiploads of young women from Holland, who should take the places of the delinquents, and who were bound to serve out their time by rigid contracts, which the councillors had pledged their wives in private should not be again abrogated.

III

Prominent Pioneer Women

Peculiarities of the Names—Marriage of Annekje Jans—" Annekje Jans's Land "—Dominie Bogartus—Tryntje Jans—Dr. Kierstede—The First Market—The Wilden's Gift—The Old Dutch Bible—The Nickname of Stone Street—A Slaap-bauck—The Kraeg—Labbadist Missionaries—The Phillipse Manor—Cornelia Lubbetse—The Two Governors.

AMONG the first settlers of the island of Mana-ha-ta were several remarkable women, who are the ancestresses of the principal families of the colony, and who, by their influence and connections, largely controlled all the affairs political, social, and domestic of the province.

Annekje Jans, Annekje Lockermans, Cornelia Lubbetse, Margaret Hardenbroeck, and Catarina de Boorgh were the principal women of this group of pioneers, and although their names may be unfamiliar to the ears of their descendants, it must be remembered that they were merged in those of their husbands and that only the latter were transmitted to posterity.

It has been mentioned that one of the first women to reach the plantation was Maryje Jans, or Jonas. She was sent to the colony at the expense of the company,

Prominent Pioneer Women

and arrived with the first emigrants. She was accompanied by her son, who was called Wolfert Webber, and two young and handsome daughters. It is stated that these young people were the grandchildren of William IX., Prince of Orange, and with the peculiar fashion of the day the last name of the family is spelled and rendered capriciously, sometimes being written Jans, at other times Jonas, while the son of Maryje Jans is called by the name of Webber.

The Christian name was, at that time, usually followed by the baptismal name of the father, and generally with the addition of "se," thus, Mary, the daughter of John, would call herself Maryje Janse, and perhaps add the name of the place or town of her birth, or that of her husband. The nobility alone had surnames, and these were affixed to the Christian name as in modern days, and were inherited by the whole family, as at present. Notwithstanding the confusion in the names it is a well-authenticated fact that Annekje Webber (Jans) was the daughter of Maryje Jonas, and that soon after she reached the shores of Mana-ha-ta she was wooed by and wedded to a young fellow who called himself Roelof Janse Van Maesterlandt, or Roelof the son of James from Maesterlandt, who was sent by the Patroon Van Rensselaer to act as assistant bouwmeester (farmer) at the colony of Rensselaerswyck. The prudence and frugality of the wife soon enabled the couple to move to Mana-ha-ta, where they joined the rest of the family, and Roelof resigned his office on the manor and purchased a farm on that island of sixty-two acres of land, situated on high ground overlooking the Hudson River, which has since become the centre of many disputes in the city of New York, and has led to innumerable lawsuits. The site is variously known as the Bogartus Farm, or Annekje Jans's land, and is now held by the trustees of Trinity Church.

Four children were born of this marriage—three daughters, who survived, married, and left descendants, and an only son, who was killed at Schenectady by the Indians in 1690. Annekje Jans (as she is usually called) was a small woman with bright, sparkling eyes and quick, energetic movements. Very soon after her arrival at Mana-ha-ta she lost her husband; but she speedily consoled herself by marrying one of the most important persons of the community, which raised her from the grade of a farmer's wife to that of a government official's. Her second choice was Dominie Bogartus, a minister in the Dutch Church, who had been sent to the plantation by the West India Company to take charge of the spiritual affairs of the community, and who succeeded the two "Comforters of the Sick" who had arrived with the first settlers.

The first governor of the Dutch plantation on the Hudson River had been Peter Minuit. He was succeeded by the nephew of the first patroon, Kiliaen Van Rensselaer—Wouter Van Twiller—who arrived at Mana-ha-ta in the spring of 1633, in the Zoutberg, bringing with him his chaplain, Dominie Bogartus. The long voyage cemented a friendship between the two men, and the cleric obtained a great influence over the governor, that stood both of them in good stead during their subsequent careers in the colony as directors of spiritual and mundane affairs.

Dominie Bogartus was a very large man, with a quick temper and fond of the good things of life. A comfortable home and the devoted care of a wife, in a community where everything depended upon the housewifely qualities of the woman, were essential to his well-being, and very shortly after his arrival he courted the brisk, wealthy little widow, who was by no means unwilling to exchange her money for the social position that the dominie could offer her. The company provided a parsonage for their clergyman, which overlooked the river and was close to the little peaked-roof church that had been erected for the use of the colonists. The new house was one of the most attractive places on the island, and was noted for the beautiful vines that clambered over the low-pitched roof and the beds of gay flowers that surrounded it, all of which were due to the housewife's love of plants and her faith in the virtues of herbs and simples; and while the dominie cured the souls of his parishioners, it was to his wife that all turned for aid in sickness.

The descendants of Annekje Jans by her two husbands number so many hundreds of persons, that it has been calculated that if her farm were now sold for their benefit, and the proceeds equally distributed among the legal heirs, granting the great value of the land, no one person would receive more than a cent.

The daughters of Annekje Jans and Roelof Janse Van Maesterlandt were named Sara, Tryntje, and Tytje. These girls were carefully educated by their mother, "after the fashion of Patria," and in consequence they were notable housewives. They spoke Dutch and English, and having been born and brought up among the Wilden they had learned the Algonquin language, which they understood and spoke with fluency. When a very young girl Tryntje married Lucas Rodenburg, who, dying shortly after the marriage, left her a childless widow; and she followed the example of her mother and accepted the hand of a prosperous young merchant of the community who was a commissary in the employment of the West India Company, and had reached the colony in 1640. Johannes Peterse Van Brugh was a fine-looking, clever, conscientious young fellow whose sterling worth was recognized by his fellow-townsmen, and it was only a few years after settling on Mana-ha-ta that he was called upon to successively fill the positions of alderman, burgomaster, and schepen. Among the wedding-presents received by the young couple was a consignment of "preserved lemons, parrots, and paroquets" sent them from Curaçao by the correspondents of the groom. The bill of lading is duly entered in the town records, dated September 13, 1659.

Van Brugh built for his bride a large and, for the times, a handsome and commodious house in the Hoogh

Straat, now Pearl Street, adjoining the premises of his most intimate friend, Govert Lockermans, and near the corner of the present William Street. The burghers of Mana-ha-ta were seldom without their bouwerie (or farm), to which they could retire in summer and from which they could be supplied with country produce. Madame Van Brugh's bouwerie was at "Dominies' Hoeck," on the Hudson River, and was probably inherited from her mother; and there she superintended the manufacture of her linen and overlooked the dairy and farm when not engaged in her hospitable duties in her town-house, where the position of her husband in the government called upon her to entertain every acquaintance that came to the place either on business or pleasure.

The children of Mr. and Mrs. Van Brugh were: Helena, who married, May 26, 1680, Tunis de Key; Anna, who married Andrew Grevenerat; Catharine, who married Hendrick Van Rensselaer; Johannes, of whom there is no record; Peter, who married Sara Cuyler, and Maria, who became the wife of Stephen Richards.

The second daughter of Annekje Jans was Tytje, who married Peter Hartgers Van Wen, a magistrate of Beverwyck, the Patroon Van Rensselaer's village, on what is now the site of the city of Albany; and the eldest daughter, Sara, married a young doctor, who was an official in the employment of the company. The marriage of this couple was duly recorded in Der Trouw-Boeck or marriage-register. That was carefully kept by the dominies of the Established Church. This book was begun in 1639, and is still well preserved. The entry reads as follows:

"den 29 dicto (February 1642)

"Mr. Hans Kierstede, Chirúrgÿn, J. M. Van Maegdenburg en Sara Roelofs J.d. Van Amsterdam. beyde wonende tot N. Amsterdam."*

This celebrated doctor was nearly as prominent a person in the little settlement as was the dominie, or the governor. He had been selected by the governors of the West India Company on account of his peculiar qualifications for the office, and he had been requested to emigrate at their expense and was assured by them of a regular salary. He was also allowed many perquisites, and presented with a piece of land on the company's reservation that lay close to the banks of the East River, near their fort, and on what was called the Strand. A house was erected for the doctor on this beautiful spot, and here he and his wife settled contentedly to raise a family of eight children, beloved and respected by all around them.

If the governor was bedecked in official robes, the fashion of the times decreed that the dominie and the doctor should also wear peculiarly cut coats as insignia of their offices, and that of the latter was marked and original. His pictures represent him in a huge hat, wide-tailed black coat with enormous cuffs, dainty lace frills at sleeves and neck, black small-clothes, silk

* Both living at New Amsterdam.

stockings, square-toed shoes, and great gold buckles, and last but not least a thick and heavy ebony cane, surmounted with a massive gold top, that tradition says was bestowed upon the doctor by the great company as a mark of esteem and a staff of office.

Before coming to New Amsterdam the goede vrouwen of Mana-ha-ta had been accustomed to visit the markets in the towns and villages of Holland, where the country people were wont to gather at stated intervals, to dispose of their farm products. Poultry, eggs, butter, pigs, geese, etc., were part of the marketable wares, but the articles manufactured by the women often were more valuable than the products of the soil, and at these gatherings, laces, flax, linen, lindsey woolsey, duffles, etc., were exposed for sale and brought considerable revenue to the farmer's wife. It was, therefore, very early in the settlement of the island that the women petitioned the councillors of New Netherlands to arrange for markets to be held "after the manner of Patria." An order from council was issued September 12, 1656, commanding that Saturday should be kept as market-day and that the sale should be held in the burgh, "on the Strand, near the house of Master Hans Kierstede." All the neighboring farmers and their wives were invited to attend and exchange their products for sewant and wampum, the legalized currency of the colony. The tribes of Wilden were encouraged to bring their simple wares, which were bought freely by the colonists.

The Goede Vrouw of Mana-ha-ta

By this time the Dutch women had become well acquainted with the wild people who surrounded them and were on friendly terms with them. Madame Kierstede was particularly kind to them, and as she spoke their language fluently she was a great favorite among them, and it was owing to her encouragement that the savages ventured within the city walls to barter their wares. For their better accommodation and protection, Madame Kierstede had a large shed erected in her back-yard, and under its shelter there was always a number of squaws who came and went as if in their own village, and plied their industries of basket and broom making, stringing wampum and sewant, and spinning after their primitive mode; and on market-days they were able to dispose of their products, protected by their benefactress, Madame Kierstede. The Wilde Menschen proved not unmindful of the kindness shown to them, and several of the Mana-ha-ta family combined with their kindred beyond the Hudson River and showed their gratitude by presenting Madame Kierstede with a large tract of land on the Hackensack River.

Annekje Jans had emigrated to America in very humble circumstances, but by her thrift and industry had raised herself to one of the influential positions in the community, and, as the wife of the dominie, was an important person, and she now found herself and her children among the most respected in the colony. Her three daughters were married to esteemed citizens, and her three sons by her second husband held places under the government and had wives who were as well connected as themselves. The influence exercised by the women of this family has left its stamp on colonial affairs, although at the time it was barely acknowledged.

Annekje Jans had a younger sister named Maryje, who married three times and had one child by each husband. The eldest was Elsie, the daughter of Tymen Jansen, who became the unhappy wife of Jacob Leisler. The son by the second husband was Cornelius Van Wevereen, named after his father; and Jacob Lockermans was the child of the third husband, Govert Lockermans. The last named boy studied medicine and removed to Maryland, where his descendants still bear the name of Lockermans, which has died out in New York. Maryje Jans's third husband, Govert Lockermans, lived in William Street, next to her niece, Madame Johannes Van Brugh. She was a tender mother to the two little daughters of her husband's first wife, Maryje and Jennetje Lockermans. The former married Balthazar Bayard and the latter Dr. Hans Kierstede de Jonge.

Govert Lockermans was a Dutchman of gentle birth who came to America soon after its first settlement. From what can be gathered of the family history it seems that two brothers and one sister, having lost their parents, determined to emigrate together to the New World. Before leaving Holland Govert Lockermans persuaded a handsome young girl to marry him and share his fortunes. Among the presents to the couple was a Bible printed in German type by Paulus Van Ravensleyn at Amsterdam, 1623. It was handsomely bound in black shagreen, tooled; with clasps and cornerpieces of silver, on which angels' heads were engraved. The first entry in the Bible is translated as follows:

"Laus Deo, in Amsterdam @ 1641. Tuesday 24 February is married Govert Lockermans with Ariantie Jans."

and is followed by the notice:

"1641, 3d November, Tuesday morning at 3 o'clock is born Maria Lockermans in the ship Coninick Davit on the voyage to St. Christopher and New Amsterdam."

This Bible was presented to the American Bible Society by one of the descendants, and is carefully preserved, and is under the charge of the Lenox Library. Another wedding-gift received by Govert Lockermans's bride was a heavy gold chatelaine, from which several chains depended to hold keys, tablets, needle-case, etc., after the custom of the day. Several of these curious chatelaines, belonging to the Dutch pioneer women, are in possession of their descendants, and one of them matches very closely that belonging to Madame Lockermans, and was probably owned by Madame Johannes Van Brugh.

There was an unwritten law among the Dutch women, that some member of the family should be acknowledged as a leader, whose influence was unbounded and whose dictates were obeyed without question. The sis-

Prominent Pioneer Women

ter of Govert Lockermans was one of these autocrats, and it was mainly due to her energy that her entire family emigrated to America.

Annekje Lockermans was betrothed in Holland to a young man from Guelderland, and before the arrangements for the marriage could be completed, he received the command of a military company from the College of XIX., and was ordered to Mana-ha-ta in 1637. As the "braudt" determined to follow her lover across the sea, she persuaded her sister and two brothers to accompany her, and we find on one of the first pages of the Trouw-Boeck, immediately preceding that of Dr. Kierstede's, the following notice:

"den 26th dicto (February, 1642)

"Oloft Stephenzen J M Van Wÿck tot Dúúrstede en Anneken Loockermans   J. D. Van Túruhóut."

The initials J. M. and J. D. signify "young man" and "maiden." The captain was registered in the name by which he was commonly known at the time and for many years after, but the family cognomen was Van Cortlandt, and by that name his descendants are known. The influence of his wife induced Oloff Stevenzen to resign his military position in 1648 and embark in the brewing business, and he consequently built a large brew-house near the fort, on what is now Stone Street, but which was at first called Brower Street, after the great brewery. This street lies between Whitehall and Broad and was one of the first lanes laid out by the settlers, and was commonly known as "the Road." In

1657 it was paved with small round cobble-stones, and the circumstance created such a sensation that the country-people visited it as a curiosity, and it was one of the sights of the little dorp. The burghers laughingly nicknamed it Stone Street, which name it still retains. The improvement was effected by Madame Van Cortlandt, as she could not endure the dust that filled her tidy house caused by the heavy brewer's wains that were constantly passing her door.

The first step of Oloff Van Cortlandt had been to build a suitable house for his bride, the contract for which is still preserved. Each detail of the house is mentioned, but one thing in particular was stipulated, namely, a peculiar kind of closet, called a "slaap-bauck." This was to be built into the side-walls of the main sitting-room, and was to be provided with a shelf on which a mattress could be laid; folding-doors, that could be closed during the day, and were thrown open only at night, were hung in front of the shelf, on which a large bed piled with duvets and pillows was spread. This was a hospitable provision for travellers, who could thus be provided with a bed at a moment's notice; the family-rooms being in another part of the house and furnished with the customary bedsteads of sassafras-wood, the odor of which was supposed to prevent vermin from lodging in them. The custom of making beds of this wood was a very early one, and was learned from the Wilden, but when it was discovered that the notion was a fallacy, bedsteads were painted green; the color of the paint or its composition being credited with the same virtue; after this also had been found worthless, the housewives resorted to other remedies, and about 1700, when mahogany was introduced into the colony in large quantities, the "four-posters" were made of this wood.

Madame Van Cortlandt furnished her house with handsome furniture that she had brought with her from Holland which was part of her dower. And as soon as the home was completed the young couple gave a kraeg or house-warming. The first guests were the work-people, who were entertained at a feast of cookies, cakes, etc., washed down by large quantities of wine, beer, and brandy. This kraeg was a customary thing, and was entered in the contract as part-payment of the building. The young people also gave a more elaborate entertainment to their friends, relations, and the members of the government, and this function was one of the first social amusements mentioned in the history of Mana-ha-ta. The quaint-looking house was built after the custom of Patria, with glazed bricks imported from Amsterdam. The roof was sloping, with the gable end to the street, a fashion that struck all foreigners with astonishment, as the English and French of the day built their houses so that the snow that fell from the roofs descended in avalanches into the streets, while the Dutch built their houses so that the roofs sloped over their own enclosures, and the drippings from them were caught in hogsheads, and thus provided the housewife with a constant supply of sweet soft water. The roof was also built in steps, so that the chimneys were accessible from the outside, and could be easily cleaned by a small boy, who was able to climb up or down its capacious throat, inside of which a regular series of steps was always provided for this contingency in addition to those on the roof. A little stoep was built on the front of the house, with commodious benches on either side of the railing, which led to a door that opened in half, the upper part of which was decorated with an enormous brass knocker. This house of the Van Cortlandts became one of the centres of the petticoat government that so often controlled the affairs of the colony and overturned the best-laid plans of its officials, who would have scorned to acknowledge the influence that Madame Van Cortlandt and Madame Bogartus possessed by reason of their dominant characters and family connections.

Not satisfied with her pleasant town-house, Madame Van Cortlandt longed for her own farm, where, like her friend, Madame Van Brugh, she could superintend the various processes of pickling, preserving, spinning, and weaving, that were so necessary for the comfort of her family. She therefore influenced her husband to purchase thirty morgens* of land on the Hudson River, overlooking the outlet of the Kloch, at Canoe Place. The northern boundary of the place was the Bestevaars Killitje (Grandfather's Creek) or Minetta Water. It

---

* A morgen was about thirty acres.

was near the wagon-road to Sapocanichan, and when purchased, March 12, 1646, was a beautiful rural retreat, with a magnificent view of the harbor and Hudson River.

Perhaps the most enterprising of all the Dutch colonists, male or female, was Margaret Hardenbroeck. She had married early in life Peter Rudolphus de Vries, and followed her husband to America, where he bought a plantation from the West India Company, on Staten Island, and began a settlement there. De Vries left an account of some of his voyages from Europe to America, that shows him to have been an intelligent, thoughtful man; but he had a quick and domineering temper and was always fighting with the Wilden, his neighbors, or the authorities. As he failed to carry out the terms of his agreement with the company and establish a colony at his own expense, his manorial rights reverted to the government, and after his death his widow sold the property and invested the money in ships, in which she traded between the two continents, establishing what was probably the first line of packets that crossed the Atlantic Ocean. De Vries left an only daughter, Eva, who married Jacobus Van Cortlandt.

During one of the first voyages that Madame Hardenbroeck made as owner of a vessel she fell in love with one of her passengers, named Frederick Phillipse, a young trader who was carrying a large stock of furs to Europe. They were married in 1662.

A very interesting account of this notable Dutch

The Goede Vrouw of Mana-ha-ta

vrouw is to be found in a diary called "A Voyage to New York," written by the Labbadist missionaries, who came to America in search of homes for their co-religionists. These men sailed from Holland on Sunday, June 25, 1679, "in a small flute ship" called the Charles, "of which Thomas Singleton was Master, but the superior authority over both ship and cargo was in Margaret Filipse, who was the owner of both, and with whom we agreed for our passage from Amsterdam to New York, in New Netherland, at 75 guelders for each person, payable in Holland." The ship sailed without the owner, who overtook it in "her yacht and came on board," says the missionary, "with her husband and daughter (Eva de Vries) and a Westphalian woman (who was a widow) and a girl, both of whom were in Margaret's service."

The passengers suffered many hardships on the voyage from overcrowding, filth, and improper food, and the missionary charged the owner of the vessel with unblushing avarice.

The wrath of the passengers was aroused when the ship lay in an English port, before starting on the long voyage across the Atlantic, when Madame Phillipse "sold to the captain of an English ship a hogshead of beer, for which her little daughter was honoured with a good lump of gold and Margaret was presented with some good apples." The passengers had nearly finished their own provisions, as they had not foreseen and provided for the detention in the English ports, and they saw before them, with dismay, the prospect of a long voyage with little to eat, and they were indignant that Madame Phillipse should sell any of the provender on board of her ship (although it was her own property), fearing that they would fall short of provisions before they reached America.

The thrift of husband and wife enabled them to purchase large tracts of land in the New Netherlands that was subsequently "erected into a manor, with grants of fisheries, mines, hunting, and tenorial rights," under the English rule. This is the well-known Phillipse Manor, where a comfortable house was erected, which now stands in the city of Yonkers. They also owned a house on Mana-ha-ta, near the White Hall, or governor's mansion, and close to Madame Van Cortlandt, on the opposite side of Brower (Stone) Street. The building now occupied by the North British and Mercantile Insurance Company, No. 54 William Street, the corner of Pine Street, was part of the property purchased by Madame Phillipse, and is owned by her descendants to this day. Madame Phillipse died about 1690, and her husband married, within two years, the young and handsome widow of John Duval, the daughter of his opposite neighbor, Oloff Van Cortlandt, and by her had two sons and a daughter, Annekje, who, by her marriage with Philip French, became the ancestress of many prominent colonial women.

There were other women who were as brave and as constant as Annekje Lockermans and who followed

The Goede Vrouw of Mana-ha-ta

their lovers to the New World. Among them was Cornelia Lubbetse, a native of Amsterdam, who had fallen in love with a son of one of the French refugee families by the name of Johannes de Peyster, who was educated in her native city. This young man was a merchant of wealth and respectability, who saw an opening in the New World for a man of his energy and integrity, and by the advice of the Patroon Van Rensselaer, who was a friend of the family, de Peyster determined to emigrate and found a family in the New World.

It was with a heavy heart that he left his betrothed in Amsterdam, but with the courage of her fellow-citizens and the example of her girl friends before her, Cornelia Lubbetse, under the charge of her two brothers, followed her lover to the New Netherlands. Although only a short time in the colony, Johannes de Peyster had provided a comfortable home for his expected bride in Winckel (Store) Street, which ran parallel with Whitehall, close under the shelter of the fort and leading to the West India Company storehouse. The street has disappeared from the maps of New York, and the Produce Exchange probably covers the site of Johannes de Peyster's house.

The wedding of the young couple took place December 17, 1651, and was a gay and noteworthy function in the annals of the community. Their house was furnished with ponderous chairs and tables imported from Holland, and the silver service that was among their possessions was the most beautiful in the colony. The little house soon became too small to accommodate the rapidly increasing family, and as der Heer de Peyster was a merchant in good circumstances, he became closely connected with the government and was called upon by his fellow-burghers to hold many important municipal positions. But he found that he could not entertain his friends with the lavish hospitality that he desired, and he therefore built a larger house on Broad Street, above the present South William, which was one of the most comfortable and commodious houses on the island. Madame de Peyster was noted for being one of the most warm-hearted and hospitable women, who exercised an unbounded influence over her husband and children. The eldest son, der Heer Abraham de Peyster, became a prominent citizen, while her beautiful daughters, Maria and Cornelia, attracted attention from every marriageable man in the colony. The elder married three times, but the younger sister (whose lover was killed by the savages) refused all offers, and was one of the few women of the community who died unmarried. The husband of Catharine de Boorgh was William Beekman; he was born at Hasselt, Germany, in 1623, and came to America in 1647, in the same ship with Governor Stuyvesant, who was accompanied by his devoted wife and widowed sister. The tedious voyage cemented a life-long intimacy between the two families. Beekman was a quiet, wise, prudent man, whose opinions soon obtained great weight in the colony, and he was called upon to act as

The Goede Vrouw of Mana-ha-ta

its lieutenant-governor and also as "governor of the Swedes colony on the South (Delaware) River." Governor Beekman bought what was known as "Corlear Hoeck" from its original owner, Jacob Corlear, the city trumpeter, and he also purchased a country seat on the East River, over Cripplebush Swamp, the site of which is still commemorated by the name of Beekman Street.

IV

The First Settlement on Mana-ha-ta

The Wilden's Castle—Canoe Place—Kloch-Hoeck—Indian Industries—Wampum and Sewant—Oyster-shells and Lime—The First Tide-mill—The Catiemuts Windmill—Negro Cemetery—Earthen-ware—Windmill Sails as Signals—Flax and its Preparation—Der Halle—Weather Predictions—Iphetonga—The Great Dock—The First Exchange—Imported Cattle—The "Tea-water Pump."

THE first settlers perched their huts on the tip end of Mana-ha-ta, just where the river that they named the Hudson joined the waters of the estuary they called the East River, and they imagined that they were in a safe and advantageous situation, as they did not realize that the natives could use the rivers as highways, as well as themselves. The tribe of Wilden, from whom the locality inherited its name of Mana-ha-ta, were too wary to live on an exposed situation like the pile of rocks selected by the Dutch, which was washed by two rivers and easily approached by the canoes of neighboring tribes, and had placed their chief castle on a hill called Catiemuts, which overlooked a charming little fresh-water lake that was surrounded by high lands and shrouded in a forest of locust and nut trees, about two miles from the south end of the island and well-sheltered from surprise by hostile tribes. What was afterward named Mt. Pleasant or Bunker Hill lay to the south, while Cowfoot Hill overlooked the sheet of water from the northern side. The outlet of this lake emptied into the Hudson River. It was a deep, slow-running stream, and flowed westward, about on the line of Canal Street; and the great war-canoes of the Indians were kept close under the shelter of its banks, near the river, and from this circumstance it received the name of Canoe Place. The lake was limpid, sparkling, and deep, with tiny bays and inlets, and great trees hanging over its banks, through whose gnarled and twisted roots trout and other fish darted back and forth.

To add to the beauties of the lake there was a well-wooded island, nearly in its centre, which afforded a safe retreat for the children and squaws in time of war, and in after years was used as a hiding-place for the contents of the Hall of Records, as the colonial government, during the war of 1728, believed it to be a safe place of concealment. The city powder-house was also erected here where it was protected by the natural environments. The lake stretched to the southeast and lost itself in a swamp that was infested by mosquitoes.

The island was particularly used by the Indians as a fish-drying encampment, as on it there was little danger of the preserves being stolen by marauding savages or thieving animals.

The First Settlement on Mana-ha-ta

The Mana-ha-tas were industrious and the most wealthy of any of the river-tribes. One source of their riches was the money manufactured by the squaws, with infinite patience and diligence, from the blue part of the clam-shells, which was broken into bits and punctured with holes; this was called sewant, and was more valuable than wampum, which was the twisted end of the periwinkle-shell. The two "shells" were strung on grass, hair, or hemp, and braided into "belts" and served as currency. As the manufacture of money from shells was confined to the sea-coast, the Mana-ha-tas and their tributary tribes on Sewan-ha-ka (the Island of Shells) and the Raritans, Hoboken-Hackingach, etc., on the western side of the Hudson, were the richest red men on the continent.

Coining was not the only source of the Mana-ha-tas' wealth, however. The fish that came into the waters surrounding this island at stated seasons of the year, gave the tribe occupation and a steady income. Quantities of fish were captured in nets by the men, who generally fished together and owned shares in the nets, canoes, etc., and these spoils were consigned to the squaws, who spread the flesh, roes, and entrails on bark, or hung them on poles, to be sun-scorched. The Mana-ha-tas were celebrated for their dexterity in preserving fish, and this delicacy they bartered with the inland tribes, who were dependent on such food in winter, and unable to prepare it for themselves. Shad, cod, herring, and sturgeon were the principal dainties preserved for winter consumption, but oysters and clams were the favorite dish of the Wilden, and were prized most highly, not only for their shells but for their flesh, which was strung on reeds and sea-grass and dried with the fish.

The site of the Mana-ha-ta village was called by the Dutch Kloch-Hoeck, or Shell Point, from the quantities of bits of clam and oyster shells heaped near the encampment, that had been discarded as worthless by the squaws, who were greatly astonished to find they were still valuable, after their own money had been made from them. The thrifty Dutchmen soon converted the shells into lime, with which they plastered the inside and exterior of their houses, much pleased at getting it so readily and cheaply. The lavish use of this shell-lime was, however, as speedily discarded as it had been adopted, as it was found to act in a very peculiar way. Two or three days before a storm, the walls would exude great drops of moisture, and thus became almost as good as a hygrometer to the inmates. This absorbent quality of the shell-lime made the houses so unbearably damp, both winter and summer, that after a few years' trial its use was abandoned.

The name of Kloch finally became identified with the lake itself, and was corrupted into the word Collect, by which name this lovely sheet of water was called, until it was filled in, by throwing into it the greater part of the neighboring hill of Catiemuts; streets,

The First Settlement on Mana-ha-ta

parks, and houses now cover its site. The Mana-hatas soon disappeared before the inroads of civilization; the tribe was partly absorbed into the Dutch settlement and partly distributed among the neighboring bands of Wilden, and the site of their castle and village was appropriated by the new-comers.

A tide-mill was erected at Canoe Place, the wheel of which was undershot, and worked by the rising and falling tide, much to the bewilderment of the savages, who imputed its movement to Manitou, the great spirit.

The Dutch placed a windmill on Catiemuts, overlooking the Collect, beside the road that led north and was called the Boston Highway, on the line of William Street. The negro burying-ground was here, as it was convenient to cut holes in the side of the hill and poke the bodies into the shallow graves; and in later years a kiln for baking earthen-ware, of the soil found hard by, was built close to this lake.

The finest and the fattest fish were always to be caught in the "race" between the mill and the lake, and Indian and Dutch urchins who had succeeded in playing "hoekies" from school, would sociably congregate side by side on its banks and angle successfully with home-manufactured hooks, made of birds'-claws, locust-thorns, or chicken-bones, and the girls would swim or paddle in the water in summer, or follow their brothers over the ice in winter, on their home-made "sluys," or beef-bone skates.

The Goede Vrouw of Mana-ha-ta

The lake was popularly reported to be fathomless, but it was successfully drained and filled in about the end of the eighteenth century, to the disgrace of the greedy municipal authorities, who wantonly destroyed one of the most beautiful features of the island, which was filled with historic reminiscences and memories of the aborigines. Its locality may still be traced under the city courts and prison, and Baxter, White, Elm, Duane, and Park Streets cross and recross it. The head-waters were in Leonard Street, and the main spring is in the cellar of a house close to the beautiful building of the New York Life Insurance Company, which is situated about on the site of the old Indian fort on the Catiemuts hill.

Some traveller has called New York the city of hills. This was no uncalled-for cognomen, as the land rose and fell all along the centre of the island, forming an almost continuous ridge, that sloped gently on either side to the Hudson and East Rivers. Little brooks trickled down their sides, and great trees covered them and made bosky shelters for foxes, deer, wolves, bears, and other game, all of which were found on the island of Mana-ha-ta up to the middle of the eighteenth century.

The Dutch settlers perched their windmills on so many of the hill-tops that they formed a prominent feature of the landscape. They had been among the first edifices erected after the arrival of the Dutch on the western continent, as the Hollanders, true to their time-honored customs, always made every arrangement to make themselves independent of outside assistance, and by their prudence and foresight provided for every emergency within their own borders.

The first town-mill was built on a high hill between Liberty and Cortlandt Streets. It was hastily constructed, and the original building was soon blown away, and a new and more substantial one substituted in 1662, which remained as a landmark for nearly a century. When the sails of the mill were not twirling around with the wind, to grind the corn in the hopper, they were sometimes used as signals, and a code was established that was easily understood by those who held the key. To announce an invasion from hostile foes the sails could be set square, one arm pointing to the sky, and the opposite one to the earth. The sails set in this way, with the upper half of the mill door open, was another signal; the sails half-clothed and set askew, was a third, and the combinations were more varied and conveyed more information than the uninitiated would credit. A code of signals established between Gardiner's Island and the mainland is still in existence at the manor house.

The island of Mana-ha-ta was endowed with many rills and streams, and there was a particularly fresh and sparkling rill (as the Dutch called it) which was closer to their hamlet than that of the Kloch. This little brook was speedily appropriated by the women of the settlement, as its waters were claimed to have especial virtues. It was usually filled with flax-stalks, which were tied in bundles and thrown into it to soak and soften, so that they could be prepared for the domestic distaff, which the women who first settled Mana-ha-ta used instead of the spinning-wheel, as they clung to the traditional mode of manufacture of linen thread, looking askance at the then novel invention of the wheel.

The hill-side that sloped toward the deep, clear spring which was the head-waters of the rill, was covered with fine grass especially suited for a bleaching-ground. It was called "De claver Waytie," and as soon as the Dutch settlement was firmly established, merry parties of young girls flocked to it daily, to soak their flax or spread their rolls of linen to bleach on the clover-patch, and they wore a narrow winding path for themselves, which was dubbed "T'Maadge Paatje" and is known to-day as Maiden Lane.

A very large, handsome, wide-spreading elm-tree grew on the corner of Wall and Broad Streets. Its drooping limbs sheltered a favorite tavern named "Der Halle." The huge bole of the famous tree could only be spanned by six men with arms outstretched, and it was encircled by rustic benches, before which were placed tables. Under the shade of "der groot" tree all the Dutch worthies would gather on a summer afternoon, after their mid-day meal, and there they would sit and dreamily puff at their long-stemmed pipes and lazily watch the passers-by. These old

The First Settlement on Mana-ha-ta

Dutchmen were "weather-wise," in their own conceit, and, by constantly studying the clouds and sky, could generally predict a coming storm when they saw fleecy little clouds gather in the sky like a flock of sheep and roll toward the wisps of thin vapor that always appeared at the same time, and the clouds looked as if they were the famous flock that belonged to Bo-Peep and were in search of their discarded tails. The Dutch called these clouds "mackerel and mares' tails." When after a storm the heavy clouds broke and parted, they would say: "It will clear if there is enough blue sky to make a Dutchman a pair of breeches." On a hot summer afternoon, if the thunder-clouds banked up black and threatening behind the "Great Rocks of Wiehocken," on the Hudson River, opposite the little burgh, the Dutch worthies would sit calmly under their beloved tree and declare that the storm would not sweep their way, unless "it came up against the wind," and not even then if the tide was running out strongly in the Hackensack River, on the western side of the Wiehocken Cliff, for they knew that the "Great Rocks" would catch the storm and hurl it backward, to be attracted by the river, and by some mysterious means (supposed by the burghers to be supernatural, and not unconnected with departed Indian spirits) the storm would be carried to sea and the muttering thunder-clouds would roll away, leaving Mana-ha-ta undisturbed.

With these and other old-time theories the burgomasters and schepen of the town, and those who had the "Burgher reicht," amused themselves, when clustered in their cosey nook, under the shade of "der groot" tree, from which nearly every movement in the burgh could be watched.

This spot was dedicated to the business of the place, and has ever since been its centre. Seated in front of "Der Halle," the pipe-puffing worthies could watch the comely Dutch farm-women, who, in close-fitting caps, without hats or bonnets, and invariably in couples, would row across the East River from under the Iphetonga Cliff (as the Wilden called the high sandy bank on the opposite shore of Long Island). The farm produce was piled in the stern of the flat-bottomed, unwieldy "battoe," with perhaps a sturdy urchin perched in the bow, with a fat porker squeaking at his feet; and the two women would steadily row against tide or wind and deftly guide their "scow" to the ferry landing.

The market-place on the Strand was hard by this favorite tavern, and to the north, in the foreground, could be seen a tiny, crescent-shaped fort called a Rondel, which was part of the town's defence against invaders. The Exchange could be reached in a moment by the worthies under "der groot" tree, as it was directly in front of them and was only an open space used as a convenient meeting-place, where merchants could congregate to barter and sell their goods.

The pride of the burgher's heart, and his chief reminiscence of the beloved Patria, with its watery highways, canals, dykes, and vlys, was the great dock, which was one of the first improvements made by the Dutch, very soon after the settlement of the colony, and which lay in front of the Stadt-Huys. Beyond the dock was a covered bridge, crossing the "Graft," as the ditch was called, that flowed through what is now Broad Street and emptied into the great dock. This bridge was on the site of the present Exchange Place, and on it the merchants congregated daily, and would lean on its wooden railings while haggling over their sales. The site had been carelessly chosen, simply on account of its convenient position, which was close to the official buildings of the burgh, as well as to the great scales and the shipping; and as early in the history of the colony as March, 1670, the governor and council saw its importance, and therefore decreed that the spot should be recognized as an official mart or exchange, "after the manner of Patria," and ordered that regular meetings should be held there every Friday morning between eleven and twelve o'clock.

But although the bridge was such a favorite and convenient rallying-place for the merchants, it was a dangerous spot on which to linger on a cold winter's day, when the ground was covered with snow and ice, as a steep hill rose above it, and down its slippery sides the children of the burgh delighted to slide, and more than one staid burgher, standing on the bridge, and quite unconscious of his danger, was knocked off his sturdy legs into the Graft by a terrified youngster, whose "sluy" had run away with him when coasting "belyguthers" down the steep sides and around the sharp turns of Flatenbarack hill. To prevent such mischances, the governor issued a decree and commanded the city watch to "prevent and forbid" sliding or coasting down the hill when the exchange was in session. At other times the children were free to do as they pleased, and the merchants might look out for themselves.

The ferry to Long Island lay a little north of the Exchange and yet partly in view of the patrons of "Der Halle," and a blacksmith's forge was established at the top of the bank overlooking the landing-stage. It was owned by Cornelius Clopper, and the spot was known as "De Smits Vlye." It was a convenient stopping-place for teams crossing from one island to the other; although when Mana-ha-ta was first settled it was not the custom to shoe horses or provide the wheels of the carts with tires.

The burghers who were seated around "der groot" tree always considered it the crowning pleasure of their tranquil afternoon, to watch their cattle slowly wend their way homeward at sunset from the common, on which they had been grazing all day under the charge of the licensed town-herdsman, Gabriel Carpsey. The herd was collected at sunrise by the official guardian, who blew a few melodious notes on a twisted cow's horn fitted with a mouth-piece, which he wore suspended by a green cord across his shoulders; and this horn served as a recognized badge of office. The old herdsman was a quaint figure, with his steeple-crowned hat and long staff, as he shuffled along in his low-heeled shoes, brass buckles, and gray stockings, preceded by the sleek kine, who seemed indifferent to his presence but who obeyed the lowest notes of the horn, and seemed to recognize the different calls that Carpsey blew to direct their movements.

The "Vlacke" to which the cows were driven was the property of the burgh and set aside as the grazing-ground, for the use of its inhabitants, and covers the site of the common, or City Hall Park, and was beyond the palisades or city wall.

"De Schaape Waytie," or sheep's pasture, was the common now covered by Broad Street, above Exchange Place. The official guardians of this flock were Claes Groen and Pieter Lieresen, who herded the sheep and goats of the community at one guilden per head a year. All the animals in the town were officially examined annually, and branded, and the signs and marks were recorded in a book kept for the purpose.

The West India Company imported cattle in the first ship that arrived at Mana-ha-ta with the first emigrants who were sent under the auspices of the company, which was in April, 1625, when one hundred and three head arrived at the "Plantation." Stallions, mares, bulls, cows, sheep, etc., were carefully selected in Holland, with a view "to their breeding and multiplying." The increase of the herd were rented, on June 20, 1640, to various settlers, and the lease of fifteen cows, eight mares, and two stallions was duly recorded in the official register. The breed was, however, a poor one, and the animals small and weak, but they increased so rapidly that at one time they threatened to become a nuisance to the settlers. The Dutch traders pitched their tents on Capsey's rocks, without duly considering the important question of drinking-water. There were a few springs at the end of the island, but the water was brackish and, as the community grew in size, the supply was insufficient for their needs. There were wells inside of the fort, and others in neighboring localities that belonged to private individuals. The water was not sweet, and the vrouws complained that "it furred inside of their kettles," and the cattle sometimes refused to drink it. It was several years after the settlement of the island before sweet and wholesome water was found about Chambers Street, and this well fortunately afforded an unlimited supply. It was called the "tea-water pump," and servants were sent to it daily to fetch water for the evening brew for the good vrouw's tea-table. Pedlers also carried the water from house to house in pails suspended from yolks hung around their necks, or in barrels called "ankers," that were hung on wheels, to which dogs were hitched and driven through the streets.

Later a city ordinance was put in force by Governor Stuyvesant to prevent hogs running through the streets, "as they rooted up the wall of the fort." The disposition of swill and garbage became a serious question with householders, and the dog-carts were called into play again, and were driven from door to door to collect the refuse from each house. This industry continued until about 1870, when a city ordinance prohibited the use of dogs for carting purposes.

V

Homes of the Settlers

Birth and Christening Customs — Caudle-parties — Christening-gifts — Izer-cookies — Folk-lore — Lullabies and Fireside Tales — The Aanspreecker — Pall-bearers and their Presents — Funeral and Marriage Ceremonies — Brides and their Quaint Costumes — Dress.

THE manners and customs of the first settlers of Mana-ha-ta were naturally founded upon those of Patria, and they were piously observed and closely followed by the expatriated ladies, who cherished the traditions of their forefathers and despised all innovations.

Among the most solemnly observed of the household ceremonies were those attending the birth of a child, and each time-honored custom was followed with undeviating regularity. The infant was wrapped in swaddling-clothes and put into an elaborately embroidered pocket, which was trimmed with frills of ribbon, the color of which indicated the sex of the child. A tiny ruffled cap confined its ears closely to its head, and the baby was wrapped so tightly in its bands that it could move neither hand nor foot, and was laid in a cradle, or hung suspended from a nail in the wall, without fear of its stirring from any position in which it might be placed.

Homes of the Settlers

The birth of an infant was announced to the neighbors by hanging an elaborately trimmed pin-cushion on the knocker of the front door, the color of which denoted the sex, blue indicating a boy and white a girl. This cushion was usually provided by the grandmother, and was generally made of such handsome materials that it was handed down as an heirloom from one generation to another, to serve for similar occasions. In families where this was the custom, the name and birthday of each child (whose arrival it had heralded) were elaborately embroidered on either white or blue ribbons and sewn to the cushion, so that this peculiar fashion became the birth-record kept by the women of the family, while the head of the house kept a record of the name, age, sex, and god-parents of his child in his family Bible, which each householder possessed. The church registers were also carefully kept, and those of the Dutch and French congregations are accurate chronicles of the day.

A very formal ceremony followed the birth and baptism of a child, and this was the grand reception held by the proud mother as soon as she was strong enough to see her female friends. Elaborate preparations were always made for these caudle-parties, as they were called, and "achterlingen," cookies, krullers, and "oly koecks" were provided for the feast. The first of these cakes is a sweetened bread, cut in slices and dried, and is sometimes called rusk. The last-named delicacy is often called a dough-nut, which is a base imitation of the true "oly koeck," that always had a nut or a raisin embedded in its centre, which added greatly to its flavor.

The particular dainty that was the inseparable accompaniment of the reception, and gave it the name, was the drink that was brewed and served piping-hot to the visitors. It was called caudle, and its concoction was a secret carefully preserved in certain families, who always prepared it and sent it to the house of "the lady in the straw" as an especial mark of their favor. A family receipt that has been handed down from mother to daughter, through the descendants of Cornelia Lubbetse (Mrs. Johannes de Peyster) calls for three gallons of water, seven pounds of sugar, oatmeal by the pound, spice, raisins, and lemons by the quart, and two gallons of the very best Madeira wine.

Such a rich compound was seductive to the last degree, and the good ladies would sip and gossip, and nod their capped heads together over it with great enjoyment. Caudle was always served in huge silver bowls, around which were hung quaint little spoons, so that each guest might ladle out a portion for herself into the tiny china cups when she was handed the bowl by the servants, and dip out a fat raisin or bit of citron to flavor her "dish of caudle."

The spoons that hung around the bowls were often gifts to the baby from its god-parents. This bowl was round, and had some scriptural scene stamped on it, and about its edge were engraved the name and birthday of the child. The handle was short, curved, and sharply crooked on the end, so that it could be hung on the outside of the caudle-bowl, and it was generally ornamented by a heart, on which was perched a beautifully modelled little bird, which in heraldic parlance is termed "a cock cantant," that is, with head uplifted and open beak. Why this peculiar emblem was selected to adorn a christening-gift, is not apparent. It is true that it was symbolic of St. Peter, but the connection with a baptismal ceremony cannot be inducted. The cock was a favorite emblem with the ancients on account of its courage and endurance, and Pliny devotes some sonorous and well-rounded sentences in praise of "its proud, commanding gait and stately stride," and wrote that "a cock, with his curved and graceful tail, inspired terror even in the lion himself, that most intrepid animal." The emblem may have been selected in order to inspirit the infant, and encourage it to be brave, although the parents could scarcely have desired that it should emulate the noise of the emblematic "cock cantant." There are many of these spoons to be found among the descendants of the Dutch settlers, and the caudle-party is not obsolete, and is still held by members of old New York families.

There was another dainty that always accompanied the caudle. These were "izer-cookies," which were toothsome cakes, made of pastry, and put into an "izer" and squeezed flat, and then pushed into hot ashes and baked. The receipt of the Dutch vrouws for these cookies was copied in various localities, but, strange to say, the cake received a new name in each place. In New Jersey they were called split-cakes, in Philadelphia squeeze-cakes, and among the English settlers in New York they became known as wafers or hard waffles.

The izer, or wafer-irons, were favorite wedding-presents, and were often decorated with the coat-of-arms of the groom, together with his initials and those of his bride, and the date of their marriage. The izer consisted of two iron plates, each one about eighteen inches in circumference, and fitting exactly into each other, and two long handles hinged them together. The carving on the inside of the plates was pressed into the dough, which when baked had the design printed on the cake. A "Social History of Flatbush" records an advertisement in a local paper of March 16, 1772, which shows how universal was the use of these irons. The notice was as follows:

"Hard and soft waffle-irons for sale by Peter Goelet, at the Golden Key, Hanover Square, New York."

The care of the baby never devolved upon a servant; the Dutch ladies set a good example to the women of their day by nursing and tending their own children, who grew up straight, strong, handsome lads and lasses who loved their mothers beyond everything.

The tender "mutter" found time, amid the countless occupations of the day, to croon over her little ones, and sing them the ditties learned at her own mother's knee. The favorite song was one that is still fondly remembered, and is as follows:

>"Trip a trop a tronjes,
>   De varken in de boonjes,
>   De koejes in de klaver,
>   De paaden in de haver,
>   De eenjes in de water plass,
>   De klaf in de long grass,
>   So goot mine kinder popetje was;"

which may be freely translated as follows:

> From your throne on my knee,
> The pigs in the bean-patch see,
> The cows in the clover meet,
> The horses in the oat-field eat,
> The ducks in the water pass,
> The calves scamper through the grass,
> They love the baby on my knee,
> And none there are as sweet as she.

There was another favorite ditty of the day which has been orally handed down to the present generation, and may have become slightly altered from the original. It was—

>"Dwur zat een aapje op-een stokje,
>   Achter myn moeders keuken deur,
>   Hy had een gaatje ie syn rokje,
>   Duur stok dat schelmje syn kopje deur;"

which means that "a tiny ape sat on a stool behind my mother's kitchen door; he made a hole in his little jacket through which the rogue pokes his head." The rest of the jingle has become so confused that the Dutch words are jumbled inextricably together and defy spelling or translation.

But if the mother sang her lullabies to her babies the father was by no means silent and had his own folk-lore to teach to his children, who would sit beside him on the stoop during the long summer evenings, or cling to him lovingly on the settee in front of the wide-throated fireplace in winter. These great chimneys were characteristic of Patria. The sides were finished with pink, blue, or purple tiles, on which were painted quaintly dressed figures, over which was the number of a text which was the key to the scriptural subjects represented. The Good Samaritan, Balaam's Ass, and Lazarus were favorite pictures. Sunday evening was always devoted to singing hymns and reading the church catechism, after which the father would take one of the pictures on the tiles as a theme for a little biblical instruction, and no well-brought-up Dutch maiden or urchin could have been shaken in their belief in the legendary whale that swallowed the prophet Jonah. Even though in after life they could find no authority for the whale, when they searched the Scriptures for themselves, the graphic scene of the spouting fish was too firmly impressed on their minds to allow them to fancy that any other monster was capable of performing the miracle. Theatrical performances were unknown in the colonies, and a dramatic exhibition, after the manner of the Italian Punch-and-Judy, was the nearest approach that the children of the early Dutch settlers ever came to seeing a play. This was also a fireside pastime and was only enacted as a great treat. It was rendered by the father of the family, whose broad-tipped, spatulated fingers were decorated with eyes, nose, and mouth, painted on the ends with red pokeberry juice, which served the first settlers in place of ink. The thumb of the left hand was wrapped in a kerchief to make it look like an old lady in a cap, and the play began. It had three performers—

A Dame.—The thumb.

A Friar.—The middle finger.

A Maid-servant.—The little finger.

Dame Thumb was supposed to be seated in her best parlor, cap on head and "specs" on nose, and a visiting Friar was supposed to be standing on the stoop outside the front door, which was formed by the ring and forefingers that touched their tips together in front of the Friar, who opened the ceremonies by rapping on the fingers before him, and the parts of the three *dramatis personæ* were rendered in different tones of voice. The Friar gave his part in a deep growl, the Dame delivered hers with a simpering lisp, and the little Maid-servant squeaked her words out in a high nasal key. The play began with the rapping of the Friar on the knocker, and the father would say, in a deep sonorous voice:

"Tap, tap at the door!"

The Goede Vrouw of Mana-ha-ta

This call was answered in a small wee voice, as if by the little Maid:

Servant—"Somebody knocks, mam! somebody knocks!"
Dame—"See who it is; see who it is."
Servant—"Who's at the door, there? who's at the door?"
Friar—"A friar; a friar!"
Servant—"A friar, good dame; a friar, good dame!"
Dame—"See what he wants; see what he wants."
Servant—"What do you want, sir; what do you want?"
Friar—"I want to come in; I want to come in."
Servant—"He wants to come in, dame; he wants to come in."
Dame—"Bid him come in, then; bid him come in."
Servant—"You may come in, sir! you may come in!"
Friar—"Thank you, good dame;" and so he popped in.

This was done by ducking the middle finger under the tips of the ones in front, as if passing through a doorway, and this dénouement was always anxiously looked for by the youngsters, and the tiny act rapturously applauded.

There was another finger-play that was reserved entirely for little children, and a well-brought-up Dutch baby would consider itself defrauded of its rights if it were put into the cradle without having its own baby-entertainment, which consisted in twisting and turning a hand back and forth before its face, keeping time to a droning tune, and the following words, which are rendered phonetically just as they have been transmitted from generation to generation, without an idea of their

Homes of the Settlers

meaning beyond their having some connection with hot buttered waffles:

> "Ter roorches, ter roorches,
> She Mameche bucleche, borche
> Ter roorches, ter roorches,
> As me mither le waffles she boxes,
> De butter la door de groches,
> Ter roorches, ter roorches
> She mameche buckle che boo."

The lullaby is still sung by the descendants of the first Dutch settlers.

The funeral services of the day were lengthy, solemn functions attended only by men, and the grief of the mourners seems to have been exhausted by the attendant ceremonies, judging by the celerity with which all widows and widowers remarried during the early colonial days.

A death was usually announced by the slow tolling of a bell, which struck a number of times to correspond with the age of the departed. The professional conductor of ceremonies was a duly licensed official and was called an "aanspreecker;" he went the rounds from house to house, dressed in a long black coat and mantle, and carrying a watchman's staff, which he struck loudly on the ground as he walked. His hat was decorated with heavy folds of black stuff, that fell down his back nearly to his heels. His duty was to inform each member of the family of the death of their relative, and invite them to the funeral, which generally took place three or four days after the death. The aanspreecker superintended this important and often very expensive ceremony, when the friends and relatives met at the house of the deceased, where he received and ushered them into the different rooms set apart for the reception. The best parlor was seldom opened or used except for funerals, and was furnished with quaint high-backed chairs, with rush bottoms. These were called the "dead chairs." After a few prayers, the procession was marshalled, and twelve of the most distinguished men of the town were selected to bear the coffin to the burying-ground. A black cloth, with heavy tassels, called a "dood kleed," was thrown over it. This pall was owned by the church, which always had two or more; the worst one being loaned to the poorer members of the congregation, while the newest one was reserved for the funerals of the distinguished members of the community.

The twelve pall-bearers literally carried the coffin from the house to the grave. They were distinguished by small white cushions, that were put on the shoulder and held in place by bands that passed across the back and chest, and fastened under the opposite arm. This was the origin of the pall-bearers' scarfs, a custom that has survived to the present time.

After the interment, the procession returned to the house in the order in which it had gone, and cakes, spiced wine, pipes, and tobacco were liberally distribnted, and the assembly was often the occasion of more festivity than was decorous under the circumstances.

> "Containing lots of fun,
> Like mourning-coaches when the funeral's done."

At some funerals, a spoon was given to each of the pall-bearers, as commemorative of the occasion. The handle terminated in what was popularly called a "monkey," and the spoons were called "monkey spoons." The figure was probably intended for one of the Twelve Apostles, but was so crudely executed that it resembled an animal more closely than it did a man.

A "mourning-ring" was usually presented to all the female relations, and inside the circle was inscribed the age, name, and date of death of the deceased; or else they received a tiny brooch, made of a rim of gold holding in place a little glass lid surrounded with pearls and enclosing a tiny snip of hair. These rings and brooches were always worn conspicuously by the relatives and were most grewsome ornaments.

A widow usually bound a piece of velvet ribbon around her head, in front of the cap, and pinned the ends with the mourning-brooch commemorative of her husband's death and her own loss.

Catilina de Peyster's funeral was said to be peculiarly "edifying and solemn." Six young ladies were requested to attend as pall-bearers, who were dressed in white sarcenet jackets and petticoats, with their heads uncovered and their hair powdered and done up with white ribbon. The funeral attracted great attention, as it was unusual for women to attend them, and when the procession started from Mr. de Peyster's house in King Street, headed by the six young ladies and followed by the white coffin, over which a white embroidered pall was thrown, the whole city hurried out to watch it march up to Trinity Church. The following Sunday Dr. Vesey preached a funeral sermon, and all the young damsels who had officiated as pall-bearers sat together in a front pew in the church, close to the parents of the dead girl.

Marriages were merry festivals. The groom was required by law to take out a license, and for many years it was only possible to obtain one at Albany, Esopus, or Mana-ha-ta. The official records, therefore, of these three places are pretty accurate family histories of the Dutch settlers. The marriage-ceremony, or "inzegeening," was usually performed at the house of the bride's parents, and all the friends and relations gathered to witness it and enjoy the feast that followed.

Among the lower classes much rough play was indulged in, and the bridegroom's house was sometimes mischievously decorated with May-poles propped in front of his door, on which were hung ragged stockings, and they were not removed until he paid his tormentors to carry them away.

It was customary to have a poor-box conspicuously

Homes of the Settlers

displayed before the door of the bride, and the guests and passers-by were expected to contribute to it, and sometimes a goodly sum was collected.

On one occasion, money was solicited for building a church, and enough was subscribed to erect the Dutch Church. Some of the guests tried to evade payment of the money, declaring their signatures to the document had been obtained "when in their cups," and that the dominie had filled in the sums opposite their names; but the excuse availed them nothing, and they were obliged to pay the full sum recorded against them.

One of the first newspapers published in New York contains the following verses:

"A Receipt for all young Ladies that are going to be married," to make a

SACK POSSET.

" From famed Barbadoes on the Western Main,
   Fetch sugar half a pound, fetch Sack from Spain
   A pint; and from the Eastern Indian coast
   Nutmeg, the glory of our Northern toast;
   O'er flaming coals together let them heat,
   'Till the all-conquoring Sack dissolves the sweet.
   O'er such another fire let eggs, twice ten,
   New-born from foot of Cock and rump of hen;
   Stir them with steady hand, and conscience pricking,
   To see the untimely fate of twenty chickens;
   From shining shelf take down your brazen Skillet:
   A quart of milk from gentle cow will fill it;
   When boiled and cooled put milk and Sack to egg,
   Unite them firmly, like the Triple League;

The Goede Vrouw of Mana-ha-ta

Then covered close, together let them dwell
'Till Miss twice sings, ' You Must Not Kiss and Tell.'
Each lad and lass snatch up their murderous spoon,
And fall on fiercely like a starved Dragoon."

The dress of the bride was a peculiar one. She always wore as many petticoats as she could carry, as these were a part of her dower and a sign of prosperity, but sometimes a bride would appear scantily clothed, and with "a shift" over her dress. This was in the case of a widow whose first husband had left debts that she had been unable to discharge, and she was married the second time in this curious apparel, so as to signify that she went penniless into her husband's hands, and he accepted her without dower, and was not to be held responsible for his predecessor's liabilities. The minister of the parish when entering the marriage in der Trouw Boeck, would place in the margin some such notice as the following: " In the presence of A. B. C., etc., was Rachel Pier, *with her chemise over her clothes*, married to Albert Hendrickse Ploeg, by me Dominie Micella, April 30, 1699."

A maiden bride wore a peculiarly shaped crown, that was generally an heirloom in the family and kept for such occasions. It was sometimes of metal, and adorned with precious stones, but more usually was of pasteboard covered with silk, handsomely embroidered in gold and silver. The bride's women also wore an emblematic head-gear. They were not often maidens, but were matrons, who admonished the bride and taught her the various duties to be performed during the services, and had general charge of the ceremonies.

The staid burghers of Mana-ha-ta were visited in the council-room, December 17, 1658, by an irate woman by the name of Madame Abraham Vosbochs, from whom Annekje Leevens, the wife of Goosen Gerritse Van Schaick, had borrowed two coronets, one for herself and one for Maria Wesselsen, which had not been returned after they had been worn by the bride's women at a marriage-ceremony. The council passed an order, requiring Mesdames Van Schaick and Wesselsen " to make restitution of the same."

Sumptuary laws regarding dress were not required in the colony, but there was an unwritten law that was obeyed without hesitation. Each official had his distinctive costume. The maiden's hair was not covered by the matron's coif. Laborers wore a dress that did not impede them in their work. They never wore long coats—those were reserved for the upper classes; but every workman and craftsman donned long leathern aprons, both in the house and in the street. One corner of it was invariably tucked under the belt when the wearer was not working, but otherwise it fell nearly to his feet. The leather was often dyed red with the bark of the chestnut or oak tree.

The peasantry pushed their hair straight back, and covered it with a close-fitting cap. The usual dress was "a short gown and petticoat," and it was the pride of the thrifty housewife to have spun and woven the stuff for these skirts herself. They were generally of linsey-woolsey of the natural gray color, but were sometimes dyed blue with a mixture of red-maple bark and copperas, or the stuff was colored red with alder-bark. These dyes had been taught to the Dutch women by the squaws. By these distinctive dresses each class could be distinguished. Even the crafts could be noted, and the married women were recognized at a glance from the maidens.

From the side of the matron always hung a chatelaine, sometimes of gold and handsomely ornamented, but more frequently of brass with steel chains, from which dangled keys, scissors, pin-cushions, and a tiny case called a house-wife (and pronounced *hussuf*), containing thimble, needles, and bodkin. The church-book, with corners and clasps of gold and silver, also hung by long chains to match, from the chatelaine or girdle.

In the "History of Flatbush" there is a curious account of one of the Lefferts family, who, during the Revolutionary War, changed all her money into gold pieces, which she sewed into a round pin-cushion and hung by her side. A party of English soldiers once entered her house, and after destroying many of the good lady's valuables, slashed at her cushion with a sword, and "cut the ribbon by which it hung, and the whole party had a boisterous game of ball with the pin-cushion, which once or twice fell into the fire-place." It was finally tossed on one side, when the poor woman eagerly and

Homes of the Settlers

quietly seized it and hid it away, and the soldiers never discovered its precious contents.

Contemporaneous portraits show that when the good people put on their best clothes, they could be very fine, and the stuffs of which they were made were of the handsomest and richest materials. The portraits at the manor houses of Rensselaerswyck, Livingston, Van Cortlandt, etc., are those of fine-looking men and sweet-faced women. The coats of the former are of velvet, silk, or satin, trimmed with handsome lace, diamond buttons and buckles, and sometimes with rare furs. Around the throats of the men were wrapped yards of fine muslin trimmed with lace, which were called "Steinwicks," after the gallant soldier of that name; and the ladies were by no means behind their husbands in the richness of their apparel.

VI

Habits, Amusements, and Laws

The Dutch Learn from the Wilden—Samp-Mortar Rock—The Wilden's Industries—Houses and Furniture—Education of Children—Strange Laws and Punishments—The Kermiss—The First Clubs—Games—The First Hospital and Orphan Asylum—The Rattle-watch—Brant—The Fire Brigade—Light in the City.

THE first settlers on Mana-ha-ta adapted themselves to their surroundings in a remarkable way. They studied the habits of their wild neighbors and were not too proud to learn from them their secrets of dyeing, preparing tobacco, or planting maize. The time for this, according to the Wilden's doctrine, was "when the birch-tree leaf was the size of a mouse's ear." The savages taught the settlers their fashion of pounding corn into "hominy," which was the Wilden's name for cracked corn. It was done by making a hole in the stump of a tree, or in a rock, into which the kernels were thrown and then beaten with a heavy pestle. A round excavation in a promontory overlooking Fairfield, Connecticut, is still called Samp-Mortar Rock, samp being another name for the ground corn; and tradition declares that the spot was always resorted to, in the autumn, by the squaws, for the purpose of pounding their corn, which was done to a musical croon that kept time to the thud of the pestle.

The leaves of the corn were woven into mats or tied into brooms, when not used for fodder for the cattle.

The breakfast of the first Dutch settlers was generally prepared at sunrise, and was of "suppone," which was mush mixed with milk, buttermilk, or "strop," as they called molasses, and if they had tea they drank it without milk. The noonday meal was buttermilk and bread, and the supper consisted of flat cakes baked in the ashes, and sometimes a bit of bacon. Sugar was made from the sap of the maple-trees, and Mr. Knickerbocker, in his amusing, but not always veracious, account of Dutch customs, declares that a large lump of sugar was always suspended by a string over the table in a Dutch kitchen, and each one would sip his tea, chocolate, or coffee, and bite a bit off the suspended lump of sugar, which was swung from one to the other.

The Wilden were, at most times, freely admitted in small companies within the "palisadoes" of the little burgh, and they brought many commodities to barter. They were cunning weavers of baskets that were waterproof, made of a species of dogsbane, and could make candles and soap of bayberries, or brushes from a block of oak, which they ingeniously split into thousands of bristles.

The wild people were not pleasant companions, as they followed a native custom and, according to the history of the Rev. Charles Wolley, it was their habit to "rub oyl of Fishes, Fat of Eagles, and Grease of Rackoons" on their skin to keep it from blistering and repel the attacks of gnats and mosquitoes. They seldom washed their bodies or even their faces and hands, and in consequence the Dutch vrouwen, who were neatness personified, thought they were irreclaimable savages, and, although invariably kind to them, did not encourage them to take up their abode within the settlement, except under certain restraints.

The Algonquin name for the Dutch was "Swan Nak Wak," but the Indians also called them "Assyreoni," *i.e.*, cloth-weavers; "Charistonin," or iron-workers; sometimes "Sauk-hi-canin," or fire-makers; while the contemptuous epithet of "Materiooty," or coward, was sometimes bestowed on the planters.

The Wilden taught the settlers to look for the great annual flight of pigeons, which, early in April, always flew north to eat the wild carrot. This flight invariably took place at dawn and never after ten o'clock in the morning. It was so heavy as to darken the sun, and so low that stones, clubs, and like missiles were thrown at the birds, which were slaughtered by thousands.

The Indians had many medicines made from plants, roots, barks, and herbs. They understood the virtues of stramonium, smut-wheat, golden-rod, elderberry, etc. They would brew catnip-tea for the sick or strengthen an invalid with a decoction of strawberry-leaves. An Indian, if ill, eschewed meat, unless it were that of a female animal, and he understood the virtues of vapor-baths. Their great remedy for cuts and bruises was Seneca-oil, which we now use in the form of vaseline or cosmoline.

As time went on and the savages became more domesticated, almost every household had one or more of the wild men or women hanging around the kitchen-fire. They never made good servants, but would do "chores" for the vrouwen, such as cutting and piling the kindling-wood, or lifting heavy kettles on the great swinging cranes, in return for food and a lodging in the barn or under the back stoep.

The houses were built with long, sloping roofs, and if possible, on a side-hill, so that the front stoep was approached by a few steps, but the kitchen-door at the back of the house was always flush with the ground. It was wide and high, and was built in this way to allow of a horse being driven in every morning, hauling, by means of a long iron chain, a huge bock-log, which made the foundation of the fire that was never allowed to die out entirely. Everyone went in and out of the kitchen-door, except on occasions of ceremony. The front parlor was a sacred apartment that was kept tightly closed except on gala days, and woe to the mouse or the "kackerlack" (cockroach) that entered it. On the opposite side of the hall, that always ran from the front to the rear of the house, was the family sitting-room. The bed-rooms were large and filled with ponderous mahogany bureaus and four-post bedsteads, under which was "een slaapbauck op rollen," or trundle-bed, which was pulled out at night, and into which was tucked from two to four children. The lower classes used great boxes with boarded bottoms for beds, which were filled with sacks of hay, corn-silk, or dried leaves. A great brass warming-pan usually hung on the walls.

The children of the first settlers were well trained in household duties, as was needful in a place where there were few servants, and each woman undertook much of her own house-work. The boys were made to carry water from the well or run errands to the wood-house, the smoke-house, and the brine-barrel in the cellar. The girls had their daily "stint" inside of the house, and, as there was always "a stretch" on the loom, an idler was often "set to do a yard" as a punishment. As time went on and better servants were to be obtained in the colony, the arduous duties of the house-wife fell on them, but every maiden, whatever her station in life, was thoroughly instructed in the details of house-keeping, and she was not considered eligible for matrimony until she could show her "kos" full of linen, spun and woven by herself, and daintily marked with her initials in cross-stitch.

The Dutch councillors were wise men whose rules were simple and hardly amounted to laws. They met in solemn conclave at least once a week, and any person might appear before them without ceremony, and state his grievance or complaint. The defendant was summoned, and both parties were usually requested to make their plea and defence in writing. This was often handed to a third party, with a request that he would try to make the two persons agree, but if this were impossible, the councillors again took up the case and pronounced judgment, from which there was no appeal. Crimes were few in the peace-loving community; the principal cases were the charges of the "Schout" against persons caught tapping (*i.e.*, drawing beer for sale) after lawful hours or on Sunday; delinquent debtors, etc.

On May 12, 1664, Jan Willemsen Van Iselstyn, "for expressing abusive language and writing an insolent letter to the magistrates of Bushwyck," was fastened to a stake at the place of public execution, with a bridle in his mouth, rods under his arms, and a paper on his breast with the inscription, "Lampoon writer, false accuser, and defamer of its magistrates," and afterward banished, with costs. One man was put into a sack and thrown into the river for committing a horrible crime—a punishment that he richly deserved; and his fate prevented the recurrence of such deeds for many a long day.

On April 12, 1658, Nicolas Albertsen, for "deserting his ship and his betrothed bride after publication of banns," was sentenced "to have his head shaven, then to be flogged and have his ears bored with red-hot irons, and work two years with the negroes." Other men were banished from the colony; but there were comparatively few crimes, and, with these exceptions, the punishments were generally of a mild character.

The worthy Dutchmen and their vrouwen were intensely practical in all arrangements for their home-comforts and the proper maintenance of their families, but they by no means neglected social duties and were noted for their hospitality. Besides fireside amusements, they desired more public gatherings, and, looking backward to the pleasures of Patria, they recalled its yearly festival, or Kermiss; the great open-air market that attracted the country-people from far and near. The burghers of Mana-ha-ta therefore yielded to the entreaties of their wives and determined to inaugurate a similar function, at which cattle could be exhibited, farm-implements sold, and the fruit of the loom, the distaff, and the needle of the house-wife might be exposed for sale; and in connection with the market, dances, trials of skill, and other amusements might be indulged in by the lads and lassies, so that all the farmers and their wives might be attracted to the burgh, to spend their money for the profit of its denizens.

Wisely laid plans were therefore adopted by a committee, which, under the sanction of the government, arranged that the first kermiss should be held on Mana-ha-ta, October 20, 1659. The council commanded "that for all fat cattle brought to the market not slaughtered," posts should "be placed by the side of the church, att the market-house and plaine afore the fort," which was therefore arranged for the accommodation of the public, and in nowise interfered with the weekly market held at the Strand, by the house of Master Hans Kierstede. The kermiss lasted six weeks, and became an institution; and from that day to this a yearly industrial exhibition has been held on "the island by the sea," sometimes under one name and sometimes under another, but always with the same general purpose.

The kermiss was first held on the spot that the governor used as a parade-ground, an open space directly north of the government enclosure, on one side of which was the church and on the other the official buildings. The spot soon became known as "D'Marck Velt." Booths were ranged on one side of the open space, and the cattle were tied to the posts by the fence of the first church-yard (a tiny enclosure that had, early in the history of the colony, become too small for its needs and was abandoned for other burying-grounds on the island). The kermiss became the great social festival of the year, and was enjoyed with zest by old and young. The goede vrouwen of the community lent their aid by inviting all their country cousins and friends to stay with them in their cheery, comfortable homes, and a round of merry-making ensued.

Unfortunately, as the reins of government relaxed, this kermiss, which at first had been so decorously conducted and widely enjoyed, degenerated into a gathering of town-loafers and rude country-boors, who seized on the chance of indulging in rough games or coarse plays, that soon made the function a saturnalia; and then those of the families whose homes overlooked the green importuned the government to interfere, and demanded to have a stop put to such excesses, declaring that they demoralized the community and were particularly hurtful to their carefully trained domestics and young people. The kermiss was therefore reorganized, all rough games were prohibited, and the meeting-place was removed to the common, which is now the City Hall Park.

"D'Marck Velt," being thus deserted, became a weed-grown and unsightly lot, and it was not until 1732 that several citizens found a use for it, and formed themselves into the first organized club of the city, and petitioned the governor and council to permit them to sod the little triangle and use it for a bowling green. The founders of the bowling club were John Chambers,* Peter Bayard,† and Peter Jay, and the spot was a favorite rallying-place for many years. The club received a regular lease of the ground for eleven years from the city authorities, on the payment of "one peppercorn per annum." In a garden belonging to a tavern near Canoe Place there had been a bowling green for many years, but it was considered

---

* John Chambers and Peter Jay married daughters of Jacobus Van Cortlandt and Eva de Vries.

† Peter Bayard married Blandina Kierstede, daughter of Dr. Hans Kierstede.

too far out of town to be convenient; and the new bowling green was well patronized, much to the disgust of the innkeeper, who had been frequently reproved and fined by the authorities for permitting his patrons to play the game on Sundays, but who paid the fine without protest, and encouraged the use of his grounds on account of the large revenue he received.

Backgammon was a favorite game among the early settlers, and there is a minute in the town records regarding the arrest of some sailors, who were at play in Jan Backus's tavern, August 4, 1660, after the inn should have been closed for the night. The "schout" of the town also arrested people for "playing golf in the streets," and an ordinance was passed December 10, 1659, to prevent such a recurrence.

As a general rule, backgammon, chess, dominoes, and checkers were played only in taverns, and the better class of Dutch colonists seldom permitted such games in their own homes. Billiards were also played, but young men who indulged in the game were looked upon as dissipated and depraved. Cards were sometimes seen, but the games played with them in those days were games of chance, or gambling games, such as lansquenet; and the pack itself was of German manufacture, with seventy-three cards, on which were painted grotesque, emblematical figures, that were rudely sketched on cardboard and colored by hand. There was no queen in the pack, her place being filled by a cavalier, who, with a knecht, or hired-man, attended the king.

The pips resembled those used in German cards of the present day, and were acorns, cups, leaves, and hearts. The pack contained, besides the suit-cards, twenty-one "Atouts," that resembled those in the Italian decks, and they had their own significance and use in the game. Whist was not invented for nearly a hundred years after the colonization of America. The children of the day played marbles, but their favorite game was "knuckle-bones," which were made from sheep-knuckles, and their rules were similar to those of the children of our times in their game of jack-stones.

The people of Holland were noted for their care of the aged, sick, orphans, and prisoners, and the humanity shown to the unfortunate and oppressed was greater in the Netherlands than was the custom in any other of the partly civilized European countries of that day.

The Dutch in the New World were not behind Patria in these respects; and as early as 1658 a hospital was provided "in a clean house, with fires of wood, and a nurse was engaged to look after the sick," and the establishment was put under the superintendence of Dr. Jacob Hendricksen Varravanger, who was the city physician, with the famous Dr. Hans Kierstede as the chief in authority; and our present New York Hospital can point proudly to the fact that its organization is older than any other of the kind on this side of the Atlantic Ocean. There were few paupers in the burgh, but in 1685 "Topknot Betty" was given three shillings a week from "the chest." Soon after the middle of the seventeenth century, the council made the necessary arrangements to take charge of, and provide for, all the orphans of the community at the public expense, and certain revenues were set apart for this purpose.

In the same year, a Rattle Watch consisting of four men was established, which was uniformed in blue dapple, turned up with orange facings. These officers were armed with lanterns, rattles, and long staffs, and their duty was to patrol the burgh by day and night, and call out the state of the weather, the hour, and any news of great importance that had been received at the city gates. This custom was continued until the beginning of the nineteenth century; and old people remembered hearing the news of Burgoyne's surrender being called out mournfully by the British sentries, who had, for the time being, taken the place of the city watch.

In case of fire, the watchman sprung his rattle, and called "Brant! Brant!" This cry was in use all through the time that the English governed the colony, and until the town watch was superseded by the city police, although it was the Dutch word for fire. It happened that a famous Indian chief had adopted the name of Brant. He was a great warrior and frequently on the war-path, and the worthy denizens of town or country never slept peaceably, as they dreaded being scalped at night by the savage and his tribe. Nurses used the name of Brant to terrify their charges into submission, and the same old lady who remembered hearing the watch report the defeat of the British and surrender of

The Goede Vrouw of Mana-ha-ta

their bragging general, also recalled how she would cower and bury her head under the clothes of the trundle-bed when she heard the watch run through the streets shouting "Brant! Brant! rouse ye! rouse ye!" and saw her father spring from the high-post bedstead beside her, to run to the fire; as she believed most firmly that Brant, the Indian sachem, was coming to claim her in punishment for some childish peccadillo.

As early as August 15, 1658, according to the minutes of the council, two hundred and fifty buckets, with ladders and hooks, were ordered from Holland. These were hung beside the Stadt-Huys, but in addition to these public arrangements, each householder was required to keep a number of leather buckets always hanging in a row under the "bock stoep." They were marked with the owner's name, and at the call of "Brant!" each man would seize a long pole and string his buckets on it. They were filled at the nearest pump and passed from hand to hand to the burning building. After the fire was extinguished, the buckets were thrown in a heap, and returned by the servants the following day. One of these buckets has lately been presented to the New York Historical Society; it was marked Rufus King, and had seen service as lately as 1815.

The streets of the dorp were irregularly lighted on dark nights by lanterns hung out on a pole from an upper window of every seventh house, and the town was not lighted by the authorities until 1762, and even then on moonlight nights the lamplighter did not go his rounds.

VII

Rensselaers of the Manor

The First Patroon—Prince Maurice in Amsterdam—Governor Wouter Van Twiller—The First Gold Thimble—Arent Van Corlear—Colonization of Rensselaerswyck—The Dorp of Beverswyck—Size of the Manor—Signatures of Sachems—Jealousy of English, French, and Dutch—Piety of the Patroon—Map of the Manor—Death and Will of the First Patroon—Successors to the Title—Der Groot Director—Charles Stuart and the Dominie.

WHILE the little colony on Mana-ha-ta was being settled under the wise superintendence of the great West India Company, a principality was founded at the head-waters of the Hudson River by one of the members of the society.

Kiliaen Van Rensselaer was a governor in the East India Company, of Holland, and had advocated its extending its plantations to America, as well as the formation of a branch of the original society to look after its affairs, and had become one of its principal stockholders. He belonged to a powerful family in Holland whose ancestors had fought in the wars of the Crusades, and for their bravery in battle they had been granted an augmentation of arms by the Knights of St. John, the cross of which community was placed on the shield of the Van Rensselaers. It is silver on a red ground, and was used with the motto, "Niemand Zonder" (no man without a cross).

The family were noted for their bravery in battle and their wisdom in council. History relates that after the victories of Prince Maurice he made a triumphal entry into the city of Amsterdam, which was magnificently illuminated in his honor. One of the most gorgeous of the decorations was on the estate of the Van Rensselaer family, which was on the principal street of the city, surrounded by high stone walls, which, together with the roof of the house, was closely set with large iron baskets called "cressets," that were filled with inflammable materials and set on fire. The brilliant effect produced by this illumination astonished Prince Maurice, who was pleased at this opportunity of showing his gratitude to a family who had lavished money in his behalf and for the honor of their country. So he summoned the Heer Van Rensselaer from the crowd of mounted gentlemen who were escorting their prince in his triumphal procession through the town and congratulated the gratified heer on the novelty and beauty of the decorations, and said that the family should adopt the motto of "Omnibus Effulgeo," "I outshine all," and take for their crest the flaming cresset. The motto and crest were accordingly at once adopted by the head of the family, as, at that time, an augmentation of arms was more highly prized than any other reward.

The family estates of the Van Rensselaers are in

Holland, three miles southeast of Nykerk, in the province of Guelderland. It was a "Reddergoed," or large tract of land sublet to vassals, the terms of whose lease required all males to follow their lord to war, and the possession of which conferred nobility. The estates were called Rensselaerswyck, the significance of which was deer's-park or deer's-lair, and the property retains the name to the present time. Numbers of buildings cover the demesne, and their quaint gable roofs are surmounted by numerous weathercocks of the arms and crest of the family. The graveyard beside the church is filled with stones, on which are the names of many of the young men of the family who were killed in the service of their country.

Der Heer Kiliaen Van Rensselaer, the founder of the Dutch patroonship in America, was a man of strong character and considerable wealth. He had inherited the family estates called the "Rensselaerswyck Reddergoed" in Guelderland and also the beautiful house and grounds in Amsterdam. He married twice; first, Hillegonda Van Bylant, by whom he had one son, Johannes; and secondly, Anna, the daughter of Johannes Van Weely. The only sister of the first patroon was named Maria. She married Rikert Van Twiller, and became the mother of Elizabeth, who married her cousin Johannes Van Rensselaer, and of the celebrated Wouter Van Twiller, the second governor of the New Netherland colony.

Kiliaen Van Rensselaer, a son of Johannes, had four

daughters, Maria, Hillegonda, and Elenora, who died unmarried; and the youngest one, Susanna, who married Jan de la Court. Der Heer Van Rensselaer also had four sons by his second marriage. They were Jan Baptist, who married his cousin Susanna Van Weely; Jeremias, born 1662, married Maria Van Cortlandt (from whom all the family in America are descended); the Rev. Nicolaus Van Rensselaer, who married Alida Schuyler, and Rikert Van Rensselaer, treasurer and staadtholder of the North Viaeuen estates, from whom are descended the Holland members of the family; but the name died out in that country early in the present century, and is only continued on this side of the Atlantic.

Madame Kiliaen Van Rensselaer was noted for her beautiful needle-work, and has been immortalized by a curious honor that was bestowed upon her. According to the Dutch chronicles Madame Van Rensselaer was in the habit of sitting at her window to sew, and attracted the attention of a young goldsmith whose shop was opposite her house. The young man was indebted to the old lady for many slight deeds of kindness, and was anxious to prove his appreciation and gratitude by presenting her with some article of his own manufacture. He noticed that she used a clumsy ivory thimble without a top, which was like those now used by tailors, and he therefore made one of gold, which he presented to his benefactress on her birthday, with the wish that " she would wear the *finger hat* as a covering to her diligent and beautiful finger." This invention of a metal thimble with a crown on it has not been forgotten in Amsterdam, the native city of the industrious lady, as is proved by the following extract from the "Pall Mall Gazette," November, 1884, in which was the translation from a Dutch paper of the day, as follows: "A bi-centenary of a curious kind has recently been celebrated at Amsterdam, being nothing less than the invention of the *thimble*. It is just two centuries since, last October, that the first European (gold) thimble was made by Nicolas Van Benschoten, a goldsmith, who devised the article for the protection of the finger of Madame Van Rensselaer."

In order to colonize in America, Kiliaen Van Rensselaer selected Arent Van Corlear to superintend his affairs and gave him the title of "Director of the Colonie," and caused him to emigrate in 1630.

The choice could not have fallen upon a better man. The new governor proceeded at once to collect a number of families who were qualified to make good colonists, and all sailed for the western continent in vessels belonging to Heer Van Rensselaer, and bearing his pennant. It is stated that the first company arrived in the ship Goede Vrouw. The settlers were accompanied by a company of soldiers under a competent leader, and the ships were filled with all the necessaries for the foundation of a colony, and returned laden with furs for der Heer Van Rensselaer, which encouraged him to proceed with his venture. The new-comers established themselves at the Manor of Rensselaerswyck, a property that had been selected by the agents of the patroon. It was at the head-waters of the Hudson River, and surrounded the site of the Indian castle of Laap-haw-ach-king, a place where the Wilden of the North were accustomed to gather yearly to exchange their furs for the clams, fish, and wampum offered by the members of the ocean tribes.

This "castle" had been purchased from its owners previous to the "erection of the manor"* by the West India Company, and the site became the cause of much contention between the governors of Mana-ha-ta and the directors of Rensselaerswyck, as the settlers built close to the walls of Fort Orange and called their village Beverswyck (or the "house of the beaver"); and as the property of the patroon included the village and many miles on either side of the river, its ownership was always a cause for dispute. This was of no consequence so long as der Heer Van Rensselaer was the guiding-star of the Amsterdam Chamber, but after his death it led to many vexatious squabbles, that were only settled on the usurpation of the English, who cut the Gordian knot after their invariable custom, by claiming ownership of the entire territory, and requiring the patroon to sue for new manorial rights. By this proceeding and its consequent fees they reaped great advantages for the home-government. The Manor of

---

* "Erection of the manor" signifies the purchase of the land and the granting by the government of manorial rights to the proprietor with the title of patroon.

Rensselaers of the Manor

Rensselaerswyck covered what is now divided into the counties of Albany, Rensselaer, and part of Columbia, in the State of New York. The tract of land was twenty-four miles in breadth by forty-eight miles in length, and it contained over 700,000 acres. A beautiful range of hills bounded the demesne to the east and west, which was watered by between thirty and forty streams emptying into the Hudson River, which flowed through the centre of the territory.

The agent of the patroon called upon the Indian owners to name their own price for the land selected, and formally bound them to the sale of their property, by requiring the sachems of the tribes to place their marks or signatures on a legally drawn deed of sale, which was fully and carefully explained to the vendors. This deed is still in existence; it contains the names of Kottomack, Nawanemit, Abantzeeme, Sagiskwa, Kanaomeek, and the villages they sold were called Semessarse, Petanock, and Negagvnse, together with the Indian castle of Moeneminues.

After purchasing the lands from the savages, the patroon completed his bargain, first with the College of XIX., and then with the West India Company, and received from them the patent of the manorial rights, the original of which is dated August 13, 1630, and is deposited in the royal archives at The Hague.

It was in this quiet way that a principality was created in the New World, independent of all other plantations, and subject to no government but its own, and widely separated by untrodden forests and deep streams from any of the European settlements.

To the north, beyond the River St. Lawrence, there was a French colony. An English settlement was far to the eastward, on the edge of the Atlantic Ocean, and at the mouth of the river, nearly two hundred miles to the south, was the New Netherland plantation of the West India Company, while westward was a wilderness sparsely inhabited by wild men.

There seemed every reason that the Europeans should live in harmony and strengthen their positions in their new homes by supporting each other in their self-imposed exile, but each one of the three colonies looked with envious eyes on the central manor, which, however, throve and prospered under the wise management of its directors, with provoking indifference to the encroachments of French, Puritans, and Dutch, who were always ready to be aggressive, in the hope of obtaining control over the rich and independent principality settled so quietly and contentedly in their midst.

The first years after the purchase of the manor saw one hundred and fifty adults settled at Rensselaerswyck, as the new purchase was named, after the estate in Holland. The head of each family was permitted to select a tract of land on which a house was built for him, and he was encouraged to clear and cultivate a portion of the ground, after having signed a lease for a term of years and renewed the vows of fealty and allegiance to the patroon that had been taken before the departure from Patria. One of the few stipulations made by the directors in their leases was the wise one that the emigrants should settle close to each other, not only for their better protection from the Wilden, but also that each community might be near a chapel in which religious services were conducted by dominies selected by the patroon and paid for by himself. The leases of the settlers were granted on very low terms, and sometimes with peculiar conditions. One of them, dated January 14, 1649, for "the old Indian maize lands at Catskills," was rented to Jan Dircksen, of Bremen, and is translated as follows: "The tenant is to read a sermon or portion of the Scriptures every Sunday and high festival to the Christians in the neighborhood, and to sing one or more Psalms before and after prayers agreeable to the customs of the Church of Holland."

Owing to the energy of the directors and the liberality of the patroon, the "Colonie of Rensselaerswyck" was planted within four years after the land had been purchased from the savages, and the men were as busy at their ploughs and the women at distaff and loom, as if they had never been transplanted but had been born and bred amid their new surroundings, which at once assumed a home-like, comfortable appearance. In the archive-house of the manor is a map drawn by John R. Bleeker in 1767; the names of the manor tenants are recorded on it.

The Goede Vrouw of Mana-ha-ta

"Kiliaen Van Rensselaer, Patroon of the Manor called Rensselaerswyck," petitioned their High Mightinesses the States General of Holland, on February 5, 1641, for a *veniam testandi*, in order "to enable him to dispose by last will, according to his pleasure, of the aforesaid Manor or feudal estate." This petition was granted the day it was received, and the will disposing of the American estates was accordingly at once drawn up. In it the colonial property was devised to the sons on whom and to whose male heirs the estate was strictly entailed. As the children were minors, the patroon appointed as their guardians, his wife's brother, Johan Van Wely, and also his nephew, Governor Wouter Van Twiller, who were soon called upon to administer to the estate, as Kiliaen Van Rensselaer died in 1645, very soon after executing the instrument.

It is doubtful if the great American estates were ever visited by the first owner, the Patroon Kiliaen Van Rensselaer. But, as has been mentioned, he was at first represented at Rensselaerswyck in the management of affairs by Arent Van Corlear, a man whose gentle manners and keen sense of justice made him beloved by all who knew him. The savages revered him, and adopted his name as a term of respect which they afterward bestowed on each governor in turn. He was a public-spirited man, and encouraged the settlers to push their plantations beyond the bounds of the Rensselaerswyck principality, and helped to found Schenectady in 1661. He married Antonia Slagboone, the widow of Jonas

Rensselaers of the Manor

Bronck, who left his name to a little stream in Westchester County, New York. Van Corlear was drowned in a squall on Lake Champlain, and was succeeded in the directorship by Brant Arentse (the Eagle's son) Van Slechtenhorst, and after the patroon's death, one son after another, as he became of age, was sent to the colony to look after the interests of the family and assume the title of "Director of the Colonie of Renaselaerswyck."

Johannes Van Rensselaer, the eldest son, made one trip of inspection to America after succeeding to the estates, but returned to Holland, where he died, leaving an infant son named Kiliaen to succeed to the title of patroon. This boy died unmarried, and was succeeded by his uncle, Jan Baptist Van Rensselaer, who had emigrated as early as 1651, and was director of the colony for many years during the non-age of the youthful heir.

A quaint little church was erected at Beverswyck at the expense of the patroon. This was decorated with stained-glass windows on which were the arms of the family and the name of the director, Jan Baptist Van Rensselaer. His only child died in infancy, and on his own death the title and estates passed to the third son of Kiliaen, the first patroon. This was Der Groot Director Jeremias Van Rensselaer, who was born in Amsterdam, and had moved to America when very young, where he married an accomplished and charming wife. She was a native of Mana-ha-ta, of Dutch parents, and was a beautiful, tall, black-haired woman, with sparkling eyes and a neck and arms of dazzling whiteness. Maria Van Cortlandt was the daughter of Oloff Stevenzon and his wife, the energetic pioneer Annekje Lockermans. The wife of der groot director was born in New Amsterdam while that place was yet in its infancy, and she was closely connected with all the rulers of the colony. Jeremias Van Rensselaer was devoted to his American beauty, and must have presented her with pride to his mother and relatives in Holland.

The handsome oil-paintings that hung in the manor-house represent der groot director in a magnificent velvet coat, lavishly embroidered and decorated with gold lace. Madame Van Rensselaer wears a satin gown trimmed with lace, and the turn of her head and her cast of features show her strong character. She was unfortunately injured after the birth of her eldest child, and was so crippled that she limped in her walk for many years, and finally was confined to her arm-chair, from which she directed the affairs of her household with consummate ability.

Jeremias Van Rensselaer was the last director of the colony, as he inherited from his brother the manor and patroonship, and the estate was thenceforth governed by the owners themselves, who became residents of the New World.

The title of patroon was borne by his heirs in the male line in direct descent down to the breaking out of the War of the Revolution, when the eighth patroon,

Stephen III., who was under age, resigned his title and manorial rights, that had been held by his family for over one hundred and fifty years, to become a plain American citizen.

Dominie Nicolaus Van Rensselaer, the younger brother of Jeremias, emigrated to America in 1674, and speedily fell in love with pretty Alida Schuyler, an American-born maiden of only seventeen summers, the granddaughter of the brave Van Slechtenhorst, whose two daughters had accompanied their father to the American wilderness and settled with him in the heart of the savages' country.

It was while presiding over the director's hospitable board that Margretta Van Slechtenhorst was wooed and won by one of her countrymen who had emigrated from Guelderland at the request of the Patroon Van Rensselaer, as he wished to have the son of a neighbor, in whom he could have implicit confidence, to represent some of his vast interests in the manorial estate. This was der Heer Philip Pieterse Schuyler, who, with his lovely wife, settled near Beverwyck and brought up a family of ten children, and there are but few of their descendants who have not left their mark on each decade of colonial history.

Charles Stuart, afterward Charles II., king of England, had spent many months of his young life in Amsterdam, where he was surrounded by a crowd of English cavaliers who were always striving and contriving to place him on the throne of his native land.

The Goede Vrouw of Mana-ha-ta

There was very little ready money among the exiles, who were often indebted to the "base mechanicals of Holland," as Queen Elizabeth termed them, for food and lodging. Among those who extended their hospitality to the young prince were the Van Rensselaer family, and Nicolaus became intimate with Charles and his courtiers. This son of the first patroon was destined for the church, and was a dreamy, studious youth. Nicolaus was noted for his soothsaying, but could seldom be prevailed upon to reveal his dreams or prophesy for his friends. Prince Charles heard of the predictions of the young Dutchman, which so often were fulfilled, and sent for him and begged to know his own fate. At that time England was in the turmoil of the Revolution, and yet Van Rensselaer promptly told the prince that the misfortunes which had surrounded him from childhood were nearly at an end, and that he would soon be called upon to take his seat on the English throne. Prince Charles was of course delighted with the prediction, and presented the prophet with a handsome silver snuff-box, which is still in possession of the family, and also told his Dutch friend to call upon the king of England for recognition. The dominie did not forget this royal command, but followed the king to London on his accession. Charles most graciously recognized the young man and caused him to be made chaplain of St. Margaret's, Westminster. This prophecy of Nicolaus Van Rensselaer's was so celebrated that one of the clergy of Mana-ha-ta, the revered Dominie Selyns, many years after considered it noteworthy, and addressed the following lines to the picture of his brother divine:

> Op t'Conterfeytsel,
> van D. Nicolaus Rensselaer, Propheet van
> CAREL II., Konick van Englandt.
> Is't Rensselaer, opt neit?
> Die Neerlandt onderrecht heft
> Van zeegen en verdriet,
> En CAREL's-croon verseght heeft
> Zeer lang voor zyn gebiedt.

The verses were translated by the Hon. H. Murphy in his work on Dominie Selyns's poetry:

> On the Portrait of Dominie Nicolaus Rensselaer, Prophet to Charles II., King of England.
>
> Is it Rensselaer or no?
> Who Netherland informed has
> Of blessings and of woe,
> And Charles's crown forewarned has,
> Long ere he came thereto.

It is remarkable that the two most celebrated prophecies of the dominie were fulfilled, and it is certain that his contemporaries devoutly believed in his soothsaying qualities, and he was consulted by high and low on all important occasions. Dominie Van Rensselaer was the owner of a watch which is noted as being the first one imported to America. The case was of brass, and it was regarded as a great curiosity, for even as late as the beginning of the nineteenth century watches were rare in the colonies.

VIII

Der Colonie Nieu Nederlands

The Second Governor—Nutten Island—The Murder of Brinckerhoff—Arrival of Governor Stuyvesant—The Accomplished Mrs. Bayard—Wreck of Dominie Bogartus and Governor Kieft—The White Hall—The Wilden—Swedes, French, and English—Encroachments of the Massachusetts Colony—Governor Stuyvesant and his Council—Lady Moody—The Quakers—Imprisonment of Director Van Slechtenhorst—Jeremias Van Rensselaer Assumes the Directorship.

OWING to the influence of the Patroon Van Rensselaer among his associates in the College of XIX., his nephew Wouter Van Twiller was appointed governor of the colony on Mana-ha-ta to succeed Peter Minuit.

The new governor sailed for America in the Zoutberg (Salt Mountain), and arrived at the mouth of the Hudson River in the spring of 1633. He was attended by one hundred and four soldiers, the first regiment that ever reached these shores.

The appointment of Van Twiller was important for the well-being of the colony of Rensselaerswyck, as it insured harmonious terms between it and that of Mana-ha-ta, as the latter held the key of the gateway to the Atlantic Ocean, the only road to Europe.

The colonies throve under the management of Van

Der Colonie Nieu Nederlands

Twiller, who determined to settle permanently in America, and he therefore purchased several different plantations from the Indians, among others the beautiful island that lay south of Mana-ha-ta, called by the first settlers Nutten Island, but now known as Governor's Island, after its first Dutch owner, Wouter Van Twiller. The little isle was covered with shellbark hickory-trees, which were highly prized by the Wilden, as from their nuts the natives concocted a drink which was the only brew they were acquainted with before the arrival of the Europeans, by whom alcoholic drinks were introduced. One of the few assaults made on the Dutch at Mana-ha-ta took place on this spot in 1640, when several boys from Mana-ha-ta, attracted by the fame of Nutten Island, waded across Buttermilk Channel, which divided it from Nassau (or Long Island), and began to gather the nuts. The savages resented this intrusion, and fell on the party and drove them away, but not before one of them, Dirck Brinckerhoff, was killed by a poisoned arrow. He was the son of Abram Brinckerhoff, who had lately emigrated from Drautilandt, with a wife and four children, all of whom lived to become good colonial subjects, with the exception of the unfortunate youth who lost his life for the sake of a few hickory and chestnuts.

After the death of the first patroon in 1645, the interests of the two Dutch colonies became more and more identical, although the process of consolidation was not without friction.

The Goede Vrouw of Mana-ha-ta

Governor Van Twiller was succeeded by William Kieft, a testy, quarrelsome little man, who was always squabbling with someone, and he in turn was followed by the great governor, Peter Stuyvesant.

The belief that the New World was overlaid with gold, silver, and precious stones was its chief attraction in the eyes of Europeans, and it was supposed that these minerals were to be scraped from the surface of the land. Fabulous tales of the wealth reaped by Spaniards in the conquests of the southern continent were fully credited, and adventurers from every country were eager to grow rich in the same way. In consequence all deeds and grants of lands were carefully drawn, so that the purchaser might have entire control of metals or precious stones found on them. Governor Kieft steadily pursued this fallacy, and imagined that he was about to make his fortune by discovering gold on the island of Mana-ha-ta. He also encouraged the sachems of the different tribes on Sewan-ha-ka and New Jersey to bring him specimens of ore, and fancied that he had realized his dreams of wealth when he purchased specimens of copper from mines that had been worked, time out of mind, by the savages, and from which they made pipe-bowls, arrow-heads, and a few simple household necessities. These mines were at Belleville, on Second River, and at Bound Brook, New Jersey. The governor was soon recalled to Holland, and he carried off with him a quantity of quartz and other minerals, intending to return to America with a staff of laborers and work the mines on the best-known European methods. He sailed for Europe in the Princess, in which was also Dominie Bogartus, and the first news of the travellers that was received by the colonists was that the vessel had been wrecked on the Welsh coast, and that the governor, dominie, and eighty-two other persons had been miserably drowned, and the precious ore dropped to the bottom of the ocean.

Governor Petrus Stuyvesant was a brave, noteworthy personage, who had lost a leg in his services for his country. He had been governor of the island of Curacoa, which post he resigned in order to return to Europe, in hopes that the superior surgical knowledge of the men of his own country might alleviate the suffering caused by his wound. He was too valuable a man to be allowed to remain quietly at home, and the government of the States General of Holland urged his acceptance of the government of the colony on Mana-ha-ta.

Governor Stuyvesant was accompanied to the New World by his wife and a widowed sister, Anna—Mrs. Samuel Bayard. No one could know the accomplished sister of Governor Stuyvesant without admiring her. She had lost a devoted husband in Bayard, and, having few ties in Holland, determined to follow the fortunes of her brother when he was appointed governor of the New Netherlands, and make a home for herself and her little family in America. She brought a tutor with her, for she wished her children to be accomplished and well-educated, but the tutor fell in love with a young

The Goede Vrouw of Mana-ha-ta

woman after he reached the colony, and, as he became useless as a teacher, Madame Bayard released him from the bond that bound him in her service for a term of years, and herself undertook the education of her children.. In this she succeeded so well that her eldest son was soon called upon to become clerk of the council, being one of the few young men in the colony who thoroughly understood Latin, French, Dutch, and English.

The first governors had been content to live in a small house, next to the chapel inside of the fort. This was now turned over to the chief secretary, and Governor Stuyvesant selected a beautiful site at the point of Mana-ha-ta, and ordered a large stone house built for the gubernatorial use. It was constructed of a gray stone, and from its color was named "The White Hall." The ladies of the family planned the lovely gardens that surrounded the mansion. They laid out prim, straight walks, bordered with box, behind which were beds of lavender, peonies, roses, tulips, and other flowers. Rows of fruit-trees surrounded a vegetable garden. To the north an imposing gateway opened on "The Broad Way." The governor's periagua and yacht lay south of the house at the Indians' "safe landing place," Capsey's rocks, and on this spot took place all the official receptions of visitors from foreign shores.

When Governor Stuyvesant assumed his office, the two Dutch plantations had been colonized little more than fifty years. They had gone through many thrilling experiences, for notwithstanding the good intentions of the officials, and the benevolence of the pioneer women to the Wilden, who encompassed them on every side, there were always causes for complaint against unruly adventurers, who defied authority and pushed their way into the wilderness in search of game, etc., and who often treated the aborigines with great brutality. It was not to be expected that the savages could distinguish between the various colonies from Europe which had settled so unexpectedly in America, with their different languages and different creeds. Dutch, English, French, Swedes, all were alike to them, nor could the wild men always be pacified after they had received some insult from a European, even though they recognized the fact that one colony was not responsible for the misdeeds of another. They brooded over their wrongs, and outbreaks were always imminent, although the Dutch were always conciliatory in their treatment of their wild neighbors, and constantly called the tribes together and tried to keep them in good humor by making them handsome presents.

Besides the mutterings of an Indian war, always to be heard near the Dutch settlements, the Swedes on the South (*i.e.*, Delaware) River quarrelled with the people of Mana-ha-ta; and even as early as 1627 Governor Bradford, of the Plymouth colony, wrote to the Dutch governor and questioned his right to assume control over the settlement of the New Netherlands, and declared that the property belonged to the king of England.

The Goede Vrouw of Mana-ha-ta

The log of the Mayflower records the fact that the emigrants were bitterly disappointed that at the end of their long voyage they had not struck the mouth of the Hudson River, instead of Cape Cod; and they would willingly have continued their trip until they reached the Dutch settlement, had not the captain and owner of the vessel refused to carry them any farther, and hurriedly placed the discontented passengers "on the stern and rock-bound coast," and departed for Europe, leaving the Pilgrims to grumble on their desolate situation and struggle for life itself, in the wilderness that surrounded them; opposed by such foes as savages, cold, hunger, and poverty, and with no hope of aid from any mortal.

The Pilgrims were in a plight indeed, exiles from their mother-country, outcasts from its established religion, scorned by the government, who were glad to see such turbulent persons pass out of their jurisdiction. They had wandered to Holland in search of homes, and then restlessly turned their faces toward the New World, where they hoped to be autocrats and autonomous.

Unlike the Dutch settlement, which was planned with prudence and judgment, with all wants foreseen and provided for, the Pilgrim settlers emigrated with few of the requisite tools, and were unprovided with materials or workmen to provide them with homes. The greater number were villagers or towns-people, and had no idea of how to cultivate the soil or provide for the necessaries

Der Colonie Nieu Nederlands

of life in a wilderness. A more hap-hazard, foolhardy undertaking was never conceived, and it was not surprising that all but a handful of the most hardy of the emigrants died during the first few years after the settlement was planted on the rocky coast of New England. The women were not helpful housewives, like those of Holland. They had learned much from their hosts during the sojourn of the congregation among the Dutch, but they were not capable of providing for their family food, clothes, etc., as the Dutch women had been trained to do. It was no wonder that the whole community cast envious eyes on the thriving Dutch plantation, and longed to oust the possessors from the comfortable homes they had established and fill them with their own families; and, with the domineering disposition they always displayed, the Massachusetts colonists tried to wrest the lands on Mana-ha-ta from the Dutch, who had discovered the territory, and lawfully purchased it from the aborigines, and, failing in the attempt, pioneers from Massachusetts encroached on the Dutch possessions wherever it was possible, and, when once settled within its confines, it was impossible to drive them away.

Between the turbulent Swedes to the left, the encroaching English to the right, the marauding Indians and French on the north, the dread of invasion by way of the sea, and the squabbles and dissensions within the precincts of Mana-ha-ta, Governor Stuyvesant had a busy life.

The Goede Vrouw of Mana-ha-ta

The chronicles of the day record his journeying to Connecticut to repel some English settlers who had built on the Dutch possessions, or sailing to the "South" River to conquer the Swedes; and the records of the "Honorable Council" are filled with his letters to that board of municipal governors describing his adventures. When at home he was constantly called upon for the decisive vote in the council, and intricate law cases were submitted to him for jurisdiction.

A close study of the records of New Amsterdam throws some light on the domestic and political life in the colony. The council was composed of the most noteworthy or esteemed men of the place—Beekman, Van Teenhoven, Johannes de Peyster, Charles Brown (a renegade Englishman who afterward left the colony. In the records his name is given as Carel Van Brugh, but he seems to have been no relation to Johannes Van Brugh), Govert Lockermans, Jacobus Kip, etc., with Governor Stuyvesant as presiding officer. All affairs, great and small, were brought before the council, who were forced to enact city ordinances—one of which was against the hogs of the East India Company, as these hogs wandered at will through the streets and preferred to uproot the walls of the fort to disposing of the garbage, as they should have done. The question of bakers' bread was a serious one, that took much of the time of the councilmen, as complaints were loud and frequent from the towns-people that the bread was under-weight, or not made of properly bolted flour.

Der Colonie Nieu Nederlands

The question of the proper quality of sewant and wampum was frequently a source of contention, as the pious settlers of the Massachusetts colony were not above mingling the native currency of shells with beads of glass, wood, and iron, and passing the worthless coinage as the true currency.

One amusing case came before the council when Madame Geues accused Goody Huybert of stealing linen napkins that were bleaching on the former's lawn. The Goody was brought into the court-room and loudly protested her innocence, and, on being remanded without bail, tried to steal off in a boat to Beverwyck. The schout (sheriff) was too quick for her, and arrested her and brought her again to the Stadt-Huys, where the whole council — governor, schepens, burgomasters, schout, fiscal, etc. — were assembled to try the case. The napkins in question were brought into court and identified by Madame Geues, and after some discussion, as the lady was by no means implacable, and only demanded that the napkins be restored to her, Goody Huybert was ordered to depart to Beverswyck, never to return to Mana-ha-ta on pain of imprisonment.

Among the peculiar persons who were attracted to the Dutch colony was an Englishwoman by the name of Lady Moody. She had been driven from the Massachusetts settlement, as Roger Williams and so many other worthies were, and she was forced to seek refuge at Gravesend, or Nassau, on Long Island, where the modest house that she had erected for herself overlooked the harbor and was opposite the plantation of Margaret Hardenbrook de Vries, on Meta Kooseka (Staten Island).

The religious views of Lady Moody are incomprehensible in these days, but she held them with tenacity, and was contented to expatriate herself in order to be allowed to believe them in peace. She was a studious woman, and surrounded herself in her isolated home with a collection of books which at that time was the most valuable on the continent. Mrs. Stuyvesant persuaded her husband to pay with her an official visit to the recluse and extend to her his gubernatorial protection. The governor and his wife were charmed with the learning of Lady Moody, and the ægis of their friendship enabled her to live in peace and contentedly to the end of her life in her lonely home.

But the governor was not equally lenient to the Quakers, who flocked to his settlement from that of Massachusetts, and he ordered them away and treated them with great harshness. One of them was ordered to be whipped, and "endured the lash until he fainted, for several days in succession, and was thought to be near his end." He was then ordered to "work at the wheel-barrow," which he refused to do. It was then that Madame Anna Bayard, who was a woman of very enlightened views, interfered in behalf of the unfortunate man. She implored her brother to release him, and importuned him so persistently and

Der Colonie Nieu Nederlands

effectually that at last the governor was induced to liberate him.

Director-General Stuyvesant's harshness to the Quakers was reported to the States General of Holland, and the governor was reproved for his severity and commanded to tolerate all religious beliefs, after the manner of Patria, to whose shielding arms Huguenots, Labbadists, Quakers, Puritans, etc., were wont to flock, sure of finding protection and tolerance within the borders of Holland.

The governor, balked of his little amusement of frying and boring holes in the Quakers, after the example of his English friends in Massachusetts, turned his attention to Fort Orange, and brewed a quarrel with Brant Van Slechtenhorst, the director of Rensselaerswyck. The dispute arose over the boundary-line between Fort Orange and the surrounding hamlet of Beverswyck, which was undoubtedly on the manor lands. There were two wrongs and no right to the discussion, which waxed hot and fierce, and Governor Stuyvesant started for Rensselaerswyck in his yacht. He had a stormy voyage up the Hudson that lasted a fortnight before he could land his army of about twenty men at the Fuyck,* as the Dutch called the disputed territory. Director Van Slechtenhorst was seized and

---

*Fuyck is the name of a fishing-net that is very large at one end and tapers to a point at the other. The disputed property was of this shape, and hence the nickname. At one time the city of Albany was always called De Fuyck.

imprisoned for refusing to strike the flag of the patroon to the governor's signal, and also for defending the manorial rights of his master, and was carried off to Mana-ha-ta by the orders of Governor Stuyvesant, where he was imprisoned. During his absence, Jeremias Van Rensselaer, the son of the patroon, was ordered to assume the directorship of the manor. Governor Stuyvesant always meant well, but generally allowed his hot temper to lead him to do wrong, and this high-handed deed led to much confusion, which took time and trouble to set straight, and it was not until the colonies passed into the hands of the English that commissioners were appointed by their new owner, the Duke of York, to decide on the title of the patroon and the rights of the director of the colony of Rensselaerswyck, with the result that the fee of all the land seized by Stuyvesant was restored to the manor, and Van Slechtenhorst was honorably acquitted, although not compensated for his unwarrantable arrest and imprisonment. Among the commissioners that arbitrated this dispute, was John Churchill, afterward the celebrated Duke of Marlborough, and it was said that the fees that he received on this occasion laid the foundation of his fortune.

IX

New York vs. New Amsterdam

Alarming News—Visit of Governor Stuyvesant to Rensselaerswyck—Indian Outbreak—The Brave Governor—The English Fleet—The Earls of Stirling and their Property in America—The Birth of New York—Feast Days and Holidays—The Predicament of Governor Nicoll—Colonel Lovelace's Reception at Rensselaerswyck—Refinement of the Dutch Families—Anecdote of the Ambassador of the Court of St. James—Recapture of Mana-ha-ta—Sunday Observances—New York and Its Cosmopolitan Inhabitants—The First Assemblies.

THE ladies of Mana-ha-ta exerted all their influence over the governor and his council to persuade them to rest at peace with the other colonies, even at the risk of losing some territory, and they gained the consent of the authorities to allow all persons to exercise their religious beliefs in freedom and quiet, after the manner of Holland, which was the most enlightened country of the day in those matters, where each person might follow his own religious convictions without question from neighbors or government; and it was with a sense of relief that the women of Mana-ha-ta discovered that their husbands and fathers had yielded to these entreaties, and were busily employed in a new and quite harmless pursuit, and that the meetings of the council were now occupied in selecting a device for a flag for the colony. In this the women were only too glad to aid them, and did so, by making a silk banner embroidered with the selected device, which was the arms of the New Netherland Company, and they presented it to the governor for his own use, while a less elaborate banner was made by a milliner, under the direction of the council, which was to flaunt from the flag-pole in the fort.

Up to the middle of the seventeenth century the colony on Mana-ha-ta had received no official cognomen; even the spelling of the Wilden's name was eccentric and changeable. The place was at first such an unimportant trading-post that it was hardly worthy of the honor of a title. Then as it grew in importance and was regularly colonized by the West India Company, all the country at the mouth of the Hudson River was vaguely designated as The New Netherlands. But as time wore on, and the company was rent with internal dissensions, the States General of Holland gradually assumed protection over the plantation, and they determined to encourage the settlement on the island of Mana-ha-ta by taking it publicly under their care and bestowing on it a more distinctive name than the Towne of Mannados, as it had sometimes been called. It was therefore arranged by the governor and council, under instructions from the home government, to hold a grand and formal function on one of the feasts of the Church, and accordingly, on Candlemas, February

New York vs. New Amsterdam

2, 1653, amid firing of guns and general feasting at White Hall, and rejoicing among the towns-people, the new silk banner was unfurled on the governor's house, and the seals of the town (which had been carefully arranged by the best heraldic authorities in the colony) were duly impressed on the parchment which proclaimed that the tiny "dorp" had developed into a "burgh," with properly authorized officials, and that the name of the new city was to be henceforth and forever New Amsterdam.

The good people flattered themselves that the name would be as imperishable as the government that they instituted, and indeed for eleven years all went fairly well, and the town throve and grew in importance; but, even during this time of seeming prosperity, the Dutch burghers were troubled by rumors from Europe that warned them that the English government (egged on by the envious settlers at Massachusetts) were arranging to invade their settlement and annex it to the other British possessions in America.

New Amsterdam was in no condition to repel an invasion. Its fort was a wretched structure that could not even withstand the attacks of the city hogs, but was crumbling under their daily onslaughts. Nor had the town any money to repair it, or throw up new defences, or even to pay an army to occupy and defend it, much less provision it against a siege.

Governor Stuyvesant did what he could to put the city in a proper condition. He ordered the breeches in the fort to be filled with earth; he sent to the neighboring farmers, and commanded them to hasten to New Amsterdam with all the provender that they could spare, and set his own servants to work to gather his crops, intending to take them inside the walls, and devote the products of his farms to the welfare of his subjects, and so provision them against a siege. But the governor needed money, and was forced to turn for help to the rich and prosperous principality that adjoined his settlement, and write to the colony of Rensselaerswyck for assistance; and although, after the high-handed treatment received by Director Van Slechtenhorst, there was little cordiality between the two governments, Stuyvesant was forced to eat humble-pie and beg the present director (Jeremias Van Rensselaer) to aid him in the dilemma.

A landsdaght, or diet, was convened in New Amsterdam in the early part of 1664, over which "der Groot Director" was requested to preside. The members were called on to deliberate on the unprotected state of the colony, and the Manor of Rensselaerswyck was asked to loan money to erect proper fortifications on Mana-ha-ta. The modest sum requested was 5,000 or 6,000 guelders, and Stuyvesant urgently demanded this in a letter dated July 8, 1664, addressed to his "Honorable and dear Heer Van Rensselaer." The director positively refused to advance the sum required without security, and the irate governor was forced to board his yacht and brave the perils of a voyage up the Hudson River to Rensselaerswyck, hoping to soften the heart of the director and persuade him that it was to his own advantage to defend New Amsterdam from the English, not only by giving money, but also by ordering out the reserves of the colony in its defence. This the director was quite able to do; he had a large sum of money at his command from the resources of the colony, and he also had a good private fortune. Madame Van Rensselaer was also rich and the daughter of one of the wealthiest citizens of New Amsterdam. The governor was received on his arrival at Rensselaerswyck with all the honors befitting his office, and der Heer Van Rensselaer and his wife gave a grand entertainment for him, but the weighty errand on which Stuyvesant had come was politely put aside and ignored.

The director could have called out a goodly troop to rally under his flag had he been so disposed, as every tenant on the manor was bound by his oath of allegiance to the patroon to obey a call to arms at the shortest notice; but Madame Van Cortlandt in New Amsterdam, and Madame Van Rensselaer, her daughter, at Rensselaerswyck, threw all their womanly influence into the scale to prevent calling out the troops, or advancing money. The ladies dreaded a war beyond all things, and they seemed to imagine that they could avert it if they could prevent the defensive preparations for it. As things turned out, perhaps they were wise in stopping warlike demonstrations that would have been insufficient and ineffectual, and they certainly prevented bloodshed. Their argument was "that they cared nothing about who were called the lawgivers or rulers in Europe, as long as they commanded at home," and while they were disputing the weighty question with their lords, armed only with their womanly weapon, the tongue, they conquered before their lords and masters realized what was going on.

It was no wonder that the ladies wanted peace at any price; they had only lately recovered from the terrors of an Indian outbreak, and hardly yet slept comfortably in their beds. The Masquaas, on the west side of the Hudson, and the Machicans, on its east, had gone on the war-path to revenge the murder of a young brave who had been wantonly killed by a drunken, worthless scamp, who had wandered to Mana-ha-ta from another colony. The Wilden did not separate the unauthorized deeds of an outcast from organized attacks of a government, and they simply revenged their wrongs on the first defenceless person that they could find, and, after murdering several trappers who were quietly pursuing their work in the forests, the savages finally fell on the scattered settlements on Staten Island, Pavonia, and Hoboken, and murdered men, women, and children in their sleep. The "up-river" tribes joined in what they determined should be a war of extermination, and the massacres extended to Esopus, a settlement on the Hudson River, half-way between Mana-ha-ta and Rensselaerswyck, the inhabitants of which were murdered in cold blood, while a terrific encounter took place on Nutten Island;

New York vs. New Amsterdam

and although the Indians were driven to their canoes, it was not without considerable loss of life among the colonists, who, while defending the Mana-ha-ta settlement on the south, learned, to their consternation, that Madame Stuyvesant, with her children and a few attendants, were at their "bouwerie," some miles north of the city walls, and with no adequate means of defence. The governor was absent on one of his many missions, but the brave lady sent word to the burghers that they need feel no alarm on her account, and quietly sent for a number of Frenchmen who had lately come to the colony in search of work, and engaged them to defend her house, which she prepared for a siege. The savages fortunately did not attack her, and gradually returned to the interior without doing any further damage, and the community settled shudderingly down to something approaching repose, and prayed that they might be left in peace by Indians and Europeans.

But their tranquillity was of short duration, and the people of New Amsterdam were startled from their beds early in the morning of August 22, 1664, by the booming of guns which they knew could not come from their ruined fort, and they were terrified when they learned that their foes were upon them, and that four English war-vessels were in the lower bay, just below "the Narrows."

Governor Stuyvesant was again away enjoying the hospitalities of his kind hosts at Rensselaerswyck, and the few troops that were at his command were either in attendance on him or were supine and without a leader in the worthless fortifications.

This English marauding expedition was commanded by Colonel Richard Nicolls, a groom of the bed-chamber to James, Duke of York, lord high admiral of England and brother of Charles II., king of Great Britain, Ireland and Wales. The Stuarts were always impecunious, extravagant, and unscrupulous, and they lost no opportunity of enriching themselves at other persons' expense. When one of the common herd took other persons' property in those days, he was punished by death or transportation, and his crime was called "theft," but when the same deed was committed by royalty, particularly if it was done by English royalty, it was commended as an honorable action by the loyal subjects and the historians, however the victims might protest and nations remonstrate. An iron arm silenced all objections, and the "king ruled by divine right."

The enterprise against the Dutch colony was quietly planned. The English had no real dispute with them, although at war with Holland, a country which was at that date "masters of the sea." So, after the fashion of England, it turned its arms against the little Dutch settlement at Mana-ha-ta rather than the well-defended ports of Holland, and the small English fleet slipped past the Dutch men-of-war in the European waters and sailed across the ocean to take possession of a colony that had not the power and scarcely the will to defend itself.

New York vs. New Amsterdam

The Duke of York, in his position of lord high admiral of England, was able to direct naval expeditions and turn them to his own advantage. The diary of Samuel Pepys, who was one of the naval board at that time, shows the corrupt condition of all the government departments under the misguidance of Charles Stuart, and particularly that of the naval, which was controlled by the brother of the king. The Duke of York determined to make a kingdom for himself in the New World; he had seen how his servant William Penn was becoming rich and independent; he was well acquainted with the success of the colony at Rensselaerswyck, and had looked with envy at the growth and increase of the Mana-ha-ta plantation. By a curious and ingenious process of reasoning, the Duke of York considered that the island of Stirling, Nassau, or Long Island, as it was variously termed, belonged to himself, together with what are now known as the States of New York and New Jersey. It is true that the duke had bought the land from Henry, the third Earl of Stirling, but, with characteristic forgetfulness, he had omitted to pay any part of the purchase-money, and had acquired no title whatever to the lands in question; but that was of no consequence in the eyes of his royal highness.

In order to arrive at any understanding of the question, it is necessary to revert to the ancestors of the earls of Stirling and their early connection with the house of Stuart.

The family of Alexander traces its descent from Alexander McDonald, a younger son of John, Lord of the Isles, by his marriage with Margaret, daughter of Robert II. of Scotland. The clans of McDonald, McAllister, etc., are of this descent. The seat of the ancient barons is at Meustrie, five miles east of Stirling, in Scotland, at the base of the Ochiel Hills, on a small stream in the shire of Clackmannon. It had been occupied since 1485. Alexander Alexander (which name was a corruption or variation of McAllister) was fifth Baron Meustrie. He died February 10, 1580, leaving a brother, John Alexander, who inherited the estates of Gogar, and a son, William Alexander, who inherited the estates of Meustrie, and was created, in 1633, Earl of Stirling, Viscount Canada, and Lord Alexander of Tullibordie.

William Alexander, sixth Baron and Laird of Meustrie, was a man of education and accomplishments far in advance of most of the Scotchmen of his time. When a young man, he had made the tour of Europe with his cousin, the Earl of Argyle. It was an unparalleled journey to make in those days, and conferred an air of distinction and breeding on the young traveller that could not have been acquired in the fastnesses of his native land. William Alexander had also acquired a reputation as a scholar and a poet, and as he was " a sprightly youth and possessed of elegant manners," he was soon introduced into the highest court circles, where he became a general favorite and the intimate friend of King James VI. of Scotland. The young men had met by chance on a sporting expedition among the cliffs of Ben Cleugh, and the king invited Alexander to Stirling Castle, with the result that the boyish acquaintance ripened into a well-cemented friendship.

James consulted his friend on all occasions, and implicitly followed his advice. It is said that "he esteemed him greatly as a wise and learned man," and his majesty was pleased to prefer him to the "Master of the Requests," and made him a knight. In one of the king's letters, he calls Sir William Alexander "my well-beloved companion and philosophical friend." The king was somewhat of a pedant, and loved to be considered wise, and he found it convenient to have always at his elbow a well-informed person on whose accuracy and learning he could depend; and his majesty often quoted Sir William Alexander's opinions as if they were his own, greatly to the amusement of the scholar, who, while recognizing the source of some of the wise sayings of his king, only bowed in humble admiration of the learning of his master, as a good courtier should do.

In 1621 the Laird of Menstrie became greatly interested in the exploration and discoveries on the American continent, and he succeeded in inflaming the king's curiosity about the New World. After some debate, the laird and his master concluded to colonize, and concocted a scheme by which they might enrich themselves with little trouble or expense. By quietly ignoring the claims of other nations of prior discovery, and overlooking as worthless the ownership of the aborigines, they decided that the king of England was sovereign of all of America above the fortieth degree of latitude and below the St. Lawrence River. Under these conditions, James granted to his "well-beloved friend" a royal charter under the great seal, dated at Windsor Castle, September 10, 1621, which gave to the laird of Meustrie all the territory lying to the east of the River St. Croix and south of the St. Lawrence River. Sir William, in return for this large grant of land, undertook to colonize it at his own expense, and accordingly, in March, 1622, the first expedition of settlers left England for the New World. The vessel in which they set sail only succeeded in reaching the shores of Newfoundland, and, after the emigrants had suffered incredible hardships, the enterprise was abandoned. But Alexander by no means relinquished his project, into which the king entered most heartily, and between them they arranged a new plan of colonization, which would accomplish the purpose at no expense to themselves. This was, to divide the country into large tracts that should carry with each estate a title, after the fashion of Holland, where certain demesnes were called "Reddergoeds," the owners of which bore as a title the name of the land. The purchasers of the estates were required to pledge themselves to colonize at their own expense, within a certain period, under pain of the forfeiture of the property, and were to be permitted to select an appropriate title for themselves and their purchase, on the payment of a certain sum of money to Sir William Alexander.

It was under this arrangement that the knights baronets of England were created in April, 1625, by Sir William Alexander, and all the patents were signed by him; and one hundred and fifty baronets were thus created under his own patent, which proves how greedily the bait was seized by the wealthy men of England, who gladly purchased a title that carried with it large grants of land on what they fancied were easy terms. It proved so indeed, as none of the baronets carried out the provisions of the purchase, which were to colonize the new country as soon as possible, and, in consequence, the estates in Nova Scotia reverted to the original grantor, while the gentlemen retained their titles, which was all that they desired to have, and remained residents of their native land. The king and his "philosophical friend" found themselves enriched by the sale of these titles and the land that they had acquired without effort or expense. The first baronets were styled "of Nova Scotia," and the initials N. S. are still to be found in the peerage after the names of the one hundred and fifty first creations.

The affection of the royal family for Sir William Alexander did not cease on the death of James I. His son and successor, Charles I., gave Sir William the privilege of coining small copper money, and also made him secretary of state for Scotland, which office he filled for fifteen years, for which he was created a peer and made Earl of Stirling, a title that was selected by the king himself and bestowed as an especial mark of the royal favor, as it was that of his own hereditary stronghold, the great Scottish castle of Stirling.

In 1628 Alexander had received a fresh grant of territory that covered all the country that lay between the St. Lawrence River and the Delaware River, from the Atlantic to the Pacific Ocean.

There is in the office of the Herald King of Arms a letter from the king, dated March 15, 1632, addressed to Sir James Balfour, Lyon King of Arms, ordering him to marshal the arms of the lately created Viscount Stirling, and in January 28, 1635, the arms of the earl were again augmented, by order of his majesty. In January, 1634, the land (or continent) granted to the Earl of Stirling had been most particularly confirmed to him, with the additional specified tract, which, in the words of the original deed (now on file in the Land Office), is as follows: "That part of the Main land in New England, from St. Croix (River) adjoining New Scotland, along the sea-coast to Pemaquid, and so up the river to the Kenebequi, to be henceforth called the County of Canada, also the Island of Matowack or Long Island, to the West of Cape Cod, to be hereafter called Isle of Stirling."

The son of the first earl who bore the title of Viscount Canada pre-deceased his father, and the title was inherited by a young child who did not long survive, but died three months after his grandfather. The title then reverted to Henry, the second son of the first Earl of Stirling, who had married Mary, the daughter of Sir Peter Vanlooe, an alderman of London. The third Earl of Stirling died August 16, 1664, but before his death he had found his estates in America a most troublesome possession. By his commands, an agent by the name of Forrester, Forest, or Farett, as it is variously spelled, had emigrated to the Isle of Stirling in order to look after the interests of the English proprietor. Under authority from the Earl of Stirling, Major Forrester had sold a considerable amount of property to settlers who had wandered there from other colonies and who were glad to receive what they considered good titles for the land they occupied and already had under cultivation, and also to consider themselves under the protection of England. The Isle of Wight, now known as "Gardiner's Island," was bought from the Indian owners, but it also received a title from Major Forrester, as agent of the Earl of Stirling.

These transactions came to the ears of Governor Stuyvesant, who believed that the land in question belonged to his masters, the States General of Holland, and were under his jurisdiction. The governor therefore quietly sent for Major Forrester, who unsuspiciously went to a conference held at Mana-ha-ta, where he was seized by order of the governor and put on a vessel bound for Holland. The governor, no doubt, thought that he had easily disposed of a troublesome person who was encroaching on his prerogative, but, as it happened, the vessel on which Major Forrester was transported was wrecked on the English coast, and he made his escape from his captors and proceeded to London, where he laid his case before his employer, Lord Stirling, who at once carried his grievances to the ears of the king. It was under these circumstances that the Duke of York offered to buy out the rights of the Earl of Stirling, who gladly sold them for the sum of £7,000, and the Duke of York, without going through the formality of putting down the purchase-money or acquiring the necessary title-deeds, immediately sent the expedition to seize on the Dutch plantations in the New World. The expedition was quietly planned, and the colonists had hardly received warning of the project before their foes were upon them.

Governor Stuyvesant rushed from Rensselaerswyck to New Amsterdam as speedily as possible, only to find matters beyond his control. He had no defences, no soldiers, no provisions, and no money at his command. The burghers, incited by their vrouwen, declared their intention of capitulating, as they preferred to keep their houses, property, and lives intact, and they saw that there was but little hope of successfully defending their unprotected situation. The governor, however, showed fight, like the brave warrior that he was, and he ordered the guns to be manned and fired on the enemy, but here again he was balked, and this time by the dominie, who laid his hand on the governor's arm and commanded peace.

New York vs. New Amsterdam

Worried and harassed on every side, unsupported by his council, defied by the petticoat government, the poor governor could only submit and sign articles of capitulation, and then retire disgusted to his bouwerie.

September 8, 1664, saw the untimely end of the Dutch burgh of New Amsterdam and the birth of the city of New York, which sprang, like Minerva, full-grown from a warrior's head. Down came the ladies' silken flag, and was carried off (to be used as a bed-spread by one of the thrifty dames), and up went the banner of St. George, and for over one hundred years the colony was doomed to be oppressed by the misrule and avarice of the rapacious English government, with only a brief respite during the few months in 1673 when it returned to the order and tranquillity that prevailed under the rule of the States General of Holland, before being again brought under the English government.

Johannes Van Brugh, burgomaster and schepen of New Amsterdam, was one of the first of the Dutch worthies to bow his neck to the yoke. He lived in a stone house on Hanover Square, and some of the handsomest trees on the island shaded his house, which was large and well-furnished, after the manner of Holland. At the suggestion of Madame Van Brugh (who was the daughter of Annekje Jans) they gave a large entertainment in honor of the new arrivals, and invited all their friends to meet Governor Nicolls and his suite, as the good lady hoped to conciliate the English in this way; and as she and her husband were among the oldest inhabitants they considered that the duties of hospitality fell on their shoulders in the absence of the official representative of their countrymen. It was unfortunate that the entertainment was not received in the spirit in which it was tendered. The new arrivals were haughty and overbearing in their manners, and, it is said, misbehaved themselves toward their hosts and their guests, so that the well-meant efforts of the good lady resulted in making a breach between the governor and the people of the town, for which his excellency was heartily sorry when he began to realize how much he had lost by his rude behavior. After-efforts toward reconciliation (which, to do the governor justice, he did his best to make) never completely healed the breach caused by the first outbreak at this entertainment. The officials were obliged to meet Governor Nicolls at occasional formal entertainments, but the staid and older members of the town, particularly the ladies, would have nothing whatever to do with his excellency or his court, and they were quietly ignored in all the pleasant entertainments which were constantly being given on the sociable little island of Mana-ha-ta.

Apparently the ladies were correct in their opinion that a change of name and owners would make but little difference in the happiness of the community. It was many years before they realized that it had not been for the good of the people, as at first they believed it to be. The English rulers could not speak the language of their subjects, and almost all were retained in the official positions that they had held previous to the conquest, and the place apparently remained a Dutch settlement, and the new governor was a thing apart from the home-life of the colonists, and had no influence over their social customs. The Dutch vrouwen controlled their households as before, and governed their husbands with silken threads. The "good man" was permitted to make the acquaintance of the English, and the young folks to mingle in the amusements devised to conciliate and amuse them by the new governor, who was accustomed to the life of a court, but the worthy vrouwen held aloof and bided their time.

There were many feast-days and holidays that were always observed by the Dutch. Paas was a cherished one and never forgotten, nor was Candlemas overlooked. New Year's Day was the grand festival of the year, and its observance, inaugurated by the first settlers, was handed down to their descendants, and was followed until about 1870, when the size of the city of New York rendered its further observance impossible. The Dutch ladies always made grand preparations for the great feast of "Nieuw-Jaar," and that of 1667 was more rigorously observed than usual, as they wished to mark their adherence to their time-honored customs. Each burgher rose early and dressed himself with care, prepared to go the rounds of the city and call on every lady of his acquaintance, to wish her a happy new year.

The governor's wife and his sister, Mrs. Bayard, received the honor of the first visit. They sat in state in the best parlor of their bouwerie, clad in their handsomest robes, and received sluy after sluy load of visitors. The best part of the function was the tasting and sipping of various cordials prepared by the matrons themselves after secret family receipts. The wine was handed with the remark, "Credencense!" and accepted with a deep bow and the wish of "A happy new year," after which each gentleman bowed himself out, to be succeeded by nearly every man of the little town who wished to pay his respects to the governor's wife, while the first-comers hastened back to the city to greet every lady of his acquaintance with the same good wishes.

It sometimes happened that among the festivals which the Dutch patronized in memory of Patria all were not held under proper supervision, and they therefore degenerated and became like the kermiss—too much of an orgy to please the proper women of the town. One of these was called the Feast of Bacchus, and the revels became so unlicensed that the attention of the governor was called to them, with the entreaty that he would take measures to repress its celebration. It was denounced as "unprofitable, unnecessary, and censurable," and it was called a "pagan feast, tho' it may be tolerated and looked at thro' the fingers in Patria."

The hospitality and simple pleasures wisely instituted by the Dutch made the city of New York unique among its neighbors, and, down to the outbreak of the Revolution, its inhabitants were noted for their kindness to strangers. "All felt it, all praised it," says a contemporary writer; "nothing was too good and no attention too engrossing for a stranger. That name was a passport to everything kind and generous. All who were introduced to the new-comer invited him to home and board, and treated him like one of the family." The houses even were planned like those of Madame Van Cortlandt, with a "slaap-bauck" in the sitting-room ready to be offered to a stranger at a moment's notice.

The sixth of December (St. Nicolaus's Day) was especially honored the year the Dutch city had capitulated to the English fleet. It was the saint's-day of the burgh, and was always celebrated with peculiar ceremonies. All the Dutch citizens were decorated by their vrouwen with new orange-colored bands or ribbons, on which were inscribed the old Dutch war-cry, "Orange Boven." This afforded much quiet amusement to Governor Nicolls and his English officers, who felt that they could afford to allow such a harmless exhibition of loyalty to Holland from burghers who went no farther in their demonstrations. But in spite of the seeming security and supremacy of the English governor, who proclaimed the "duke's laws" and instituted many changes in the government, he was in fact in a mighty precarious position. From the time of his arrival in the colony he had received no support from the home government, no provisions, and no clothing for his soldiers, and they were few in number and utterly inadequate for his needs. He tried to fill his empty "chest" by building a tavern adjoining the alley beside the

The Goede Vrouw of Mana-ha-ta

Stadt-Huys, on Pearl Street, opposite Coenties Slip. A covered way connected the two places, much to the horror of the Dutch worthies, who thus saw "tapping" and drinking encouraged by the governor, when it had always been hitherto the practice to frown on or prevent it. The Duke of York had been willing enough to seize on the American colony when it cost him nothing, as he hoped to get a large revenue from it at no expense to himself; he wanted money from his new possessions, but had no idea of spending any, even to insure his retaining them. The town, which had been poorly fortified against his attack, was no stronger than at its capitulation. The English governor was surrounded by enemies—passive and peace-loving ones it might be, but still quite willing to return to their allegiance to Holland, and on the slightest encouragement to send him to a rural retreat after his predecessor, Governor Stuyvesant.

Two tribes of savages on the northern border went on the "war-path," and Governor Nicolls was distracted with anxiety. Of course the worthy denizens of the colony were well-acquainted with these difficulties, and hoped that they would disgust the English and force them to leave the plantation. Nicolls tried to coerce his subjects into contributing money for his expenses, but as he had no means of enforcing commands when he issued them, he was no better off than he was before.

The small English army quartered in the battered fort were barely sheltered from the elements, and only provided with coarse and dirty straw for bedding that had been discarded by the Dutch soldiers as worthless, and the old vrouwen of the place shook their heads over the thriftlessness of a government that failed to provide for the health and comforts of its dependents, and the ladies were delighted when they heard of a letter the English commander had written to his superiors, in which he said: "Such is our straits that not one soldier to this day, since I brought him out of England, has been in a pair of sheets." To the Dutch vrouwen, who knew how dependent their husbands were on home comforts and cleanliness, this state of affairs meant defeat and the probable abandonment of the enterprise by the enemy, who had so far gained nothing by their capture; since the women concluded that the soldiers would rebel unless their wants were better attended to. The soldiers, however, were forced to remain, and it was Governor Nicolls who resigned and, determined to beat a retreat, demanded his recall from the home government. Colonel Francis Lovelace soon arrived to take his place.

The new governor found many vexed questions awaiting his arrival for adjustment, and among others, the dispute on the northern borders with the savages. Nicolls carried Colonel Lovelace in the gubernatorial yacht to Rensselaerswyck, and the governors spent a week at the manor-house, and were fêted by the patroon and his wife. The hospitality and courteous manners of the Dutch families keenly impressed the soldier-governor, who found, in what he supposed would be a wilderness, more refinements and luxuries than he was accustomed to at home. King Charles had particularly recommended him to be friendly with the Patroon Van Rensselaer, to whom and to whose family the king had been so greatly indebted during his exile; and Governor Lovelace, after being entertained at Rensselaerswyck, wrote a private letter to his sovereign, in which he said, "I find some of the people have the breeding of courts, and I cannot imagine how such is acquired."

There was another ambassador connected with the Court of St. James, who was at the same time discovering for himself that the English were behind the Dutch in their notions of good-breeding and cleanliness. This was Sir William Temple, who had been sent ambassador to The Hague. He was one of "the most elegant and accomplished gentlemen at the court of Charles II.—a wit among the courtiers, and a courtier among the wits," says Macaulay in his "Essays." This great man, who had inherited a handsome estate from his father, Sir James Temple (Master of the Rolls in Ireland, and one of the Privy Councillors), was educated at Cambridge, and was fond of literary pursuits, and jotted down some of his experiences during his residence among the Dutch, where, says Macaulay, "he was surrounded by objects interesting in the highest degree to a man of his observant mind. The simple life of the burghers struck him with astonishment; he was accustomed to see in England great display and but few com-

New York vs. New Amsterdam

forts." "Dining one day with the chief burgomaster of Amsterdam, he noticed that every time that he spat on the floor, while at table, a tight, handsome wench, who stood in a corner holding a cloth, got down on her knees and wiped it up. Seeing this, he turned to his host and apologized for the trouble he was giving, and received the jocular response: 'It is well for you that my wife is not at home, for she would have turned you out of the house for soiling her floor, although you are the English ambassador.'"

Mana-ha-ta was destined to be captured and recaptured, time after time, without a blow being struck in its defence, and the year 1673 saw its capitulation to a Dutch fleet, which sailed into the harbor and quietly demanded that the English robbers should renounce their prey. Governor Lovelace had no option but to obey, and the burghers and their wives rejoiced greatly over the bloodless victory. The latter pointed out with pride that lives, property, etc., were intact, and all owing to the feminine judgment that had counselled submission to the English the year before, when the British fleet had been the conquerors without firing a musket, and in turn had yielded to the superior force without even a word of protest. The English had jeered at the Dutch for their cowardice, and in turn had displayed the same pusillanimity.

Now, the most worthy of the citizens of Mana-ha-ta were called on to form a government. Admiral Colve (one of the commanders of the Dutch fleet) was placed in the governor's chair; Oloff Van Cortlandt, William Beekman, Johannes de Peyster, Nicholas Bayard, and Guilian Verplanck composed the council, and occupied themselves at once in restoring to the city its Dutch laws, civic seals, and old insignia.

The dignified custom of observing Sunday was at once resumed, and the first one after the capitulation saw the worthy governor, schepens, and burgomaster meeting at the Stadt-Huys, when summoned by the tolling of the bell, clad in long cloaks and huge bell-crowned hats, marching in stately procession, striking in unison their ponderous gold-topped staffs of office, to the old church, preceded by the "bell-ringer," carrying velvet cushions to be placed in the government pew for the better ease and comfort of the worthy magistrates; while their wives and children quietly gathered in the same building, each one provided with a small square "foot-stove," which warmed their feet during the long and somewhat tiresome thanksgiving services that ensued.

But this state of affairs was not destined to last long. The Dutch colonies in America had been for years a source of trouble and annoyance to the States General of Holland, who had been forced to protect their emigrants at great expense to the state, while the profits of the colony were absorbed by the West India Company. The government could protect the water-soaked lands of Holland during the war with England with comparative ease, but it was difficult to defend a colony the boundaries of which were so undefined and of such great extent; it was little wonder, then, that, when arranging the treaty of peace between the Netherlands and England, the colony of Mana-ha-ta became a shuttlecock between the two powers, and the Fatherland finally tossed it, with a sense of relief, into the hands of the rapacious English.

Governor Colve received orders from his government to resign his seals of office to the properly accredited English authority, and on February 9, 1674, Sir Edmund Andross arrived in the colony, and Mana-ha-ta yielded again to a bloodless conquest, quietly resumed the name of New York, accepted the English officials and their laws, tucked the silken flag of New Amsterdam over the bed of the goede vrouw who reclaimed her handiwork, and settled down to the altered state of affairs with as much grace as possible.

While it is true that the inhabitants of the plantation on the Hudson River were chiefly of Dutch extraction, many of the immigrants were from other countries. Having found in Holland relief from religious persecution, many of these persons gradually drifted to the New World, where they felt more sure of a livelihood than was possible in the crowded countries of Europe, and the point of attraction in America was the Dutch settlement. Many of the wanderers had married in Holland, where the women were noted for comeliness, virtue, housewifely qualities, and these ties drew families of mixed blood to Mana-ha-ta, and the colony became cosmopolitan in its character at a very early date. As early as 1668 arrangements had been made for weekly reunions by the principal families of the town. These sociables were the first of the assemblies, or dances, for which New York has always been noted. The ladies planned the entertainments and kept the management of them always in their own hands. They were at first held at the houses of the members in turn. The quantity and quality of the refreshments were determined on by the matrons, and were simple in the extreme, and generally consisted of roast oysters, cakes, and jellies. The gathering took place at six o'clock in the evening and broke up at nine, precisely, after a nightcap of hot spiced wine, served in silver tankards. These assemblies were continued until the breaking out of the War of the Revolution, and were attended by the descendants of the original projectors, and the membership was almost considered hereditary. The principal families concerned were the Van Cortlandts, De Peysters, Kips, Lockermans, Lawrences, Stuyvesants, Bayards, Proovosts, Varleths, Schricks, etc. As the young people grew up they were permitted to join these assemblies, which became a favorite place for courting, and many matches were made at these hospitable gatherings. But they also covered political meetings, which could be held under the nose of the government without suspicion, where the men discussed affairs of state and their wives were able to throw in quiet words of counsel, that received due attention and had their weight in matters even of the gravest importance.

The first history of Mana-ha-ta, written by a native-born citizen, is worth quoting. The writer was named Daniel Denton, and his descendants live to-day in Jamaica, Long Island, as he did. He was the son of a clergyman, born at East Hampton, Long Island, and settled at Jamaica, where he became a burgomaster, and his description of the colony may be repeated in his own quaint language. It was written in 1670, and, as has before been mentioned, he refutes the derivation of the word Mana-ha-ta, given it by an ignorant English traveller who was unacquainted with the language, and who had blindly adopted some jocose remark and declared that it was derived from a "drunken orgie" held on the island by its discoverers.

This statement is declared incorrect by Denton, and, as he was familiar with the Algonquin language, he is probably right. The author describes the island of Mana-ha-ta in the following words: "Here you need not trouble the shambles for meat, nor Bakers, nor Brewers, for Beer or Bread, nor even to a Linen Draper for a supply. Every one Making their own Linnen and a great part of their Woolen Cloth for their ordinary wearing. You may travel from one end of the country to the other with as much security as if you were lockt within your own Chamber, and if you chance to meet with an Indian Town they shall give you the best Entertainment they have, and upon your desire direct you on your way. But that which adds Happiness to all the rest is the Healthfulness of the place where many people in 20 years time never know what sickness is. Which they look upon as a great Mortality if 2 or 3 die out of a town in a years time—you shall scarce see a house but the South side is begirt with Hives of Bees which increase after an incredible Manner."

X

Passing of the Pioneers

Death of Governor Stuyvesant, and His Epitaph—Death of Mr. and Mrs. Van Cortlandt—Their Children—Purchase of the Van Cortlandt Manor—The Marriage and Home of Dominie Selyns—Death of Annekje Jans—The Varleth Family—Madame de Peyster and Her Children—Marriage of Maria de Peyster and Death of Her Bridegroom—The Second Marriage—The Spratts and the "White Ladye of Baldoon"—The Food of the Early Colonists—Introduction of Vegetables into the Colony—The Wilden's Names for Fish, etc.—Patriotic Crabs—Manufactory of "Sout"—Poems on Fish.

YEARS passed by, and the goede vrouwen were beginning, sorrowfully, to discover that the change in the government was having its effects, and that a change in the manners and customs of the younger generation was taking place in a way that was by no means pleasing to the conservative pioneers. One by one the heads of the families were called to a better land, and there was no one to take their places.

The doughty warrior, Petrus Stuyvesant, died full of years, mourned by all who knew him. Dominie Selyns wrote an epitaph for the occasion in his native language, which hardly seems dignified and worthy of so great a man, and is perhaps the reason why it is not cut on the cenotaph that is now in "St. Mark's, in the Bouwerie," which simply records the name and date of the death of the hero. The lines written by Dominie Selyns were as follows, and contain two puns on the name: "Stuyft niet te seer in't sant want daer leyt Stuyvesant," which may be translated: "Stir not the sand too much, for there lies Stuyvesant."

About the date of the great Dutch governor's death the goede vrouwen of Mana-ha-ta were called to mourn the loss of one of their principal members and first settlers. This was Annekje Lockermans (Madame Van Cortlandt), who died suddenly in 1684, soon after the death of her husband, wise, kind-hearted Olof Stevenzon Van Cortlandt, who died on the 4th of April, and his widow survived only until the 14th of May, and was believed to have died of a broken heart. The worthy old minister, Dominie Selyns, was deeply grieved at the loss of two of his principal parishioners, with whom he had been on terms of the greatest intimacy for many years, and he wrote the following lines as an epitaph for the well-beloved wife and mother:

"GRAAFSCHRIFT.

Voor J. W. Anna Loockermans wede. van den Heer Olof Stephenzon Van Cortlandt, overleden den, 14th May, 1684.

IN DOMINE QUIES.

Hier rust, die sonder rust was tsedert Cortlandts doot,
   En zocht geen rust, dan haest en nevens hem te rusten,
Hy stierf. Sy leest en sterft men rust in Abrams schoot,
   En leest waer Jesus is, in ware rust en lusten.

Passing of the Pioneers

Was Anna* in Godts dienst, badt Hanna † met Godts geest,
 Maer dese was alleen, dat beyde zyn geweest."

These verses have been translated:

Here rests, who after Cortlandt's death no rest possessed,
 And sought no other rest than soon to rest by him.
He died. She lived and died. Both now in Abram rest,
 And there, where Jesus is, true rest and joys abide in.
God's will did Anna serve; God's aid did Anna pray,
 In this alone alike, that both have passed away.

With the death of this noteworthy couple the first degeneration of the true Dutch element of the burgh began. They had borne together all the earliest struggles of the pioneers, seen the birth of the little town they loved so well, aided in its erection into the burgh of New Amsterdam, sorrowfully witnessed its sudden capitulation and the beginning of the English rule, and yet allowed none of these changes to disturb them in their happy family life, and only gathered more closely around them the best elements of the colony and quietly upheld the dignity and traditions of Patria.

Mr. and Mrs. Van Cortlandt had four daughters—Maria, Sophie, Caty, and Neltjie, who were blithesome, comely damsels, and from this group der Heer Director Jeremias Van Rensselaer (who was considered the best match in the colony) selected his bride in 1662. This was one of the first weddings of a native-born American girl, and the rejoicings on the occasion had been very

* Luke ii. 36.   † II. Samuel i. 10 and 11.

great. Sophie Van Cortlandt married Andrew Teller, Caty married first John Duval, and afterward Frederick Phillipse, while Neltjie became the bride of Brant Schuyler, July 12, 1682.

The eldest son, Stephanus Van Cortlandt, married, September 10, 1671, Gertrude Schuyler, and built for her a house on the corner of Broad and Pearl Streets. He also obtained manorial grants, under the English conditions and stipulations, which were quite different from those of the original Dutch grants, as they did not require the proprietor to colonize at his own expense, nor had he the same rights over the tenants, who simply were governed by the laws of the colony and owed no allegiance to the owner, as was the case with the patroonships. One was a principality, the other was a gentleman's estate.

The manor of the Van Cortlandts was granted by patent from Governor Dongan, in 1685, and a handsome country-house was immediately erected there for the family. It is said that the land was originally purchased from the Indians, who rowed the young Dutchman in a canoe up the Hudson River, and, when they reached the selected location, which they called Kitch-a-wan, told him that he might buy for some trifles, that they named, as much land as "a man might travel in a day." To their surprise the offer was quickly accepted, and young Van Cortlandt handed them the purchase-money, and, landing on the shore, mounted a horse that he had ordered brought there and galloped off across the country, thereby covering so much ground "in his day's journey" as made him a great landed proprietor for the rest of his life. Part of the property was a neck of land jutting into the river, and called by the Indians Meanagh. The large inland tract was called Appamapagh.

A highly esteemed lady who lived on Mana-ha-ta was Margaretta De Riener; she married Cornelius Steenwyck, and lived on the corner of Bridge and Whitehall Streets. This couple were very rich, and they loved to gather around their great square dining-table all the young people of the neighborhood, and the weekly supper-parties of Madame Steenwyck were noted far and near. After the death of Mr. Steenwyck, in 1664, his widow married Dominie Selyns. Their house was a typical one of the day, and an inventory of its furniture has fortunately been preserved. The dwelling-room was provided with twelve russia-leather chairs and two velvet chairs with fine silver lace; one cupboard of French nut-wood, one round and one square table, one cabinet, thirteen pictures, and a large looking-glass, five alabaster images, a piece of tapestry for cushions, a flowered tabby chimney-cloth, a pair of flowered tabby curtains, a dressing-box, and a carpet. In the fore-room was a marble table, eleven pictures, seven russia-leather chairs, a clock, etc.

It would seem from these items that Dominie Selyns had been as fortunate as his predecessor Dominie Bogartus had been, when he married Annekje Jans

The Goede Vrouw of Mana-ha-ta

(Van Maesterlandt). This good lady had left New Amsterdam after the intelligence of the shipwreck of her husband reached her and moved to Beverswyck, where she purchased a house on the north side of Yonker Street (now State and James Streets, Albany). Here, beloved by all who knew her, the brisk little widow laid down the law, and controlled the social festivities of the dorp. Shortly before her death, in 1663, she executed a will in favor of her children, which was signed in the presence of Rutger Jacobsen Van Schoendervelt, who had been an intimate friend of her first husband, Roelof Jansen Van Maesterlandt, and had emigrated at the same time, in 1636. The other witness to the will was Evert Jansen Wendell, also an early settler of Beverswyck.

Among the organizers of the assemblies was Madame Caspar Varleth. This name vanished early in the history of the colony, as there were only female descendants. Madame Varleth had three daughters: the eldest was Maria, who married three times, and her husbands were burgomasters and schepens in New Amsterdam and Fort Orange; Judith, the second daughter, married the accomplished nephew of Governor Stuyvesant, Nicholas Bayard, and was the sister-in-law of Maritje Lockermans (Madame Balthazar Bayard), Bladina Kierstede (Madame Petrus Bayard), and Madame Meynt. With this family connection, and owing to the important official posts filled by her husband, Madame Bayard occupied no small place in the little community. Catherine Varleth married Francis de Bruyn, from whom are descended innumerable Browns and Bruens, or Brewens, of the present day, living in the city of New York.

Maria Varleth had an interesting romance at the time of her first nuptials, and her name figures conspicuously in the annals of the town. It appears that the groom had parents living in Holland, and that, being impatient to get married, he did not comply with the laws, and failed to get their written consent to his marriage. The ceremony was however performed, and then the troubles of the young couple began. The council ordered the groom to leave his bride until the parental consent was obtained. The friends of both parties interfered, and finally they were permitted to consider themselves legally married, but not until they had convulsed the colony with their petitions and suits and counter-suits. The groom did not live very long, and his widow married der Heer Paulus Schrick. Two of their children married, respectively, a de Peyster and a de Minvielle and left no descendants, but the youngest daughter became the wife of a fine young colonial soldier, Captain Anthony Brockholst, afterward lieutenant-governor of the province, and kept up the family traditions for hospitality.

As has been said, the group of goede vrouwen who did so much to plant the infant colony on a firm basis by their fine good sense and clever management, formed a centre from which all the gayeties of the place arose.

The Goede Vrouw of Mana-ha-ta

They had instituted the assemblies and oyster-supper parties, and other congenial entertainments, and the whole community lived together like one large family. The pioneers of Mana-ha-ta did not live long after the English took possession of the plantation; some had already succumbed to the hardships of their early life. Among these was Margaret Hardenbrook (Mrs. Frederick Phillipse), who died before she could settle down to the enjoyment of her well-earned home in the colony.

Madame Govert Lockermans, who had so bravely followed her husband across the sea, was soon worn out by the hardships of a pioneer's life, and died after a brief married life, but her place had been speedily filled, as was customary in those days, for no man could afford to live without a helpmeet, who was the main support of the household. Her successor was the widow Mariyje Jans, the sister of Madame Bogartus. Govert Lockermans lived on the north side of Hanover Square, and adjoining his home was one of the best houses in the town, in which lived Johannes de Peyster. It was on the corner of William Street and Hanover Square, facing the south and overlooking the beautiful river. A merry family of boys and girls grew up under this roof, happy under the government of their good mother, who was the last survivor of the original group of the goede vrouwen of Mana-ha-ta.

The eldest son was a thoughtful, steady young fellow, and succeeded his father as a prominent burgher, and was known as "der Heer" Abraham de Peyster. He

Passing of the Pioneers

married in 1687 the daughter of his uncle Isaac, Catharine de Peyster, and the same year, the second son, Isaac de Peyster, married Maria Van Balen.

Both young men were devoted to their mother, and they relied on her judgment to an unusual extent, and even their wives accepted her dictum as final in all their family affairs. The two younger brothers soon followed the example set by their elders, and selected as wives two sisters, Maria and Anna Bancker. All the young men carried their wives to comfortable homes of their own, and as each one married, the couple joined the assemblies founded by their parents, which now threatened to outgrow the houses of the members.

As her sons married and left her, Madame de Peyster began to fear that her daughters were doomed to "comb St. Catharine's hair" and remain spinsters. This indeed was the fate of the youngest sister, Cornelia, who never married, her heart having been broken over the fate of her lover, who had been murdered by Indians. But the gay elder daughter, pretty Maria de Peyster, was surrounded by lovers, all of whom she encouraged, and yet, to the despair of her family, she persisted in refusing their addresses. At last the motherly influence prevailed, and Madame de Peyster was well satisfied when the girl's choice fell on the son of her neighbor and dear friend, and the betrothal of her daughter to Paulus Schrick was announced. He was the son of Maria Varleth by her second marriage.

His father was engaged in a brisk trade between Mana-ha-ta, Connecticut, and Virginia, and was well inclined to give his son a handsome allowance on his marriage, although the young fellow was by no means poor, having made several voyages on his own account. He was quite well-off, and he made a liberal settlement on his bride that made her one of the richest women in the place. The groom at one time had lived at Hartford and also in Flushing, owning property in both places, but on his marriage he resolved to settle permanently in New York.

The bride had been carefully trained by her mother and was one of the best spinners and weavers in the colony. In consequence, her great oak "kos" was filled with beautiful linen, made and marked by her own deft fingers, and tied in packages with colored tape, and as the dowry left to her by her father was secured to her, and under the guardianship of her brothers, there was no delay over the preparations for the wedding, which took place at the home of her mother, May 11, 1686. The ceremony was performed by the Rev. Henricus Selyns, and was by him duly recorded in the "Trouw" book:

"Paulus Schrick, J. M. van Hartford in N. Engel. en Maria de Peyster, J. D. van N. York."

The young couple began house-keeping under the pleasantest auspices, in a large house built by Schrick for his bride, on what is now Broad Street, but which was then known as "Prince's Graft." This house was surrounded by gardens and sheltered by large trees; its site is now covered by the buildings No. 67 and 69 Broad Street, which were erected when the handsome old house was pulled down to make room for business offices.

The centre of the Graft had originally been a brook which was the outlet for a marsh that lay above Beaver Street. It had been drained in 1659 at the cost of about $1,000. Above Exchange Place was the Schaape-Waytie. This street had originally been occupied by shoemakers, but after the erection of Madame Schrick's house it became one of the fashionable quarters of the town, and although it had a fine title that was recorded in the town register, the sly folks dubbed it "Petticoat Lane," by which name it was generally known. The home seemed to be the centre of happiness, when suddenly it was rendered desolate by the untimely death of the bridegroom, Paulus Schrick, only a few months after his marriage. The whole community was afflicted by the bereavement of their favorite friend, and worthy Dominie Selyns, who shared the general sorrow, recorded their grief in a brief notice in the church register, the sole instance in which such a thing was done, which proves how great the general sorrow was over the death of the promising young fellow. Madame Schrick was left with a handsome fortune, it is true, but upon her devolved the responsibilities and cares of the business it had taken her husband so many years to establish. With the aid of her brothers, however, the widow bravely faced her troubles and wisely conducted her affairs in her own name, like a true Dutch matron.

Mr. Purple, in a communication to the "New York Genealogical Record," says of this lady, "that by reason of her birth and alliance she was one of the most remarkable women born in New Amsterdam, and a complete record of her family connections would include a fuller history of the civil and military affairs of colonial times than the same account of any other person born during the Dutch possession of Manhattan Island."

Such a woman could not remain long a widow, and suitors flocked around her as eagerly as when she was Maria de Peyster; and it was not long before the gossips discovered that she was encouraging the attentions of a young Scotchman, who had emigrated to America about 1680, and who was already so highly esteemed in the community as to have been appointed Alderman of the Dock Ward, a position at that date of considerable honor and importance. No one was surprised when, on August 26, 1688, Dominie Selyns was called upon to join the hands of the Widow Schrick and John Spratt.

One of the wedding-presents was a huge Bible, printed in Amsterdam by Marcus Doornick, 1682, in which are the following entries:

"$16\frac{88}{87}$.—John Spratt of Wigton, in Galloway, and Maria de Peyster of New York, were married the 26th of August.

"$16\frac{89}{88}$.—On Munday the 16th of July between 8

and 9 of the Clock was born my daughter Cornelia. Baptized on the 18th of July.

"16$\frac{77}{78}$.—February 1st Saturday, betwixt 10 and 11 of the Clock in the forenoon was born my son John. Baptized on Sunday the 2d of February.

"16$\frac{77}{78}$.—Munday the 17th of April at 12 of the Clock in the afternoon was born my daughter Maria. Baptized on the 23d of April."

John Spratt was born in Scotland. He was one of the many Scotch Covenanters who had been driven from their native land and had found shelter in Holland. A large band of Scotchmen settled with him in the Netherlands, but they found the country thickly peopled and there seemed but little chance of the emigrants being able to support themselves or their families. As was natural, the younger men were willing to wander farther afield, and, encouraged by the West India Company, many of them ventured, under their auspices, to face the long voyage and probable hardships of the New World, in the hope of making a fortune. John Spratt was one of the number, and it was not long after his arrival in the country that his education and capabilities enabled him to lay the foundation of the fortune that he afterward acquired.

The family of Sproat, or Spratt, was a numerous one in Scotland, and was noted particularly for having only male children. The head of the family lived at Baldoon, where their ruined castle is still to be seen. The Spratts were a wild set of people, leading riotous lives and squandering their property, ready for any excitement, and prominent in all the border fights of the day. They were masterful in their households and deterred by nothing when "in their cups." One of the Spratts of Baldoon earned for himself an unenviable and undying notoriety by his brutal conduct to his wife, an amiable and beautiful woman, as tradition relates that he strangled her in one of his drunken rages, and from that day to this, on moonlight nights, the "White Ladye of Baldoon walks on the ramparts of the ruined castle, moaning, shrieking, and wringing her hands."

But the name of Spratt has died out both in Scotland and America and only lives in the traditions that tell of their wild deeds in the mother-land. The John Spratt who emigrated was apparently a quiet and dignified personage, highly respected in the community. The home of Mr. and Mrs. Spratt was the centre of interest in the colony, and, owing to their mixed nationality, was a neutral ground on which all political discussions could take place; and as Mrs. Spratt was closely related to all the principal persons on the island, they naturally rallied at her house. News travelled slowly in those days, but whatever penetrated to Mana-ha-ta was sure to be learned at the house in Prince's Graft, and for many years everyone considered it the birthplace of the political struggles that now began to agitate the colony.

The principal food of the early colonists was taken from the neighboring forests and rivers. Fish were

Passing of the Pioneers

abundant in the waters that flowed before their doors, and were captured with the greatest ease; edible vegetables grew wild in the rich soil; game lingered in the neighboring forests, and were snared or shot without trouble, and the tables of the new settlers were always lavishly supplied with wholesome food.

The Wilden made use of many roots and herbs, and taught the new-comers to like them as they did themselves; and they had willing scholars, as the natives of Holland knew and valued green vegetables as food long before other European nations could be induced to eat anything but flesh or a few roots. The French at that time had learned to prize some of the products of the vegetable kingdom, but in England the use of greens was hardly known. It is a well-authenticated fact that Queen Henrietta Maria introduced "salads" into the British Isles, when she went there as Queen Consort, as she pined for the fresh greens of her native land, and the king, to humor her, had a vegetable-garden laid out at Hampton Court for her use, by gardeners brought from Holland.

The introduction of vegetables in the kitchens of England stopped the dreaded scourge of scurvy, which, before the common consumption of green-food, had been prevalent there.

The Dutch brought carrots, turnips, parsley, potatoes, fruit-trees, and many herbs and flowers to our shores. These soon strayed from the gardens and became wild; turnips sowed themselves, and carrots ran riot over the land, the lovely flower of which was called by the English settlers of Massachusetts colony, " Queen Anne's lace."

Some writers have claimed that Irish emigrants introduced potatoes into America when they settled Londonderry, Massachusetts, in 1715, as from that time their use spread rapidly through the English settlements. But the Dutch colonists used the vegetable long before that date, and the name was such a common one at Mana-ha-ta that, as early as 1654, the court minutes of the place mention a sailor who went by the nickname of " Pataddes " (potatoes); and the Labbadist missionaries, in their famous diary, state that they were regaled with a mess of " potatoes " when visiting Beverswyck.

The Dutch not only learned the use of the staple products of the country from the Wilden but also adopted the original names, many of which are still retained.

In some localities clams are called " cloppers " or " quahogs," and maize, hominy, succotash, and suppaun retain their Indian name. But the Dutch had a quaint fancy about the names that they gave to the fish that ran into the northern waters, at regular and stated times of the year, and they gave numbers to the fish as they came from the South to spawn. So the fish that we now call " shad " was by them named " elft " or eleven, not only because it was the eleventh in order that appeared in the Hudson River, but also because it invariably arrived on the 11th of March, off Sandy Hook. It was a custom among the fishermen to present the first shad of the season to the governor, and it was usual for him to order it "planked," that is to say, the fish was split and fastened on a piece of birch-bark, and cooked before the embers of a wood-fire, after the Indian fashion, and served on its bark platter at the table. The cunning fish retains its time-honored custom to this day, and always arrives on the 11th of March, and it seems a pity that the suggestive name given to it by the early Dutch settlers should not have been retained. "Der elft" was succeeded by the "seabass," which received the name of "der twaelft" or twelve, not only because it followed the shad, but also because of twelve peculiar stripes, six on each side of the fish, as if it intended to mark itself with the number "twelve."

Drum-fish were next in order, and were dubbed "dertien" or thirteen. "Steur," or, as we know them, sturgeon, were very common in the Hudson River and attained a great size. They were often captured eight feet in length, a size which has been duly recorded by the eminent Swedish naturalist Klam, in his carefully written narrative of his wanderings in America. The roe of the sturgeon was highly prized by the Wilden, who cured it and considered it as great a delicacy as the Russians do their dainty "caviare," prepared from a kindred species of fish. The spawning-ground of the sturgeons lay a little south of "Claverack," the lower portion of the Rensselaerswyck Manor, and they were so plentiful in the waters of the northern Hudson that they were nicknamed "Albany beef." This fish makes great leaps from the water in pursuit of its prey, and they are dangerous neighbors to fishermen on that account, as they have been known to plunge through small boats. The descendants of the goede vrouwen of Mana-ha-ta tell a legend of the Hudson, which they heard from their grandmothers, of an old woman who was once lazily rowing across the river in her "battoe," when a huge sturgeon leaped into it and crashed through the bottom of the boat. The ancient dame hesitated only for a minute, and then, with immense presence of mind, seated herself directly in the hole, which her capacious person (loaded with many skirts of lindsey woolsey) filled so completely, that the boat was rendered water-tight, and she was rowed safely to land. The sturgeon's "silvery leap" in the moonlight of the Hudson River has been immortalized by one of the descendants of the first Mana-ha-ta settlers, an American poet of great gifts, Rodman Drake, in his verses on "The Culprit Fay," a tale of the fairies of the Highlands of the Hudson. "Salm" or salmon were, at one time, so plentiful in the waters of the Hudson and Connecticut Rivers that servants, when signing their bond for a term of years (as was customary), stipulated that they were not to be asked to eat salmon more than once a week.

Crabs were held in great estimation by the Dutch,

who declared that they were patriotic to Patria, as their claws were of the color of the flag of the Prince of Orange, which was white and blue; and the husband of Margaret Hardenbrook records in his journal that "crabs show sufficiently that it belong to us, to people, the country, and not to the English, owing to their white and blue claws." Unfortunately, the crabs' claws have a habit of turning red when they are boiled, so the English pointed triumphantly to this changeableness on the part of the crab, and declared that it would desert the Dutch colors for the English when given the opportunity, very much as the Dutch themselves did when forced to abandon their government for the English rule.

If the Wilden taught the Dutch how to preserve the flesh, fish, and vegetables in their own peculiar manner by "scorching" them in the sun, or smoking them with aromatic herbs, the latter in return instructed the savages in the art of salting. At first, the colonists found it difficult to procure salt in sufficient quantities for their purposes, but Madame de Peyster suggested to her husband that he should import a cargo of "sout" from Curacoa, and for this timely act the lady received in private the thanks of all her friends in the community, although her share in the matter is not recorded in the town chronicles together with that of her husband, on whom great praise is bestowed for the benefit he conferred on his fellow-burghers. It was soon discovered that sea-water could be evaporated, and a factory for manufacturing "der sout" was established at Coney Island, which flourished until the great saline deposits of Central New York were discovered.

A roving Dutchman, named Steendam, was attracted to Mana-ha-ta soon after its settlement, and he was so charmed with the beauties of its situation and the quantity and quality of the game found there, that he addressed a long poem on the subject to the authorities in Amsterdam, in which he enumerates all the fish, fowl, and beasts found on the continent, one by one. The poem is a long one, but a couple of the verses descriptive of the fish bear quotation:

> "En prick, en aal, en sonne-vis, en Baars
> Die (blank en giel) u Taaff'len als wat raars
> Vercieren kan : ook Elft, en Twalft niet schaars
> Maar overvloedig.
>
> "Sleen brassen Steur en Dartien en Knor-haan
> En Zee-baars, die geen Vorst sal laten slaan,
> En Kabellen : en Salm die (wel gebraan)
> Is vet en voedig."

The following is Mr. Murphy's translation:

> The lamprey, eel, and sunfish, and the white
> And yellow perch which grace your covers dight,
> And shad not scarce, but quite
> Innumerable.
>
> The bream and sturgeon, drumfish and gurnard,
> The sea-bass which a prince would not discard;
> The cod and salmon cooked with due regard
> Most palatable.

XI

The Dutch and Their Neighbors

Boers and Yankees—Threatened Amalgamation of the Colonies—The Naming of New England—Its Delegate to the King—Revolt of New England—Confusion in New York—Train Bands—Jacob Leisler—Colonel Bayard's Arrest—Judith Varleth's Romantic History—John Spratt, the Speaker of the Assembly—Persecution of the Van Cortlandts.

GRADUAL changes began now to take place in the social life of the colony. At first the townspeople had lived together in harmony like one large family, that only grew stronger and more closely bound together as the years went on by reason of the constant intermarriages of the young people, but the arrival of the English gradually and slowly worked a change. The beloved Dutch language was superseded by English, which the older ladies could never be taught to understand. Their quaint manners, their customs, and their religion were derided or despised by the usurpers, but notwithstanding all the influences that were brought to bear on the stately dames, they steadily kept to their own ways, continued to speak only the language of Patria, to attend devoutly their own church—where the services were invariably conducted in Dutch—and rule their households after the fashion of their mothers. Such persistent and steady resistance could not but have its effect, and the result was that the impress the Dutch pioneers left on the New World is uneffaced even after the lapse of two hundred years, as some of the good old customs are still observed on the island of Mana-ha-ta.

Although the Dutch were peace-loving to a fault, they bitterly resented the encroachments of the Massachusetts colony, which now became bolder under the new rule, and which pushed its vanguards closer and closer to the Hudson River. Settlers from the East, who had for years looked longingly at the thriving Dutch villages and farms, now began to flock to them. These intruders received but a chilly reception.

A new element of discord was now to be thrown into the midst of the northern colonies of America, and there was great excitement and much indignation in the newly fledged little capital of New York when it was learned that the king of England was planning to amalgamate all his possessions (north of Pennsylvania) under one government. James, Duke of York, had lately succeeded his brother Charles on the tottering throne of England, and by his fine contempt of the ordinary rules of morals and manners, and a total disregard of truth and honesty, was already pushing over that very unstable seat and assisting at his own downfall. The king by no means realized what very incongruous elements he was attempting to mix when he arranged to class together the people of such different manners, laws, and customs as those of the plantations in the New World, and he would have cared little, if he could have been brought to understand, what antagonistic communities he sought to control simply by his autocratic decrees.

The eastern colonies had a peculiar form of government of their own invention, which differed considerably from that of the Dutch colony, the laws of which were drawn from the best ones adopted by Patria. These laws were the wisest, most enlightened, and tolerant that were to be found in Europe. They were founded on good principle and common sense, and were subsequently generally adopted for the government of the colony.

The political consolidation of the colonies proposed by the king aroused great alarm, especially as it was thought to be the ultimate aim of the king to impose the Roman Catholic religion upon them. In order, therefore, to protect their religious beliefs, they sent representatives to the Court of St. James to beg that these scruples might be respected, determined to try peaceful measures before resorting to open defiance and rebellion, as they were quite prepared to do if their respectful remonstrances were not heeded. Their agents were Sir William Phipps and Dr. Increase Mather, both of them American born, and therefore with more independent ideas than those of most of the English subjects. On the arrival of the ambassadors in England they found to their joy that James had been forced to abdicate in favor of his daughter Mary and her Dutch husband, who had already grasped the reins of power. The two Americans were keenly alert to take advantage of this new move on the chess-board of Europe, and proposed to the new king to allow the eastern colonies to be autonomous, and begged him to remove all the English representatives and also separate the English-speaking colonies from the Dutch. King William made evasive replies that were construed as concessions by the ambassadors, who returned to America and reported, as if by authority, the news that they desired to have believed. News travelled slowly in those days, and the report, authorized by the delegates, of the downfall of popery in the person of King James, and the accession of his daughter, was deftly mixed by the Yankees with the report that the king had consented to the removal of Governor Andros, and this caused an immediate revolt of the eastern colonies from the rule of the governor.

New York learned this news from correspondents in Boston, and received the contradiction of it through Virginia news-letters. No one knew what to believe or to whom to turn. They did not even know what to call themselves, as their name, style, and government had changed with startling rapidity in the last few years.

The members of the king's council in New York were, at the time, Frederick Phillipse (who had married Margret Hardenbrook and then Catharine Van Cortlandt), Nicholas Bayard (the husband of Judith Varleth), and Stephanus Van Cortlandt—all worthy men, in whom everyone had implicit confidence. They represented, either in themselves or through their wives, all the various views and sentiments of the colony. The last-named was forty-six years old at the time, and completely identified with the Dutch interests, not only by his birth but by his marriage with Miss Schuyler, the granddaughter of the old director of Rensselaerswyck, Brant Van Slechtenhorst. Stephanus Van Cortlandt had succeeded his father in his "burgher rights," and also in the esteem of his fellow-citizens, and had been a popular man with them for over twenty years. He was fond of display and extremely hospitable, in the exercise of which he was ably seconded by his wife.

Governor Andros was called to Boston by the rebellion of his subjects there, and Lieutenant-Governor Nicholson had charge of the colony of New York during his absence. Before they could receive official intelligence of the change in the English rulers, and the council take proper steps for their own protection, Sir Edmund Andros was thrown into prison by his Massachusetts subjects, leaving "New England" without authorized government, while New York staggered under a load of perplexities as to her best plan of action. One thing only was agreed upon on all sides, and that was to arm the citizens. The Dutch were in hopes that they would be allowed to return to their old allegiance to Holland; and the few French, Scotch, and

The Goede Vrouw of Mana-ha-ta

English settlers of New York desired autonomy and independence, while relying for protection on England, but there was no agreement between the parties, who were so wofully perplexed by the complicated state of affairs that they did not know exactly what they wanted, and could take no concerted plan of action.

Matters in Europe at that date were horribly confused, and in the American colonies they were so inextricably mixed that they never became untangled until the "knot" was cut by the Revolution in 1776, when a nation was added to the history of the world.

Since there seemed to be nothing to do but to raise an army for self-defence against the French, New England, and the Indians—from all of whom outbreaks might be expected as soon as they learned the condition of affairs—New York bustled about and organized "train-bands," composed of all the men of the colony who could bear arms.

A company was raised and put under the command of a young German, who had been of no importance up to that date, but who now made himself useful to the authorities in many ways, and was rewarded by being given a commission in the miniature army. This man was Jacob Leisler, who had married Elise Jans, daughter of Maryje Jans, and widow of Schepen Peter Cornelius Van der Veen, who was called "one of the great burghers." Leisler was eager to distinguish himself, and did not disdain to do many things that were beneath the dignity of the Dutch burghers.

The Dutch and Their Neighbors

Der Heer Abraham de Peyster raised a company by his own exertions, and was made its captain. His brother-in-law, John Spratt, held a commission in this company, and many of their friends became members of it.

Each day developed some new source of alarm. The Indians on the north were reported to be on the "war-path," incited by the good French missionaries in Canada, who never lost an opportunity of trying to drive all but their own countrymen from the American continent. Everyone was suspected and dreaded as a possible foe, either at home or abroad, and, as these terrors were vague and undefined, they were in consequence the more alarming, as no one knew what to expect or from what quarter an onslaught might come.

None of the burghers cared to take too much responsibility upon themselves for fear of possible consequences, and in this state of indecision the bold, adventurous Jacob Leisler pushed himself to the front, and, after occupying various subordinate positions, finally announced himself the governor of the colony.

The citizens hardly grasped the situation, and although not crediting the legal rights of the usurper, they hesitated about deposing him.

Now, party feeling began to run high indeed; families were divided against themselves, and chaos and confusion reigned supreme.

John Spratt was firmly convinced that the Protestant cause would prevail in England, and as Leisler professed to be its supporter, Mr. Spratt threw all his energies into supporting the new governor. Mrs. Spratt was conservative in the extreme, and, true to her Dutch blood, disliked all changes and innovations. She was quite unconvinced that the new ruler of England was firmly established on the throne, although she ardently desired to see the Prince of Holland in that position. She hoped that he would not uphold the Leislerian government in the colony, and she relished but little seeing her husband so closely identified with a cause that she could not believe would be a successful one.

It was unfortunate for all parties that the character of Leisler was not one to shine when the man possessed supreme power, as he might have assisted his fellow-citizens in their emergency. But the more power he had the more he wanted, and the more arrogant he became, until finally he seemed to think that he was a heaven-sent ruler from whose despotic laws it was a criminal offence to rebel. He now imagined that the men who, by their indifference, had allowed him to pass over their heads and become their ruler, were his enemies, and that they were only watching for an opportunity to depose him and place themselves in his office. He frightened his council by dictating absurd orders to them, and then suddenly turned on his first friends and supporters and cast them into prison.

The first man to suffer was Colonel Bayard, the nephew of the late Governor Stuyvesant, who had finally summoned up the courage to point out to the assembly and the people that Leisler was exceeding his authority. After a wordy war of some months' duration the usurper determined on a perfectly uncalled-for and unjustifiable step, and ordered the arrest of Colonel Bayard. This was done without consultation with his council, and was the act of a tyrant.

The country-home of Colonel Bayard was some miles beyond the city walls, near the Collect. From it a charming view of the Hudson River and opposite heights could be obtained. For many years the house was such a prominent feature of the landscape that some of the early surveys of Hoboken and Wiehawken were made from "Mr. Bayard's chimney," or Mr. Bayard's red front-door. The house was filled with costly furniture imported from Europe, and Mr. and Mrs. Bayard had lavished taste and money on its decorations. Mrs. Bayard had been a noted beauty in her youth. When quite a young girl she had lived for a time (about the year 1662) in Hartford, Connecticut, where she was arrested and imprisoned as a witch. Whether this frightful suspicion was caused by her beauty or her talents, or because she spoke Dutch, cannot now be determined. Her family entreated that she might be released, but the Connecticut people were obdurate. Finally Governor Stuyvesant was induced to interfere and wrote a letter to the authorities in Hartford, which he sent by Miss Varleth's brother, in which he says:

The Goede Vrouw of Mana-ha-ta

Worthy & honoured Sirs:

This occasion of my brother-in-law's * being necessitated to make a second voyage to aid his distressed sister, Judith Varleth, imprisoned, as we are informed, upon pretended accusation of witchery, we really believe, and from her well-known education, life, conversation, and profession of faith, we dare assure you that she is innocent of such a horrible crime, and wherefore I doubt not that he will now find your honor's favour and aid for the innocent.

After the receipt of this letter the damsel was allowed to return to New Amsterdam, where she married in 1666 Colonel Nicholas Bayard, the son of Anna Stuyvesant by her first marriage. Their town-house was in Stone Street (then called the Hoogh Straat), near Hanover Square.

On the outbreak of the troubles with Leisler, Colonel Bayard quietly retired to his farm when he found that he was getting fruitlessly embroiled with the usurper, but he was unprepared for his sudden arrest, and was one morning startled by the reports of his servants, who had seen some soldiers marching up the lane and concealing themselves in the shrubbery, near the house. Yielding to the entreaties of his wife, Colonel Bayard dropped the razor with which he was shaving himself and hid himself in the cellar, while Mrs. Bayard boldly went forward and demanded the reason for the intrusion of the soldiers. These fellows, however, rudely pushed

---

* Nicholas Varleth, who had married Anna Stuyvesant, the widow of Samuel Bayard.

her aside, tore her cap from her head, and swore at her for preventing their entrance to her house, and rushed from room to room smashing the furniture, ripping up the feather-beds with their bayonets, and prodding the family portraits with their swords, under the pretence of searching for Colonel Bayard. "When his retreat was finally discovered they treated him roughly and marched him off to the fort in the city, where, by the governor's orders, he was loaded with irons and thrown into a dungeon, where he remained for many months."

The colonists were dismayed by the tidings of Colonel Bayard's arrest, and they felt as if no one was safe. Leisler was a new-comer in the colony, a man of obscure birth, with a detestably jealous temper that made him disliked abroad and feared by his family, who were only kept in subjection because they dreaded his terrible outbreaks of temper. He had no friends, no relations of his own, and no position in the colony to warrant his taking the position that he did, and yet such was his power at that time that none dared withstand him.

John Spratt was then speaker of the assembly convened under Leisler, and he and his wife were greatly exercised over the brutal treatment of Colonel and Mrs. Bayard and the incarceration of the former, but they could do little to mitigate their sufferings. Mrs. Bayard was the aunt of Mrs. Spratt's first husband, Paulus Schrick (de Jonge), and the whole family were up in arms against Leisler, although none now dared openly to oppose or defy him. Fears were now entertained that the tyrant's arrogance would lead his adherents into trouble, and everyone on the island began to think of his own safety. No one knew whose turn it might be next, and Stephanus Van Cortlandt wisely determined to remove to a place of safety and carry his family to the manor-house, as in his official position he had steadily opposed Leisler's arrogant proceedings.

The illness of one of Mrs. Van Cortlandt's children obliged her to return to town, but even her cares and anxieties did not protect her from Leisler's insults. This boorish man had not been received into the family of his wife with any cordiality, and he was now rejoiced at having an opportunity of revenging himself for fancied slights. The connection with Stephanus Van Cortlandt was not a close one, and was only through the marriage of Leisler's mother-in-law, Maryje Jans, to Govert Lockermans, the brother of Mrs. Van Cortlandt, but it might have been sufficient to protect the unhappy mother and wife when she was in such grief over the illness and subsequent death of her child, who lost its life in consequence of the exposure during the hurried flight to the manor-house and forced return to the city, whither Mrs. Van Cortlandt returned for medical advice with the more courage, as she fancied that she had nothing to fear, for there was only a difference of opinion between her husband and Leisler, and no one believed that the latter would push matters to extremities and wantonly insult a helpless woman. Van Cortlandt learned of the death of his child at his retreat at Hartford, where he had gone to consult some of his friends as to what measures they should take to protect themselves against this new enemy that had arisen in the colony.

XII

New York in Infancy

Robert Livingston, First Lord of the Manor—His Scotch Ancestors—The "Queen's Mary"—The Rev. John Livingston—His Retreat to Holland—His Marriage to Mary Fleming—Her Piety and Benevolence—Plans for Emigration—Robert Livingston Arrives in 1674—The Patent of the Manor—The Price Paid to the Indians—The Marriage of Robert Livingston—His Eldest Son—Mrs. Philip Livingston's Wedding-gifts—The Marriage-chest—Guysbert Livingston—Robert "Second" and Clermont—John Spratt—Mary Leisler's Marriage—Arrival of Governor Slaughter—Leisler and Milborn Hanged—De Smit's Vlye and the New City Hall—The First Dutch Church and Its Bell.

THERE was another distinguished refugee who had sought shelter at Hartford, and who was sharing the retreat of Stephanus Van Cortlandt. This was his brother-in-law, Robert Livingston, a Scotchman who had come to America in 1672, and who had soon become identified with the interests of the colony by purchasing large tracts of land on the east bank of the Hudson River. Robert Livingston was the descendant of a long line of Scotch ancestors, and was connected with the houses of Callendar, Bruce, Hepburn, etc.

The family-tree of the Livingstons stretches back to 1124. They were Lords Livingston and Earls of Linlithgow. The fifth lord, Alexander Livingston, was minister of Monnebrock, County Stirling; he married Barbara Livingston, of the house of Kylsyth. He was a firm adherent of the king, who put his daughter Mary under the personal guardianship of Lord Livingston, and she was brought up under his eye. Mary Livingston (the laird's eldest child) was the playmate of the princess and one of her most intimate friends. On the marriage of the Scotch heiress to the French king, Mary Livingston was appointed one of her maids of honor, and accompanied her royal mistress to France; and we may quote from Chalmers's "History of England" the following rhyme:

> Last night the Queen had four MARIES,
> To-night she'll have but three;
> There were Mary Seton, and Mary Beaton,
> And Mary Livingston, and me.

Lord Sempell married Mary Livingston and carried her away from the court of France, where the gossips of the day declared that she was greatly admired by his Royal Highness Henri II., King of France and husband of Catharine de Medici. The brother of "the queen's Mary" was the father of the Rev. John Livingston, who was the father of Robert Livingston, first lord of the manor. The portrait of the Rev. John Livingston, painted by Frans Hals, is now in the possession of one of his American descendants, and shows a shrewd, handsome, clever face, with twinkling eyes and large mouth, and the pointed beard of the period, shaded by the huge flapping-brimmed hat that was then the fashion.

The Rev. John Livingston was a man of considerable note and influence in his own community, and was of course devoted to the cause of the exiled princes of the house of Stuart, and he was appointed by the Scotch kirk in 1649 to go to Breda and invite Charles Stuart to return to the home of his ancestors and resume the crown of Scotland. The exiled prince received the commissioner with great cordiality, and went so far as to partake of the communion at the hands of Dr. Livingston as a proof of his good faith, and took the oath of fidelity to "the holy league and covenant" by the direction of the cleric.

The Rev. John Livingston is generally known in family parlance as "Mass John," from the stand that he took against the introduction of the Roman Catholic mass in Scotland. His outspoken views got him into trouble with the authorities and obliged him to beat a hasty retreat with his fellow-non-conformists to Holland, where he soon gathered around him a large congregation. Dr. Livingston possessed the gift of eloquence to a marvellous degree, and crowds of his fellow-countrymen flocked to hear him preach. He must also have acquired the language of the Dutch, for many of his hearers were drawn from the native families. The tale of his courtship and marriage to a lady of Rotterdam is very quaint and may be found in his own words in a rare book written by one of his descendants, Mrs. Joseph Delafield. It was as follows:

"She [Mary Fleming] had been recommended to me [as a wife], and for nine mos. I had been seeking direction from the Lord, who provided an occasion for our conference. I foregathered with her on my way to Meeting, and consulted with her anent the text of the Discourse I was to preach. I found her confidence so spiritual that my mind was much cleared, and I saw that it was the Lord's will that I should marry her."

Mrs. Livingston was indeed a pure-minded and lovely character, and charitable to an extreme degree. Mr. Watson, in his "Historic Tales of Olden Times," states: "I have seen an autograph letter from Robert Livingston's Mother, written from Amsterdam when in her 80th year, and providing therein for his receiving out fifty of that people at a time (*i.e.*, members of her late husband's congregation, who wished to join his son in the new world) as his working men, to serve seven years apiece for only food and raiment, all for the sake of freedom and liberty of conscience."

These emigrants were assisted to come to America out of the widow's private purse, and the sum that she disbursed was not intended to be repaid to her, although it came to a considerable amount.

During his life in Holland Dr. Livingston became a great favorite with the rich Dutch burghers, and apparently was intimate with the first Patroon of the Manor of Rensselaerswyck. This acquaintance led to the discussion of the advisability of the removal of the Scotch congregation to the New World. The patroon was always willing to assist worthy people to emigrate, and he encouraged their settling on his estates. Dr. Livingston had a large family to provide for, and he was most anxious to emigrate and desirous that his congregation should accompany him in a body. The arrangements for such a wholesale emigration were expensive and complex, and the dominie made two fruitless attempts to reach the "promised land," as he called it, but he died in 1672 without leaving Holland, and on his death the enterprise was partly abandoned, although many of his flock moved to America at different times. Several of his family married and settled in Holland, which was partly their native land, not only by birth and adoption but also from their descent on the maternal side. Some of the sons removed to Scotland, and one daughter became the wife of Andrew Russell, a Scotchman who was living in Rotterdam.

It is more than probable that Robert Livingston emigrated by the death-bed advice of his father, for he almost immediately left his widowed mother to the care of his elder brothers and sisters and sailed for the New Netherlands, where he arrived about 1674, at the same time that the Rev. Nicolaus Van Rensselaer came to settle on his father's American estates, armed with additional authority from King Charles II. to act as his majesty's chaplain in the colony. The young men seem to have been friends from early life and they continued their friendship when they met on the bank of the Hudson River.

On July 22, 1685, Robert Livingston obtained the patent of the manor of Livingston from Governor Dongan. It contained 160,000 acres and was beautifully situated on the Hudson River, half-way between Mana-ha-ta on the south and Rensselaerswyck on the north, and opposite to the possessions of the patroon in the Catskills. The manor carried with it no title, as was the case with the Dutch plantations. Its owner was styled " Lord of the Manor," after the English fashion, but this title was not bestowed by the government, nor was it hereditary. The manor had been lawfully purchased from the Indian family that owned it on July 12, 1683, and the price given to them was fully stated in the title-deeds, and included blankets, duffles, shirts, stockings, axes, adzes, paint, twenty little scissors, twenty little knives, twenty little mirrors; the last being an especial gift to the women of the tribe which highly delighted them, but which caused a good deal of trouble to the proprietor. For whenever one was broken the squaw would return and demand that it be exchanged, and would take up her quarters in the great kitchen of the manor-house, and there she would remain; no coaxing or entreaties were able to move her until the "Laird" himself, with appropriate gravity and formal speech, presented her with a new one.

Robert Livingston was a pious man, who had been carefully taught by his Dutch mother and had received an especial training for the life of a pioneer. He understood surveying, had studied both Dutch and English law, and was in every way fitted, both by temperament and education, to manage the large estate which his thrift had enabled him to purchase, but he lived on his wild lands alone and had no wife to aid him by relieving him of the manifold cares of the small establishment that he maintained before making his great purchase of the manor.

The romantic story of his marriage has been related by "a lady of the family of Livingston" in an unpublished sketch entitled "The Livingstons of the Manor." It seems that the Rev. Nicolaus Van Rensselaer had married Alida Schuyler soon after his arrival in America. This lady was a native-born American woman, her father, Philip (Pieterse) Schuyler, having married the daughter of the director of Rensselaerswyck, Brant (Arentse) Van Slechtenhorst, and Madame Van Rensselaer was the sister of Madame Stephanus Van Cortlandt, and also had five brothers, all of them prominent in colonial affairs. After some years of a childless married life the dominie and his wife were one summer's day voyaging in their yacht from Mana-ha-ta to Rensselaerswyck, a trip that sometimes took a week to accomplish. Dominie Van Rensselaer was noted for his soothsaying and second-sight, and several of his prognostications had been fulfilled, notably the one, already mentioned, that predicted the accession of Charles Stuart to the throne of England when he was a homeless wanderer in Holland, and the dominie's words were received with awe and credulity. Dr. Van Rensselaer was suddenly taken very ill on board of his yacht, and he declared that he had received a summons to the land of spirits, and hurriedly determined upon making his will, and insisted that his wife should not wait until they reached Rensselaerswyck, but that she should send at once for a lawyer to execute the instrument according to due form. The terrified woman ordered the yacht to be headed for the nearest shore, and a messenger was dispatched to search for a lawyer through the sparsely settled shores of the Hudson River.

Madame Van Rensselaer was pleased to receive in answer to her summons her well-known friend Robert Livingston, who hastened to the bedside of the semi-unconscious man, who was lying in the cabin. What was the dismay of Madame Van Rensselaer when her husband raised himself on his elbow and gazed with glazed and fixed eyes on Mr. Livingston, and " then cried in a full tone: 'Bring any other man; this one will become the husband of my wife.' No doubt the prediction produced the fulfilment," continues the account, "for it was not long before the marriage took place of the first lord of the Manor of Livingston to the widow of the poor dominie, who had been laid to rest in the grounds of Rensselaerswyck."

Tradition says that it was owing to the ambition of this daughter of the Schuylers that the purchase and erection of the manor was made. She had enjoyed the position of "Lady of the Manor" as Madame Van Rensselaer, and she could not bear to return to the simple position she had held previous to her first marriage.

The record of the wedding of the laird of Livingston is in the family Bible, and is in the handwriting of the groom. It is in the Dutch language, of which this is a translation: "1679 on the 9th day of July (old style), I Robert Livingston was married to my well beloved helpmate, Alida Schuyler, widow of Dr. Nicolaus Van Rensselaer, in the Presbyterian Church of Albany, America. May God be with us and bless us."

Every entry in the Bible is followed by a short prayer. In recording the birth of Robert (his second and favorite son) the prayer is, "May the Lord bless him, that he may grow up in might, and be brought up in the Presbyterian religion."

Mr. and Mrs. Livingston had a family of four sons and two daughters, and the enumeration of their descendants would include the name of every well-known and influential family of New York.

Their eldest son was Philip Livingston, named after his grandfather, Philip Schuyler. The first-born son married Katharine Van Brugh, the granddaughter of the oldest burgher of New Amsterdam. Her father, Johannes Van Brugh, and mother, Sara Cuyler, had both of them inherited property from their parents, who were among the first settlers of the New World, and among the largest landholders on the island of Mana-ha-ta. The dower of Mrs. Philip Livingston was a handsome one, and, in addition to the lands and money that were carefully settled on her, Mr. Van Brugh sent to Delf for a complete set of china, which included dinner, breakfast, and tea sets that would be priceless in these days, and gave it to the bride as a wedding-gift. Pieces of this china are still preserved by her descendants.

Katharine Van Brugh was well brought up, according to the thrifty ways of those days and after the customs of her Dutch ancestors. She had been taught all the customary household duties, and, like the maidens of her day, had forestalled the needs of house-keeping and spun and woven quantities of linen. This was placed in a great "marriage-chest," also imported from Holland by her doting parents. This "kos" or "koff" is still in existence, and is in the possession of one of the Van Rensselaer family, having descended to its present owner through the marriage of Stephen Van Rensselaer III., eighth Patroon of the Manor of Rensselaerswyck, with Katharine Livingston, the granddaughter and namesake of Katharine Van Brugh. The "kos" stands about twelve feet high, and is broad in proportion. It is of oak, and handsomely carved on the outside, and is filled with curiously contrived secret drawers and receptacles, and has ample room for the linen and silver of the household and of its mistress. The key-hole is concealed under a swing-cover of wood, which, when in place, looks like part of the ornamental carving; and the great iron key, with its crooked wards, seems more fitted to unlock a fortress than a marriage-chest.

The descendants of Mr. and Mrs. Philip Livingston were numerous, as they had six sons and two daughters, and every one of them took a prominent part in the government of the colony, and aided in the construction of the new country, which took its place among the nations of the world as "the United States of America."

Robert Livingston's third son was called Guysbert (or Gilbert). He married Cornelia, the daughter of Henry Beekman, and was the founder of the Poughkeepsie branch of the family. The fourth son of Robert Livingston was his father's namesake, and is usually known as "Robert Second," to distinguish him from a nephew of the first lord of the manor, the son of an elder brother of the same name, commonly known as Robert Jr.

"Robert Second" was sent to Scotland to be educated, and a Scotch aunt wrote to the proud father as follows: "Your son is very like you, comely, and fond of being fine." After studying law at the Temple, London, "Robert Second" returned home "an accomplished gentleman," and opened a law-office in Albany. We may quote from Mrs. Delafield's history of her ancestors, page 122, to show the quick wit and courage for which the Livingstons were noted:

"The first summer that young Robert passed with his father at the manor, his attention was attracted one afternoon to what seemed to him an unusual number of negroes skulking around. That night, after he was in bed, he heard a noise in the chimney, and presently a pair of legs appeared. Robert jumped from his bed and seized the fellow, exclaiming: "Villain, confess!" The man, utterly confounded, acknowledged that he was one of a band of thieves who had fixed upon that night to rob and murder the whites. Robert's father was so much pleased with his son's intrepidity that he gave him the lower end of the manor, a tract containing about thirteen thousand acres. This son was afterward called Robert of Clermont, after the name given to the new house that he built, and his property was called "the Lower Manor," although not legally entitled to the name.

But to return to Robert Livingston, the first lord of the manor, and his dispute with Leisler. The laird was opposed to the usurper, who, in order to annoy Mr. Livingston, demanded his books and vouchers, so that they might account for the public money lodged in Mr. Livingston's hands, and endeavored to attaint the laird without waiting for him to put in a defence. Mr. Livingston refused to appear personally before Leisler, and quietly wrote to the council that it was impossible for him to produce his books and vouchers, for the very good reason that, as Leisler had already seized them and had them in his possession, it was impossible for the rightful owner to hand them over to the authorities as requested, and he therefore could not be held responsible and attainted for not producing them. Such a sensible reply enraged Leisler, who threatened to imprison Mr. Livingston as soon as he could be captured.

With Colonel Bayard in prison, Stephanus Van Cortlandt and Robert Livingston in voluntary exile, and most of the bewildered denizens of Mana-ha-ta too demoralized to take any active steps for his overthrow, Leisler thought that he was securely placed in the governor's chair, and he issued proclamations and manifestoes, as if his dictates were infallible.

It was with infinite relief that the unhappy colonists learned, through private sources, that King William had not confirmed Leisler's self-assumed patent as governor. Official confirmation of these tidings was slow in crossing the seas; and although the imperious tyrant heard the news that predicted his downfall, he had gone too far to retreat, and found himself in a perilous position, surrounded by men of standing and wealth, every one of whom he had antagonized at one time or another by his brutal conduct, either directly or through their relations and friends. There was no hope of support at home, and none to be looked for abroad.

It had been with a great deal of hesitation that John Spratt had accepted the position of speaker of the assembly; it was, of course, a post of considerable honor, but one that might involve him in trouble if the government of Leisler was not confirmed by the Lords of Trade in England. The post, however, was not one in the gift of the governor, and therefore Mr. Spratt believed that by accepting it he was acting for the best interests of his king and his fellow-citizens, as he hoped that he would be able to restrain the impetuosity of the self-styled governor, and curb the assemblymen in their desire to free the colony from all connection with England. The time was not ripe for autonomy, and the graver and more thoughtful members of the colony were not ready to cut themselves free from Europe.

It was now that Mrs. Spratt showed her wisdom. She counselled her husband to great caution, and begged him to conciliate the persons who might consider themselves in opposition to him owing to his official position, by showing them all possible leniency on every occasion, even at the risk of embroiling himself with the testy governor. She also withdrew herself from any intimacy with the governor's family, and exerted herself to exercise unwonted hospitality and kindness to all.

Matters dragged along heavily and there was little sociability or amusement in New York during this period of suspense. Leisler continued to show his boorishness and brutality to everyone within his reach, and went so far as to pick a quarrel with the inoffensive Dominie Selyns, who had ventured to differ from some of the opinions of the usurper. Leisler thereupon publicly slighted the dominie on every occasion. But the gossips were fairly electrified when they learned one morning that Leisler had carried his tyranny to extremes in his own family and had commanded his daughter to marry, without delay, or publishing of banns, or such ceremony, his henchman and subordinate Jacob Milborne. This fellow had been a servant in Connecticut (according to the records of the day) and he had run away from justice, as he had been accused of stealing from his master. He had wormed himself into the confidence of Leisler and now threatened to betray some important secrets if not bribed to silence. Leisler had little money at his command, and he thought he could effectually silence Milborne if they were more closely allied and their interests made identical, so pretty, blue-eyed Mary Leisler, much against her will, was secretly married, without bann, license, or the blessing of good Dominie Selyns, to the vulgar, elderly groom, for whom she did not attempt to conceal her aversion; and all the old Dutch ladies shook their nodding caps and declared that no good could possibly come of a match not consecrated by their beloved dominie.

But sudden relief from the tyrant's rule was at hand. The servants of the town woke their masters early on the morning of March 19, 1692, with the news that they had heard the report of cannon in the lower bay, and this was speedily followed by the announcement of the arrival of the ship Archangel, which anchored at the Narrows, off the "Watering Place," at Staten Island. On board this ship was the newly credited governor, who had been hastily despatched from England by the king, to take charge of the turbulent colony of New

New York in Infancy

York. The chief men of the city crowded into their yachts, or chartered the public pereauguas, and sailed down the bay to welcome his excellency and lay their grievances before him. Leisler shut himself up in the fort and would not order the customary salute of welcome to be fired to announce the arrival of the new official, as he refused to believe that he was properly commissioned by the king.

Henry Slaughter, the new governor, on being informed of the chaotic condition of affairs, embarked with great state in the pinnace of the ship and proceeded to the government landing-place at Whitehall, and from there, amid tumultuous greetings from the populace, he proceeded to the old Stadt Huys, and although it was nearly midnight by the time he arrived there, he took the oaths of office that night, and immediately sent to demand entrance to the fort.

The tables were now turned : Leisler and Milborne were committed to the prison from which Colonel Bayard was released, and after due trial, at which both Leisler and his subordinate were found guilty of treason, Governor Slaughter signed their death-warrant, and they were speedily hanged. It is said that the governor would have shirked the responsibility of condemning the usurper to death, and would have transported him to England to receive sentence from the king, but there were too many influential men in the colony who, with their families, had suffered from the inhuman persecutions of Leisler, to allow him to escape so easily, and they contrived to have the death-warrant laid before the governor after a hearty carouse, and secured his signature and saw that it was carried into effect before he could become sober and repent of his action. It has been the custom of late years to try to exculpate Leisler, and to endeavor to show that he was a hero and a martyr, by diligently suppressing all his cruelties and persecutions, and exalting the few services to the colony that could be discovered. Some historians have nearly persuaded themselves that he was an ill-used man who met with an unjust fate at the hands of an ungrateful public, but the government documents of the period do not warrant this assumption.

The family of Leisler made a bitter outcry over his death, although it was openly said that they regretted the confiscation of his property more than his ignominious departure from life. The widow and sons petitioned the English government to such good purpose that the estates were restored to the family, and his daughter soon dropped the hated name of Milborne and married Nicholas Gouverneur, duly honored by bann and license, and became the ancestress of one of the most respected and notable families on Mana-ha-ta, and one that is particularly distinguished for having inherited the beauty of "pretty Mary Leisler."

Mrs. Spratt was deeply interested in all these proceedings and was well satisfied when she found that her husband would not suffer for the position which he had taken under the late government, and that, although under English rule, the Dutch burghers were not overlooked in the distribution of the city offices, and she and her family were much gratified when her brother, der Heer Abraham de Peyster, was appointed mayor of New York, 1691.

The newly created official was a native-born citizen, with inherited "burgher rights," which, in those days, carried great weight and influence. He loved his birthplace and was much interested in its well-being and improvement. To signalize his elevation to the mayoralty, he donated a piece of marsh-land to the city for dock purposes. This meadow was called "Smit's Vlye," as it had originally belonged to Cornelius Clopper, the first blacksmith. "Vlye" signified "wet or marsh land," and the word is still used in the same sense, in many parts of New York where the inhabitants are the descendants of the original Dutch. The reclaimed land was partly filled by a dock, at which the farmers of Long Island could land and display their produce for sale on the "Vlye," which gradually became used for a weekly mart, and was finally officially recognized and became known as the "Fly Market"; and the people of to-day firmly believe that it received the name because of the flies that were attracted by the meat and other things that were exposed for sale, and entirely ignore or have forgotten the derivation of the name, with its widely different meaning.

Mayor de Peyster also presented to the city the valuable lot where the United States Treasury now stands, in

Wall Street. This celebrated site was first used for the grand new City Hall that was soon erected, with its colonnades that stretched over the pathway, which was the successor of the picturesque and ancient Stadt Huys, which had overlooked the Strand and the East River. On the steps of the new building the inauguration of General Washington took place when he took the oaths of office as first president of the United States, and these steps with the iron railing were preserved when the building was demolished early in the nineteenth century, and were placed in front of Bellevue Hospital, where they still remain.

The first Dutch church had been built within the enclosure of the fort, for the better protection of the worshippers from surprises from the Wilden; but these had now wandered far from the settlements of the whites, and sudden surprises were not to be apprehended. The congregation had outgrown its narrow quarters, and took the opportunity, while der Heer de Peyster was in office, to urge the necessity of moving to another site, for, since the arrival of the English, the Lutheran belief was no longer the established religion, and it was no longer of importance that the church should be beside the dwelling of the governor. It was determined that a new and more capacious building should be erected on Exchange Place. This edifice was built after the latest fashion and was considered a very handsome building. It was decorated with stained-glass windows that displayed the arms and insignia of all the principal members of the congregation. The bell that hung in the new belfry was the original one that had been subscribed for by Johannes de Peyster and his fellow-citizens, and cast in Holland. For many years it had summoned the burghers to prayer, had called the citizens to the court of justice, had given the signal to rise and to rest, had announced a funeral, a wedding, or a christening, and its deep and well-beloved note had been the signal for all important events in the little place. The silvery tone for which it was distinguished was given to it during casting, as the schepens and burgomasters of Amsterdam had attended the ceremony and had thrown into the molten metal silver pieces of great value, which had made the bell a more precious one than was usually the case. The original bell is still owned by the church and is hung in the belfry on the corner of Fifth Avenue and Forty-eighth Street, where careless citizens pass it heedlessly by and never give a thought to the old bell that has seen every change which has taken place in the history of New York.

Mayor der Heer de Peyster signalized his accession to power by other beneficent acts. Chief among them was one that was inspired by the women of his family, who drew his attention to the dirty condition of the streets and begged him to order them cleaned. The Dutch ladies were noted for their cleanliness, and they had long been exercised over the filthy condition to which the streets, lanes, and roads had degenerated since the advent of the English. The prim, neat, well-kept roadways, bordered by low hedges or wooden fences, had become slovenly looking, weed-covered, rutty quagmires, and every visitor tormented the cleanly housewife by bringing a quota of mud on her tidy, well-scoured stoep. In vain they made their servants braid mats of cornshooks and lay them on the top steps; in vain they added scrapers, or hung a broom beside the front door. Scraping and sweeping were useless, and the goede vrouwen wisely turned their attention to improving the condition of the streets, as some goede vrouwen have done two centuries later, and they succeeded in having an ordinance passed in 1692, which required every householder to keep the street clean in front of his own door, while the public authorities were required to dig up the weeds and keep the sidewalks, or rather pathways, clear. Laurens Van der Speigle, a respectable baker, was appointed the first public street-cleaner. One of his daughters married Rip Van Dam, who, in course of time, became governor of New York, and another daughter married the son of the first brewer of Mana-ha-ta, Isaac de Forest.

A new governor arrived in New York, August 29, 1692, and was welcomed as all governors are bound to be by citizens who hope for better administration with every change. The Dutch ladies were greatly amazed at the fresh importation of English manners and customs. The governor tried to impress his new subjects by appearing in a magnificent coach drawn by six horses.

His wife and daughters were stylish ladies who aspired to hold a court, while at the same time they were not quite sure that the inhabitants of the colony were good enough for such superior people as themselves to associate with. Mrs. Spratt concerned herself but little with these affairs. She was contented and happy at seeing her husband quietly immersed in his commercial affairs, and safely delivered from the complications that his loyalty to his mother-country, as against the Dutch interests of the colony, had drawn him into under the misguidance of the unhappy Leisler. The influence of Mrs. Spratt's family had been sufficient to shield him from any ill-effects that his connection with Leisler might have drawn upon him, and all were now content to settle down to their quiet family life and wonted hospitable festivities among the old settlers, who completely ignored the mimic court, that had few attractions for a people who did not understand its language or admire its customs.

The town of New York was still but a small place where everyone was related to everyone else, and the whole community were deeply interested in an important social event in 1694, which commanded all attention. This was the marriage of Mrs. John Duval, who had been left a widow some time previously and now became the second wife of Frederick Phillipse. She was the daughter of Oloff Van Cortlandt and the sister of Stephanus Van Cortlandt, and during the reign of Leisler she had been absent from the island, sometimes staying with her sister, Madame Van Rensselaer, wife of the "Groot Director," Patroon Van Rensselaer, at Rensselaerswyck, or else with her nieces, who had lost their mother, Mrs. Brant Schuyler, in February, 1689, just at the time when the colonists were distracted by political affairs. All these persons had been bitterly opposed to the Leisler government, and they were happy to return to the comfort of their homes and forget and forgive past differences and discussions.

Mrs. Phillipse was quite as remarkable in her own way as her predecessor, Margaret Hardenbrook, had been, although totally different. The new Mrs. Phillipse was charitable to a degree, and she also took an immense interest in the natives, who had now degenerated into a shiftless class of persons who were content to live in a state of dependence on the whites. In order to educate them and ameliorate their condition, Mrs. Phillipse undertook to provide a school for the children and also had a church erected near her manor-house, in which she took the deepest interest, and forsaking the amusements of her town-life, she retired into the country, and tradition states that she rode her gray mare every day to watch the workmen build the church, which she subsequently endowed with a considerable portion of her own fortune.

New York at this time was intensely cosmopolitan, and it is on record that in 1664 there were eighteen different languages spoken within its limits. But the Dutch was still the one in most general use—in which church services were held, and law cases tried, and news-letters exchanged.

An interesting law-case came up in 1693 which related to the title of Govert Lockerman to the open space in front of his house, which was then a common but is now known as Hanover Square. The oldest inhabitants were called upon to testify concerning it. They were Johannes Van Brugh and his wife. He remembered forty-six years back, and she remembered fifty-six years, or to 1637, and they both declared that the spot had always been open ground and a common, and they refused to agree to its being fenced in or built over; and the tiny triangle remains to-day, a mute witness to the vigorous defence it received from the lips of Tryntje Jansen, the daughter of the famous Annekje Jans.

XIII

The Pirate and His Escapades

Governor Bellomont and " My Lady "—Captain Kidd—Money Pond on Montock—The Quidder Merchant—The Isle of " Wight "—Captain Lion Gardiner—Kidd's Visit to the Lord of the Isle—The Treasure Unearthed—Kidd Hung in Chains—Lord Bellomont's Coffin-plate.

THE whole of the island of Mana-ha-ta was now beginning to be covered with signs of habitation. The little "dorp," which at first was merely a cluster of traders' huts perched "at the place of safe landing," Capsey's rocks, on the very end of the island, was now growing and spreading over the land. Villages were clustering in various convenient spots, and pretty farms lay on the slope of many of the hills, the tops of which were often crowned with great windmills, whose flapping arms gave an air of motion to the landscape that, together with its situation on the rapidly flowing rivers, made it look like a gigantic vessel sailing pleasantly down the stream. The country-houses of the gentlefolks of the dorp peeped from under their great sheltering trees all along the borders of the Hudson and the East Rivers. The chief features of the place were still entirely Dutch, and these were only lost by very slow degrees under the British rule. The English gave the colony what was called the "Duke's Laws," which were about as confusing and poor a code as could be well imagined, but they could not alter the daily habits and customs of the people, and, indeed, the example set by the English governors and their staff was one to be shunned and not followed. The unfortunate colonist had enough to do to untangle the intricacies of the laws and the evil consequences that ensued after their administration without permitting interference in the more sacred church and household customs.

Governor Slaughter was not a success as ruler of the colony. He was convivial in his habits, and the Lords of Trade were obliged to recall him, and in 1698 they despatched a new governor to New York. This was Richard Coote, Earl of Bellomont and Baron of Coloony, in the County of Sligo, Ireland. He was over sixty years of age, and had a wife to whom he had been married when she was only twelve years old. She had been living in London for many years while her lord was absent in one of the West Indian colonies, where he had held an official position. Lady Bellomont had refused to accompany her husband on his distant mission, and had remained in England, where she had distinguished herself by gambling and leading such a fast life that her family had felt obliged to notify her lord of her extravagance, and request that he would return to England and put a stop to her disgraceful behavior. Lord Bellomont, in consequence, resigned his position and hastened home, where he found matters were even worse than had been represented to him.

After settling affairs to the best of his ability, Lord Bellomont solicited the post of governor of New York as the best way of repairing his impoverished fortunes, as it was an acknowledged fact that the post carried with it considerable emoluments for a ruler who was not over-scrupulous, and he carried his wife with him to America, in spite of her bitter reproaches against such an exile, which she considered would be worse than death to a woman accustomed to the dissipations of life in London. Notwithstanding the misconduct of "my lady," Lord Bellomont was excessively fond of his beautiful wife and very jealous of all attentions that were paid to her. He discouraged the men of the colony from visiting at the executive mansion, and shut his wife up and would not allow her to associate with the ladies of the place. Miss Younge has written a very interesting history of this lady called "Love and Life," and gives in it a graphic account of her escapades in England, which would seem to prove that she was rather out of her mind, and is by no means complimentary to her, although probably true in all respects.

His lordship came to America filled with good intentions, which took the line of allowing no one to get rich at the expense of the colonists—except himself—and openly avowed himself "a reformer;" but his first step was peculiarly in the wrong direction, although

The Pirate and His Escapades

it was not his fault, as he acted entirely by the direction of his masters, the Lords of Trade. There was no navy in those days that was capable of defending the long coast-line of the American colonies, and it was deemed advisable to raise one in these waters, for the better protection of the merchantmen, which were often captured by pirates when nearly at their haven. To try to secure the safety of these vessels of commerce, the governor issued licenses to certain masters of sailing-craft, as privateersmen, and he induced Robert Livingston and many of the citizens of New York, as well as his majesty the king of England, to invest their money in this species of amateur navy.

Unfortunately for the reformer and his colleagues they intrusted one of their principal vessels to the charge of a well-known New York skipper by the name of William Kidd. He had married, May 16, 1691, as her third husband, Sarah, widow of John Oorst and daughter of Samuel Bradly. They were quite wealthy people for those days, and Captain Kidd owned several vessels of his own, in which he was accustomed to make voyages to Europe. There is a notice in the city archives of the indenture of a servant that he brought from England with him, who was formally bound to Mrs. Kidd on her arrival in America and agreed to serve a number of years in return for her free passage across the ocean. It is probable that Lord Bellomont thought that he had made a very safe selection when he commissioned Captain Kidd as an official privateersman, but it is probable that the captain had been in the habit of doing a little poaching on his own account for several years, although no one seems to have suspected him at the time that he received the commission from the government. It is certain that he was in the habit of concealing ill-gotten treasure in various localities on the Hudson River, the Long Island Sound, and at different places on Long Island. There are manuscripts in what is believed to be Captain Kidd's handwriting, which give directions for finding certain treasure that was hidden near Flushing, which it is believed was discovered many years ago, although the find was kept quiet at the time. There is also a pond on "Montock," the extreme east point of Long Island, which is called Money Pond, from a report that Captain Kidd sank two chests of gold in it about 1699. Near this sheet of water, by the north side of the island, is a medicinal spring. It is exceedingly cold, but it bubbles and boils as if over a hot fire. The Montauk Indians believe that its waters are a sovereign cure for consumption, and also consider it haunted and bewitched, as it is a fresh-water spring and yet is within a few feet of the ocean—a thing, however, that is not very uncommon on the shores of Long Island. This spot is believed to have been a favorite hiding-place of the captain's, when his fellow-citizens fancied that he was cruising in very distant waters.

Matters culminated when Captain Kidd was ordered to sea to protect some valuable merchantmen that were expected from India laden with spices, carpets, silks, and precious stones. The privateersman fell in with one of the expected vessels soon after he rounded Montock (as the end of the island was then called). The ship was The Quidder Merchant, named after Philip Schuyler, who had received the nickname from the Indians, who could not pronounce his name, and it had attracted attention from its oddity and had been bestowed on the vessel, which is now supposed to have belonged in part to Mr. Schuyler.

Captain Kidd boarded The Quidder Merchant, and, after disposing of her crew, he secured the cargo and sailed into the mouth of the Sound to what the Dutch called "Kromme Gouw," but which is now known as Gardiner's Bay. Kidd landed on the isolated island (which is nearly opposite New London, in Connecticut), at the entrance to the sheet of water that separates Long Island from the mainland. The Isle of Wight (which is the true name of the place, having been given to it by one of its first owners) is now called Gardiner's Island, after the lords of the manor, who have handed the property down intact from father to son for over two hundred years. It was purchased from the Indians by Captain Lion Gardiner in the year 1640, and the title was ratified by Major Forrester, agent to Henry, fifth Earl of Stirling, and the original parchment title-deeds are still preserved at the manor-house, with its attesting signature.

Lion Gardiner was a gallant soldier who had been invited to emigrate to America by the rulers of the Massachusetts colony, who found that they required men well versed in the arts of war to defend their settlements from the savages who surrounded them. Lion Gardiner was of English birth, and, as a very young fellow, he had fought against the Spaniards in Holland, where, like so many of his countrymen, he fell in love with a Dutch lady, the daughter of Dirck Williamson, whose wife's maiden name was Hachin Bastiens. Gardiner was an extremely handsome young fellow and reputed to be the best engineer officer of his day. Governor Winthrop, in his diary, records the arrival in America of the gallant soldier and his bride in the following words:

"November 28th, 1635. Here arrived a small norsy bark of 25 tons sent by the Lord Say and Seal with one Gardiner, an expert engineer, to begin a Fort at the mouth of the Connecticut River. She came through many tempests, yet through the Lord's great Providence, her passengers 12 men and 2 women and goods all safe."

The second woman mentioned as having braved the perils of the voyage with Mrs. Gardiner was her maid, an indispensable luxury to a Dutch lady of the period but an unnecessary one in the eyes of the Puritans, who were not accustomed to live in the comfort that the Dutch were; and unfavorable comments were made as to the luxurious habits of Mrs. Gardiner by the stern New England matrons in consequence of her having an attendant. Captain Gardiner remained some time in the service of the Massachusetts colony, and then, becoming disgusted with their cruelty to the Indians and with their over-righteous ways, he resigned his position, and while resolving to settle in the New World, determined to move beyond their jurisdiction. With the acumen of a soldier he selected an island for his home, named by the Wilden Manchannock, and pronounced by them "Man-shon-o-noc," or "place of great sickness," as he thought that if surrounded by water he would be tolerably free from surprises from the savages. The price paid to the Wilden for their island was "one large black dog, one gun, some powder and shot, some rum, and a few blankets." Captain Lion Gardiner also bought large tracts of land on Long Island, and his purchases were erected into the manor of Gardiner by the English governor, and is the only one of the manors that remains undivided just as it was bought from the aborigines and in the hands of the descendants of the first proprietor.

Gardiner's Island is about three miles long by one wide, and is covered with deer and game of all sorts, which are carefully preserved by the "proprietor" or "lord of the manor." The great oaks that cover one part of the island have never been cut, and are part of the original forest. The southern end was swept by a tornado in the beginning of the nineteenth century, and there are few trees remaining on it. The windmills that daily grind the meal for the table of the "lord of the isle" are those built for the first owner over two hundred years ago, and are still in a perfect state of preservation.

The Goede Vrouw of Mana-ha-ta

The grandson of Captain Lion Gardiner was living like a patriarch amid his flocks and herds when he was one day dismayed at receiving a visit from a stranger, who announced himself as Captain Kidd. It is doubtful if Mr. Gardiner had ever heard of his visitor or of his commission from the governor to maintain a private navy. But Kidd soon told Mr. Gardiner all that it was convenient that he should know about himself, and then informed him that he (Captain Kidd) had landed a quantity of goods on the island which was concealed in a hollow about half a mile west of the manor-house, and Mr. Gardiner was asked to allow it to remain there untouched until such time as Kidd could return and claim his booty. Before leaving the island Kidd threatened the "proprietor" with vengeance if the treasure was unearthed, and showed himself in his true colors. The privateersman was short of provisions and water, and he swaggeringly ordered Mrs. Gardiner to command her servants to kill and roast a pig for him. In reward for this he presented the lady with a beautiful piece of brocaded silk interwoven with gold threads, and dropped a handsome diamond into the pitcher in which the servant served him with cider. No doubt these were part of the booty from the ill-starred Quidder Merchant, and they are still preserved as relics at the island. After providing himself and crew with provisions for a long cruise, Captain Kidd sailed away from the island the same day, and the terrified owner was thankful to see him depart.

The Pirate and His Escapades

After cruising for a short time Kidd was bold enough to venture into the harbor of Boston, believing that his piratical deeds were still undiscovered, but the non-arrival of The Quidder Merchant had aroused suspicions, and Kidd was detained by the authorities. Kidd at once boldly sent to the governor of New York and demanded his release as an accredited official of the government, but that gentleman found that Kidd had much exceeded his license and became rather alarmed as to his own position in the matter. Kidd became desperate as he saw that the authorities in Boston were determined to hold him responsible for the terrible losses sustained by their merchants, and he declared that if he were guilty of piracy the governor of New York and the king of England were equally so, as they had often been glad enough to accept a share of his plunder without inquiring too closely as to how it had been obtained. Finding that bluster and threats had no effect on the magistrates, who would not permit him to be released, Kidd wrote a private letter to the governor begging that he would intervene in his behalf. Governor Bellomont, finding that he was likely to get into trouble through his connection with Kidd, determined to abandon him to his fate, and on January 5, 1699, wrote to the Lords of Trade in London:

"Captain Kidd sent his gaoler to me a fortnight ago, to acquaint me that if I would let him go to the place where he left the ship Quidder Merchant, and to St. Thomas Island, and Curacoa, he would undertake to bring off three score thousand pounds which would otherwise be lost; but I sent him word he was a king's prisoner, and I could hearken to no such proposition. But I bade the gaoler try if he could not prevail with Captain Kidd to discover where his treasure lay hid—but he said nobody could find it but himself, and would not tell further."

Threats and persuasions were brought to bear on the prisoner, and he finally confessed that Mr. Gardiner could disclose the whereabouts of the treasure of The Quidder Merchant, which had been concealed on the island, and the Boston authorities immediately sent two agents to ask Mr. Gardiner to show them the hiding-place. The adventure with the pirate had nearly faded from the mind of Mr. Gardiner, who had scarcely credited the tale of the buried treasure, and he was surprised and alarmed at the appearance of the detectives. At first he would not believe in their authority, and it was a long time before he could be persuaded to guide them to the place which has ever since been called "Kidd's Hollow," near "Cherry-tree Harbor," and then only on the condition that, if any treasure should be discovered there, he should accompany the agents to Boston and receive a receipt, not only from the government but also from Kidd himself; and he was astounded at the value and quantity of the booty that was dug up. There were bags of silver, gold, and precious stones, bales of merchandise, and many other valuable things, and they were all carefully packed and carried to

The Pirate and His Escapades

Boston by the commissioners and Mr. Gardiner, and delivered to the authorities there, who caused an inventory to be made and duly set forth, on a huge sheet of parchment, to which the signatures of the council were appended, as a receipt in full; and this receipt is still carefully preserved at Gardiner's Island.

There are many localities still pointed out as the hiding-places of Kidd's treasure, but there is no historical evidence that any was ever discovered, except the buried treasure on this island. Probably the finders, if there were any, were not as honest as Mr. Gardiner.

The fate of Captain Kidd was the usual one of those days, when piracy on the high seas was always punished as severely as possible, as it was such a menace to all life and property on the ocean; and the captain soon swung in chains on the gibbet at Boston. Soon after the sudden death of Kidd, his widow married Christopher Rosby, her fourth husband. The only daughter of the unfortunate man assumed the name of one of her stepfathers, of whom she had quite an assortment, and tried to obliterate as far as possible all connection with her disgraced parent. She married, and her descendants are still living in the city of New York. The second husband of Mrs. Kidd was William Cox, to whom she had been married April 17, 1685. He was drowned off Staten Island in 1690. It is not known what name the daughter of Kidd adopted in order to conceal her identity.

After an uneventful career as governor of New York,

his excellency Lord Bellomont died in the city, February, 1701, and was buried within its limits, in the old church-yard. Many years afterward his coffin was exhumed at the opening of some of the streets in the lower part of the town and the plate on which the governor's name, title, earl's coat-of-arms, coronet, etc., were displayed was wrenched from its place and sold to the keeper of a museum. The plate was of silver and uncommonly large. It was kept on exhibition for many years, until the proprietor of the museum failed, when "my lord's" coffin-plate was melted into—teaspoons.

XIV

Society Under the English Rule

Death of John Spratt—Marriage of His Widow—Colonel Provoost Made Mayor of the City—Death of Mrs. Spratt-Provoost—Colonel Provoost's Troubles—Madame Knight's Journey to New York—Lord and Lady Cornbury—The Court of Their Excellencies—Miss Van Cortlandt as Maid of Honor—Escapades of the Governor—Mr. Bedlow and His Island.

THE quiet home in Prince's Graft was for the second time rendered desolate by the sudden death of the ex-speaker, John Spratt, who succumbed to a prevalent fever and the medical treatment of the day. He died in 1696, leaving his widow with an infant daughter named Catharine, a child of two years of age called Mary, a son John who was barely seven, and Cornelia, the eldest daughter, a child a little over eight years old, who bore the name of her grandmother Mrs. de Peyster.

The brave widow faced this second desolation in her home with characteristic courage and pious resignation, and she tried to carry on the business that she had inherited from first one husband and then another, and also endeavored to attend to the wants of her little family. In this Mrs. Spratt was greatly aided by her mother and maiden sister Cornelia, who lived in the old home of Johannes de Peyster, within a stone's throw of her house. But even when aided by their advice and the counsel of her brothers, Mrs. Spratt found the responsibility too great to be borne alone, and was forced to look out for a partner to share her business cares. In those days business usually took precedence of sentiment, and it was with little surprise that the friends of Mrs. Spratt learned of her marriage to Colonel David Provoost (the third of that name), a wealthy widower and an esteemed citizen. His grandfather had been one of the first settlers of Mana-ha-ta, and was an intimate friend of Govert Lockermans. "Both men were hated by the English," says Mr. Purple, in a communication to the "New York Genealogical Record," "and David Provoost was a thorn to them, who dreaded the influence he wielded over the Indians, and his success among them as a trader, by what they termed "a crooked and pverse waye." Colonel David Provoost was the grandson of this gentleman, who married Margaret Gillis Van Brugge. The colonel had already filled several municipal positions, and was now a portly widower with a large family of children for whom he was anxious to provide a home, a governess, a maid who would make all the clothing they required (which in those days could not be bought and was always made by the lady of the house and her maids, under her superintendence), and last, but not least, he desired a wife for himself, with a comfortable fortune and home. And all these were combined when he took to himself as wife the "comfortable widow of John Spratt, of blessed memory."

The records of the Dutch church show the date of his marriage to Mrs. Spratt, and the pious groom also recorded it in the Bible of his predecessor, thus: "In the year 16$\frac{33}{34}$, the 20" of January, I, David Provoost, was lawfully joined in marriage with Maria de Peyster, widow of John Spratt of blessed memory."

This year also saw the elevation of the bridegroom, David Provoost, to the office of mayor of the city of New York, succeeding in this position the brother of his bride, der Heer Abraham de Peyster; and their home became the centre of social life in the province. Two families of young people could not fail to make a gay household, although the children of Mrs. Spratt-Provoost were not of an age to enter in the formal entertainments of their elders. But Mrs. Spratt-Provoost followed the example shown by her mother and instituted a series of weekly receptions at her own home, where all her friends were welcome. These friendly meetings were more enjoyed than the formal assemblies to which all the Dutch families belonged, and which were kept up with unabated success, and into which the conservative matrons would allow no foreigner to penetrate.

All the sociables and assemblies were rudely stopped toward the spring by the death of Mrs. Spratt-Provoost, as nearly every family in the town was connected with her, and all were deeply affected by her death. And the next entry in the Bible was: "In the year 1700, on the 5th of May, died in the Lord, my beloved wife Maria, in the afternoon, between six and seven of the clock, aged forty-one years, seven months, and twenty-nine days, of which we lived together two years, three months, and three days. Until the Lord separated us. She was buried in Col. Abraham de Peyster's Vault in the Church yard."

A good deal of confusion ensued on the death of Mrs. Spratt-Provoost, as she left three young children motherless, and Mr. Provoost had his own large family to take care of, who were again left without a proper protector. He naturally desired to continue to live in the luxurious home in the Prince's Graft, which he had hoped was secured to him and his family for their life, but the relations of his wife by no means approved of this arrangement, and indeed it would seem, by the lawsuits that followed on the death of Mrs. Spratt-Provoost, that the widower was desirous of making the allowance provided for the children of his second wife (who were quite wealthy for those days) cover the expense of clothing and educating those by his first marriage.

This arrangement was by no means approved of by the guardians of the Spratt children, and they required a rigid accounting, which left the worthy ex-mayor somewhat in debt to his late wife's estate. In July, 1710, having unwarily confessed judgment for four thousand pounds, although he afterward declared that his real debt was only a little over four hundred pounds, Mr. Provoost was put under the custody of the sheriff, at the suit of der Heer Abraham de Peyster, the trustee of Mrs. Spratt-Provoost's estate. This was a severe blow to an influential citizen who had been a member of the assembly, mayor of the city, and a member of the king's council in 1709; and as he was at this date reelected to a position in the government, the confinement to his own house under the charge of the sheriff prevented him from attending to his duties. On July 2, 1711, Colonel David Provoost addressed a letter to the speaker of the assembly, reciting the fact of his election as one of the representatives for the city and county of New York, and praying for enlargement.

At the same time a petition was presented to the house from Cornelia, John, and Mary Spratt, children of John Spratt, deceased, setting forth that David Provoost, their "father-in-law," was declared in custody to the sheriff on their behalf, he not having paid their portions, and praying the house would consider their case, they being orphans.

Governor Hunter, who was at that time in office, referred to this petition in his message to the assembly, November 23, 1711, as "a dispute between the de Peysters, as guardians of their nieces and nephew, and the Provoosts." And in his letter to the home government of May 7, 1711, the governor mentions it as a case requiring the intervention of the Court of Chancery, as he says " there is no address at common law." The difficulty was finally adjusted before April 30, 1712, at which time Colonel Provoost took the oath of office and his seat in the assembly.

New York had a very agreeable visitor in December, 1704, in the person of a Boston lady, who left a sprightly account of her travels from one city to the other, which was published under the *nom de plume* of " Mme. Knight." The lady was apparently a widow, who was forced to take this journey at the beginning of winter in order to collect some money owing to her late husband. She must have been a brave woman to undertake such a long and hazardous trip by herself, and also must have had a superior education for the time to be able to narrate her adventures in the agreeable way that she does. She says:

"The Cittie of New York is a pleasent well compacted place, situated on a Commodious River which is a fine harbour for shipping. The Buildings Brick Generally, very stately and high, though not altogether like ours in Boston. The Bricks in some of the Houses, are of divers Coullers and laid in Checkers being glazed, look very agreeable. The inside of them are neat to admiration, the woodwork, for only the walls are plastered, and the Summers and Gist are plained and kept very white scour'd, as so is all the partitions if made of Bords. The fire-places have no Jambs (as ours have) But the Backs run flush with the walls, and the Hearth is of Tyles, and is as far out into the Room at the ends as before the fire, wch. is Generally Five Foot in the Low.r rooms, and the piece over Where the Mantle tree should be, is made as ours with Joiners work, and as I suppose, is fastened to iron rodds inside. I went to a Vendue where I bought about 100 Rhems of paper, wch. was retaken in a fly-boat from Holland, and sold very Reasonably here. some ten some Eight shillings per Rhem by the lott wch. was ten Rhem in a lott. And at the Vendue I made a great many acquaintances among the good women of the town, who curteosly invited me to their houses and generously entertained me. The house where the Vendue was, had Chimney Corners like ours, and they and the hearths were laid with the finest tile that I ever see, and the staircases laid all with white tile, which is ever clean, and so are all the walls of the Kitchen wch. had a Brick floor.—The English go very fashionable in their dress. But the Dutch especially the middle sorts, differ from our women in their habett go loose, were French Muches wch. are like a capp and a head band in one, leaving their ears bare, which are sett out wth. jewells of a large size and many in number, and their fingers hooped with Rings, some with large stones in them with many Coulers as were their pendants in their ears, which You should see very old women wear as well as Young. They have Vendues frequently and make their Earnings very well by them, for they treat with good Liquor Liberally, and the Customers Drink as Liberally and Generally pay for't as well, by paying for that which they Bidd up Briskly for, after the Sack has gone plentifully about, tho' sometimes good pennyworths are got there. Their Diversions in . Winter, is Riding Sluys, about three or four miles out of Town, where they have Houses of entertainment, at a place called the Bowery, and Madame Dowes, a Gentlewoman that lived at a farm House, who gave us a handsome Entertainment of five or six Dishes, and choice Beer and Metheglin Cyder &tc. all of which she said was the product of her own farm. I believe we mett 50 or 60 sluys that day—they fly with great swiftness and some are so furious that they'll turn out of the path for none except a Loaded Cart."

The Goede Vrouw of Mana-ha-ta

Such, then, was the pleasant life in the province of New York when William of England died and Queen Anne succeeded to the throne, and was crowned April 23, 1702.

The queen had a horde of the poor relations of her mother (Anne Hyde) to provide for, and, among others, had a graceless cousin, whom she was glad to get out of England, and she therefore despatched him to New York as its governor, regardless of his enormous debts, his profligate character, and his total disqualification for such a delicate and onerous position.

Edward Hyde, Lord Cornbury, arrived in the colony May 3, 1702, with his wife, who was a lady of small intelligence and a limited education. She was not his equal in birth, and had never had any beauty to speak of, but she had a beautiful ear, and my lord had fallen in love and married her on account of its peculiar shapeliness. Unfortunately, the ear soon ceased to please, and then the wife was neglected. My lady was much pleased with her position among the nobility of England and her close connection with her majesty, and willingly overlooked the neglect of her husband for the sake of the position that he could give her. She was as extravagant and as unscrupulous as himself, and made herself useful to him by suggesting and executing plans for raising money, when they were in their most desperate straits, which it is probable even such an unprincipled person as the governor would have hesitated to carry out. The couple had been forced to leave England secretly, in order to evade their creditors, and they had accepted the position in the colony simply to enrich themselves by extorting money from their subjects, and were perfectly unscrupulous and barefaced in their methods.

His excellency and his lady had very expensive habits and no money, and they condescended to many unworthy devices in order that they might be able to keep up a court in the style that they deemed befitting their rank; and Lady Cornbury invented a scheme for securing free service that was commendable only for its ingenuity.

On the arrival of his excellency, the people of the colony hastened to White Hall to pay their respects to the new governor and his lady, and were delighted with their gracious reception, which was so different from what was generally accorded to them by the English rulers. They little suspected what the suavity and graciousness concealed.

Many dinners and entertainments were given in honor of his excellency and Lady Cornbury, and a particularly notable function was given by Madame Van Cortlandt. Soon after this, Lady Cornbury made a selection from the young ladies of the principal families of the colony, and invited them to take up their residence with her at the governor's mansion, and act as her maids of honor. At first this was esteemed as a great distinction, and the worthy members of "her majesty's council" and the other officials of the government were proud to have their daughters attend the governor's court; but, little by little, the young ladies discovered that their position was no sinecure. Lady Cornbury had a large allowance from her husband—on paper—for her household expenses, but she never could get her husband to pay her the money. She therefore resorted to the most peculiar devices in order to keep up appearances before the world. One of her economies was to keep no servants, and her maids of honor were required to sweep and dust, help in the kitchen, act as seamstresses, as waiting-maids to her ladyship, and were never permitted to leave the house. The indignation of the Dutch burghers, when they learned how they had been entrapped into turning their daughters into servants for the English lady, passed all bounds. The girls were carried away from White Hall, sometimes by force, and generally after a very stormy interview with her ladyship, who would screech and scream, and rave around the rooms, and even try to scratch and strike her quondam maids of honor, who confessed to their parents that she had resorted to such means to keep them in servitude, and they had endured their captivity, as they were afraid of what her ladyship might do to them.

Lady Cornbury revenged herself on the first deserters by abusing them and their parents to all who would listen to her. There were many such, as in all communities there are plenty of worshippers of the nobility, the wealthy, or the powerful. A new set of girls was easily secured, but, as they experienced exactly the same treatment as the first bevy had received, they also returned to their parents in a high state of indignation, and the governor and his lady soon found themselves shunned by high and low.

Among the first maidens who had been entrapped by this original scheme of Lady Cornbury's was Miss Gertrude Van Cortlandt, the daughter of Stephanus Van Cortlandt of the manor, and granddaughter of Oloff Van Cortlandt, a man who had held many positions of honor in the "plantation," and who had been one of its most esteemed citizens. It is a matter of surprise that the governor should have connived at such an unpardonable piece of arrogance toward a young girl whose family was of such prominence, and, although hardly credible, it was quite in keeping with the governor's usual behavior, as his head was quite turned by his near connection with her majesty Queen Anne, and he believed that anything he might do was pardonable in one so closely allied to royalty, and that it must be condoned by his subjects in New York.

Miss Gertrude Schuyler Van Cortlandt was afterward married to Colonel Henry Beekman as his second wife, but left no descendants. In after days, she would often relate her funny experiences as maid of honor, and would sit on the edge of her chair straight as an arrow, with her hands crossed before her, to show how the maids sat in the parlor before Lord and Lady Cornbury when they expected company; and her stories were carefully preserved in writing by members of her husband's family, and still exist in manuscript. A reference is made to them in Mrs. Delafield's "Biographies of Francis Lewis and Morgan Lewis."

There are other family traditions that recall how Lord Cornbury would sit at his table for hours at a time, drinking the good wines that he had begged from his subjects, and one evening, being somewhat intoxicated, he went into his wife's room and dressed himself in her clothes and started for a walk in the gardens around White Hall. His secretary persuaded him to return to the house, and the freak was only known to a few persons, who were shocked at the levity that prompted such undignified conduct on the part of the representative and relation of her majesty Queen Anne. But, emboldened by the success of his first experiment, Lord Cornbury soon repeated it, and this time he wandered beyond the limits of his own enclosure, and paraded up Broadway, where he was seized by the city watch while flaunting his gay satins by moonlight, and behaving in such a manner as to scandalize the old guardian of the peace. The officer was still more horrified when he found that he had in custody a man dressed in women's clothes, and was amazed beyond description when he found that his prisoner was none other than the governor of the province, in a highly hilarious condition; and the watchman could scarcely be induced to release his excellency, as he considered it the duty of the watch to carry all prisoners to the guard-house, no matter what was their degree. This excess could not be concealed from the public, and a reference to it is to be found in Mr. Smith's "History of New York;" and of course it was common talk at the tea-tables of the town.

Everyone now shunned the governor and his wife, who found themselves reduced to extreme poverty. The council and assembly prevented them from robbing the public exchequer, tradespeople would not trust them, the rich citizens would contribute nothing to their support or allow their daughters to serve as domestics at the mimic court, and the exalted pair were in a bad plight. But her ladyship was callous and perfectly indifferent to public opinion, and she hesitated at nothing when she had an end in view.

It was a custom with my lady to order her coach and start on a round of visits, when she would enter any house that attracted her attention, and after glancing about her, she would call her footman and order placed in her carriage any article that might happen to strike her fancy or please her taste, and in this way, to the disgust of the ladies, cherished bits of china, priceless lace, valuable books, etc., all vanished into her capacious coach, and were carried off by her rapacious ladyship. In the "Biographies of Francis Lewis and Morgan Lewis" is this account of her ladyship:

"As hers was the only coach in the city, the rolling of the wheels was easily distinguished, and then the cry in the house was, 'There comes my lady; hide this, hide that, take that away.' Whatever she admired in her visits she was sure to send for the next day."

To add to the aggravation of this polite thievery, Lady Cornbury would sometimes send to say that the owners could redeem their property by paying for them, but otherwise she would sell them for junk; and it often happened that the unlucky townspeople would be forced to buy their own belongings from a pedler to whom they had been sold by her ladyship. Fortunately for the citizens of New York, this lady died on Sunday, August 11, 1706, aged thirty-four, and after grand funeral ceremonies, which Dame Rumor declared were never paid for, the Lady Cornbury was laid to rest in the "English Church-yard," as Trinity Church was then called.

There was an Englishman who came to New York about this time and determined to settle in the colony. He had amassed a fortune in the East Indies and was attracted to America by the fact that Lord Cornbury was its governor, as they had had some acquaintance in early life. On Mr. Bedlow's arrival the governor gave him the privilege of victualling the fleet, a post that carried with it great facilities for making money. Mr. Bedlow died suddenly, and his excellency, probably fearing that some of the secret arrangements that had been made between him and his commissioner would be disclosed by his papers, demanded that they be placed in his hands, and by so doing quietly possessed himself of all the vouchers for the victualling department, and collected the money due on them, which he put in his own pocket. When the heirs came to look for their papers and demanded their return from the governor, he denied all knowledge of them, and the widow and children were reduced to the greatest poverty.

Mr. Bedlow purchased an island in the harbor of New York that is still called by his name. It was a convenient spot for him to store the articles required for the English fleet, and the vessels could lie close to its shores and be loaded without going to the city. This island is now covered by the unsightly monument called the statue of "Liberty Enlightening the World," a monstrosity that disfigures the entrance to the otherwise beautiful harbor of New York.

XV

Wedding-bells and Caudle-cups

Neltje and Polly Spratt—The Weddings in the de Peyster Family—The Children's "Companies"—The Marriage of Miss Spratt to Samuel Provoost—His Death—Mrs. Provoost lays the First Sidewalk in New York—Lord Cornbury and his Visit to Jamaica—A New Way of Erecting a Church—Weddings in the Van Dam Family—Recall of Lord Cornbury—Lord Lovelace and his Sudden Death—Governor Hunter—Change in the Government at Rensselaerswyck—Kiliaen the Fourth Patroon, and "Quidder"—The Governor's Visit to the Manor of Livingston—He Stands Sponsor to Robert Hunter Morris—The Indian's Summary of Governor Hunter's Character.

THE orphan children of John Spratt were carefully educated by their grandmother, Madame de Peyster, for the position in life that they were to be called on to fill. The large fortune that was left to them by their parents was husbanded for their use, and they were put in possession of it when they became of a suitable age. The elder daughter, Cornelia, was of a lovable, quiet character, fond of reading her Bible and happy in her domestic duties, the devoted companion of her grandmother and maiden aunt. But Polly Spratt was quite different from her sister, and was a daring, mischievous sprite, full of tricks that she did not hesitate to play on her grandmother and sweet aunt.

Wedding-bells and Caudle-cups

Those good ladies shook their heads over "Polly's pranks," but indulged her slightest whim, and she led the van in all the sports of her young companions, unchecked by her grandmother, who would have been horrified and indignant if anyone had dared to suggest that Polly was spoiled or indulged more than any other girl of her age in the province.

As a child Polly had delighted in coasting down the steep sides of "Flattenbarack Hill" with her daring brother Jack, all the boys in the town following her with admiring eyes when she stood upright on her "sluy" and darted down the hill-side, a feat that no boy in the company dared to perform, and that startled one of her staid uncles almost out of his wonted dignity when he found the young hoyden with dishevelled locks, who came rushing down the steep incline and nearly threw him into the kennel, was no other than his own little niece, Polly Spratt.

Time passed and the hoyden grew to be a lovely young girl. She was a comely lass with bright, sparkling eyes and ruddy cheeks, and as she was an heiress in her own right she had many suitors. There were two gay weddings in the family of her uncle, Johannes de Peyster (who had succeeded her step-father as mayor of the city), when in 1715 Betsy, or Elizabeth, de Peyster became Mrs. Jacobus Beekman, and in November of the same year her brother, Johannes de Peyster (de Jonge), married Miss Anna Schuyler. This wedding was soon followed by that of Cornelia de Peyster, another sister, to Matthew Clarkson. The daughters of der Heer de Peyster had already become the wives of Philip Van Cortlandt and John Hamilton. This large family connection always welcomed Polly Spratt at all their festive gatherings, and no merry-making was complete without her, the bonniest, brightest maiden of them all. She led the dance at all the gay assemblies, was the pioneer on the newly formed ice on the Collect, and it was her skates (made out of beef-bones, and a present from some youthful admirer) that were the first to be strapped on by one of the crowd of attendant boy cousins or friends, flocks of whom were always in her train. Polly could row or sail a boat with the ease and hardihood of long practice, and her indulgent uncles, who had never permitted any escapades in their own families, were always ready to excuse her and beg her off from the slight punishments her indulgent grandmother inflicted when Polly had committed some unusually great breach of decorum.

There was a curious custom in the early days of the colonies, when the children of the towns gathered themselves into sets or "companies," as they were called. Boys and girls in each one were equally divided, and they were usually about the same age. The children of a company always played together, and they acknowledged one of their number as leader, although there was no formal election or organization. The formation of a set was generally purely accidental, and was caused by propinquity or perhaps by the intimacy of the parents, but most generally by the age of the children, those of the same age naturally preferring to play together. Parents seldom interfered with these intimacies unless some very objectionable child was admitted in the company. These playmates grew up like children of one family and generally intermarried, and this was so much a matter of custom that matches were seldom made with members of other sets.

Mrs. Grant, of Laggan, in her memoirs of Mrs. Schuyler, "An American Lady," mentions this custom, and says:

"In Albany the Companies at a certain time of year, went in a body to gather a particular kind of berry on the hill. It was an annual festival attended with religious punctuality. Every Company had a Uniform for this purpose; that is to say, very pretty light baskets made by the Indians with lids and handles, which hung on the arms, and were adorned with various colors."

On these expeditions the girls always carried their work with them, as they were industrious little maidens and were constantly employed in knitting stockings for themselves, the boys, and the slaves of the family, and they would sit in groups, chatting, sewing, and knitting, while the boys wandered afield gathering berries or nuts, which were always carefully divided with the girls at the end of the day. In the winter the amusements were held in the homes of the children, unless they could skate or go in large sleighing-parties to the country-home of one of the members. Polly Spratt was the leader of a large company in New York that was chiefly composed of her band of cousins, her numerous step-brothers and sisters, and the descendants of her grandmother's early friends, the first settlers of Mana-ha-ta.

Neltje and Polly Spratt had been children when Lady Cornbury was forming her court, and so escaped playing the rôle of handmaidens to her ladyship, but many of their friends and the older girls of the family had served their time at court, which, although annoying and hard to endure at the time, was now told over and over again to the friends of the maids of honor, who were always ready to make merry over their past adventures. The sisters grew up in the quiet refinement of their grandmother's home, which was as far removed from the coarseness of the English court-life as was possible in such a small town, where the "door-latch hung always on the outside" (to quote a familiar proverb of the day) and where high and low mingled in every-day pursuits and amusements; and it was hardly possible to hold aloof from all contact with the governor's family any more than in the case of an opposite neighbor. But Polly Spratt, although not at court, had (as has been said) plenty of gayety, and more lovers than her anxious grandmother could keep count of, who were captivated by Polly's handsome black eyes and merry, clever speeches. It was with the greatest reluctance that her guardians permitted her to be betrothed, at the age of seventeen, to Samuel Provoost, a member of Polly's company from childhood, and a younger brother of her mother's third husband, David Provoost. This family were of French descent on their father's side, and had long been prominent members of the New York colony. Early marriages were the rule in those days, but no one wanted to see the pretty curly head of Polly Spratt covered with a matron's coif. But the wilful maiden had her way, and on October 15, 1711, she married Mr. Provoost and went to house-keeping in the handsome house that was purchased for her by her husband, who was already well established in business and considered a thriving merchant. The bride's fortune was partly invested in the business, and her uncles looked well after the interests of their ward and had the money settled on her. She had been taught the management of business affairs, after the custom of Holland, and she soon showed the capacity she had inherited from her mother and took her full share in the management of her husband's importations and correspondence.

Mrs. Provoost lost her first child, a little girl, who was born a year after her marriage, but she had two sons, who grew to manhood. These were John and David Provoost; the former born in 1714, and the latter in 1719.

It is probable that Neltje (or Cornelia) Spratt died about 1716, as the old Bible which contained so many interesting family records passed into the hands of her brother Jack on March 27th of that year. There is an entry in it, "April 15, 1705, Cornelia Spratt," under which is added the name of her brother, written in a different handwriting, "John Spratt, 1716," as if, after the death of the young girl, the book had been given to the next of age.

If the supposition that Neltje Spratt died at this time is correct (and there is no later record of her), Mrs. Provoost was not only called upon to mourn the loss of her only sister, but also, in a very little time, that of her husband, Samuel Provoost. It was well that the young widow (who was barely twenty-six) had identified herself with her husband's business, which was that of an importer, with correspondents in many parts of the world, and understood its management. She immediately assumed control of it, and, with her thrifty Dutch habits, added considerably to her fortune. She had a row of offices built in front of her house, directly on the street, with a large store on one side.

Mrs. Provoost was shrewd enough to perceive that although her shop was convenient for herself, as it was so close to her home that she could attend to her household duties and still superintend the details of her counting-house at the same time, yet, as it was not situated directly on the exchange, that merchants and purchasers from other places would not be attracted to the shop unless their attention was called to it. She therefore ordered a quantity of large flat stones to be laid as a sidewalk, not only in front of her place of business but beyond her property and up to the streets on either side of it. This was an important improvement, as the roadway had been paved, when the street was opened, with small round stones, which served to prevent carts and horses from sinking into the mud; but there was no provision for foot-passengers, whose patience was sorely tried by being obliged to stumble over the rough cobble-stones. To add to the discomforts of the pedestrian, the street was made to slope toward the middle, which formed a kennel through which water was generally running, and under such conditions walking dry-shod was no easy matter.

Mrs. Samuel Provoost's pavement was the talk of the town, and such a convenient innovation attracted many visitors, not only from relations who were proud of her ingenuity, but from all her old " company," who flocked around their beloved Polly, and thought her the wisest woman of her day. It was a capital advertisement for the shrewd little lady, as she had foreseen, and country-people and visitors from other towns would turn out of their way to gaze at the wonderful new invention, and, when once attracted to the spot, could never resist entering the counting-room, and in consequence Mrs. Provoost had large country orders always on hand. The stone "walking-side" laid down by the private enterprise of a woman was the first pavement in the city of New York. Some of the neighbors followed this praiseworthy example and laid brick walks, which were called "strookes," and, by degrees, paving and curbing the streets were undertaken by the municipal authorities, and not left to individual exertions. It was said that Mrs. Provoost wished the authorities to pave the walks for her, and they declined, saying that it was not possible to do such a thing, and that she undertook to give them an object-lesson, in which she thoroughly succeeded.

Mr. Livingston Rutherfurd, in "Family Records and Events," states that "Mrs. Provoost's store was acknowledged to be one of the best appointed in the city, and her social position was in no way affected by her business pursuits. She was for a long time the only person besides the governor who kept a two-horse coach." It is probable that Mrs. Provoost never had a thought as to her social position. She had been accustomed to being surrounded from her childhood by the most agreeable and educated people of the place, all of whom were occupied exactly as she was herself, and as her parents had been occupied before her, and there was no one enough of a snob in the city to hold himself aloof from one of their number, simply because that one invested her money in mercantile pursuits and conducted her business herself. Such ideas were foreign to those of Dutch descent, and were only the reflections of the opinions of the English, who preferred to live in idleness and on the bounty of others (if they did no worse), and pretended to despise honest labor.

The shop, its handsome mistress, and the wonderful coach were famed far and wide, and two good ladies of Philadelphia made a journey to New York to see the sights, chief of which they conceded were "the great store and the strange carriage of Madame;" and their awe and admiration are quaintly expressed in a manu-

Wedding-bells and Caudle-cups

script journal and history of their travels, which are worthy of being printed for the amusement of readers of the present day.

In 1702 yellow fever devastated New York, and its inhabitants fled far and wide. Those who had houses in the country went to them, and crowded them with all their friends and relations who had no other place to go—for those were the days of the greatest hospitality and everyone was welcome, even the poor, homeless Indians, who sometimes wandered around the country, stopping at the first house they fancied, sure of a nook in the ingleside, a warm meal, and shelter for the night. No one was ever turned away from a vrouw's kitchen; she always had food and welcome for all.

Among the other refugees was Lord Cornbury, who fled from his post at the first signal of danger and retired to the pretty little village of Jamaica, on Long Island, as Sewan-ha-ka began to be called about that time.

In those days Jamaica was beginning to be a summer-resort, and gentlemen from New York, with their families, frequently visited it for the purpose of hunting deer and shooting grouse, which abounded on the neighboring plains of Hempstead. It was convenient also to the great bay, which afforded good sport—duck-shooting as well as fishing; and Jamaica was therefore the favorite headquarters of sportsmen. But there were few houses in the hamlet that were commodious enough to accommodate Lord Cornbury and his staff, and the Presbyterian minister most courteously put his manse, which was the largest house in the place, at the disposal of his excellency. The governor accepted the courtesy as if it were his due, and, not satisfied with the pastor's residence, Lord Cornbury also demanded the use of the chapel, so that services might be conducted there according to the ritual of the Church of England; for, whatever else the governor was careless about, he never neglected his official attendance at public worship. The minister and congregation of the Presbyterian church gave up their edifice with considerable reluctance, as may be supposed, to the use of the governor, when, what was their surprise and indignation to find that the governor accepted their loan as a gift, and then quietly turned over manse, meeting-house, and glebe to the Established Church of England, and put a priest of that denomination, and of his own preferment, in charge of the establishment, under the protection of his excellency! The Presbyterian minister and his congregation were indignant beyond measure at this wholesale robbery by her majesty's representative, but they had no redress even at law, and Christ Church, Jamaica, was founded in this remarkable way, as anyone may learn for himself by reading the Colonial Documents of the day, with their reports on this subject.

In the Colonial Documents of the State of New York by O'Callaghan it is recorded that (vol. v., page 111) Governor Cornbury, in his official position, granted part of the Newtown patent to Mr. Boudinot, who had advanced money to pay for the grand funeral services held over Lady Cornbury, in discharge of £300 owing to him. It was in this way that the disreputable governor performed his duties to the colony of New York. After the citizens had recovered from their dread of the yellow fever and had settled down quietly once more in their homes, many festivities were arranged for that had been deferred on account of the prevalence of the pestilence. The Van Dam family had always been part of either Neltje or Polly Spratt's "company," for the two sisters, being of different ages, were not in the same one, and members of different families were always sorted out according to their age. The elder members of the Van Dam household had married some years before Polly Spratt had grown up. The first-born son had taken for a wife Judith Bayard; Richard Van Dam, who came next in seniority, married Cornelia Beekman, and in October, 1704, great preparations were made for the wedding of the handsome eldest daughter, Calatyntie, whose lover was a thriving young merchant of the place called Walter Tong, who duly took out a license from his excellency, who granted under seal and bond his august permission for the marriage on the 16th of the month.

Rip Van Dam, the father of this large family, was the son of an early settler of the colony. Madame Van Dam was the daughter of the first official street-cleaner of New York, and her only sister had married Isaac de Forest. It may be difficult to understand in these days of how much importance all these family connections were, as the ties have been lost sight of during the lapse of years, but in those days the bonds were strong and close, and families were most loyal to each other, members of the different companies continuing their intimacy even after marriage. So they were pretty certain to uphold each other in any important event that might be agitating the community at the time. The English governors often found themselves unaccountably thwarted in some scheme in which they had counted on support from their council, and it was often entirely due to the counter-influence brought to bear by some member of a far-reaching family or company whose views the project did not happen to suit.

The Van Dam family were one of the most united in the place, and during the subsequent colonial troubles, when Rip Van Dam was supporting the interests of his fellow-citizens against the encroachments of the English, this underlying, far-reaching net-work of family ties did much to assist him in his brave resistance against tyranny and oppression.

Mr. and Mrs. Walter Tong had only one child, a daughter, Mary, who married Robert Livingston, third lord of the manor, and this connection added to the power and influence of the Van Dam family, and drew closer together the interests of the Presbyterian and Dutch Church parties against the English and foreign influences which began to make themselves felt in the colony. Lord Cornbury had disgraced himself so thoroughly that his cousin, Queen Anne, was forced to recall him and send to her province in America Lord Lovelace, a gentleman with a better reputation than that of his predecessor, but the new governor caught a severe cold on his voyage to the colony, which left him in such poor health that he died seven months after assuming office. He was succeeded by the lieutenant-governor, who filled the office for a few months until supplanted by a fresh arrival in the person of Robert Hunter, the first governor ever sent by England to take charge of her New York colony who proved to be congenial to the colonists in temperament and tastes. Ex-Governor Cornbury was immediately thrown into prison for his debts, and there was not one person who could be found to pity or take compassion on him; and it was not until money was sent out from England that he was able to obtain his release, and he left the colony execrated by high and low.

Governor Hunter was a middle-aged man, travelled and well-read. The friend and correspondent of Addison, Swift, and other literary men of the day, the colonists highly appreciated such an addition to their circle and cordially welcomed him as their ruler, and enjoyed the strong contrast of an educated and honorable gentleman after the corrupt and ignorant persons who had been sent again and again to govern them, and his excellency was fêted on every side. One of his first excursions was to the manor of Rensselaerswyck, where he spent several days enjoying the hospitalities of the patroon.

The Goede Vrouw of Mana-ha-ta

Eighty years had elapsed since the plantation of the "Colonie of Rensselaerswyck," and they had been uneventfully passed in the peaceful pursuits of agriculture, hunting, and fishing by the patroon and his subjects. The peculiar condition of government that was provided for under the rights granted by the States General of Holland had been considerably altered and modified under the rule of England.

Der Groot Director Jeremias Van Rensselaer, having refused to assist Governor Stuyvesant with money or men at the time of the first occupation of Mana-ha-ta by the English fleet under Colonel Nicolls, had discovered to his surprise that the warning of the governor was fulfilled, and that his plantation at Rensselaerswyck was doomed to stand or fall with that of the Dutch West India Company. But the patroon accepted the change in the government with philosophy, and exchanged his rights as an independent prince for manorial grants, which he took out under the English laws. While the patroon was thus shorn of his military honors, his distinctive flag, and his independent army, he retained the ownership of the vast tract of land which his father had originally purchased, and which had been settled entirely at the expense of the first patroon. Jeremias Van Rensselaer was quite willing to abandon the empty honors of a principality in the New World for the more substantial benefits that he presumed he would receive from the support of the sister plantation of Mana-ha-ta. As the interests of the two places became more and more identical, the dividing line between the two colonies gradually faded away, greatly to the contentment of all parties, who now made common cause against the English government, which was always endeavoring to squeeze money out of the colonies, and did nothing to advance their interests, encourage their commerce, or protect them from the savages that surrounded them.

Governor Hunter's conciliatory visit to the manor-house at Rensselaerswyck was to the patroon,* and Patroon Van Rensselaer and his chief ally, Peter Schuyler, were glad to have this much-sought opportunity of laying before the chief officials their perplexities with regard to Indian affairs, and of considering the best method of dealing with the savages and keeping them friendly and willing to resist the temptations always being held out to them by the French in Canada to murder and exterminate the whites. But, fortunately for the lives and fortunes of the Dutch planters, there was one man who had more influence over the sachems of the northern tribes than any of the Jesuit priests in Canada, and this was Peter Schuyler, who was usually called by the nickname that the Indians had bestowed on him, as they could not pronounce his name—"the Quidder." It was by his influence that a number of braves had been carried to England and presented to her majesty Queen Anne;

* Kiliaen Van Rensselaer, the son of Jeremias, who had succeeded to the family estates in 1674.

and this expedition was believed to have riveted the ties between the Wilden and the colonists, and it was hoped that the savages had been overawed by the brilliancy and power of the English court, and that they would counsel their comrades to resist the temptation of going on the war-path, having been convinced of the hopelessness of fighting against such a well-equipped government.

After his visit to Rensselaerswyck, Governor Hunter dropped down the river in his yacht and stopped at the manor of Livingston, where the first lord of the manor, with his wife, had assembled a great party of friends and relations to greet him. The governor was determined to make friends with all his new subjects, and his next visit was to Lewis Morris, one of his warmest supporters, whose acquaintance he had made in Europe. The friendship was cemented on the birth of Governor Morris's second son, who received the name of "Robert Hunter," after his excellency, a name that became synonymous with all that was upright and honest in the province of New Jersey, of which place he became one of the "proprietors," and in after-life enjoyed the honor of being its chief-justice.

Governor Hunter not only made friends with the people of the colony, but he also determined to identify himself with its interests by becoming a landed proprietor, and to this end he selected a beautiful site on Raritan Bay, one of the inlets of the New York harbor, and proceeded to have a mansion erected there to which he might move when called upon to exercise his official duties in the province of New Jersey, over which he had control, as well as over New York. Governor Hunter, by selecting the hamlet of Perth Amboy for his official residence, greatly pleased the inhabitants of that plantation.

While Governor Hunter was at Rensselaerswyck, he demanded certain conditions of the Indians which he deemed necessary for the preservation of peace between the savages and the colony, but the Wilden were not willing to agree to any concessions, and a spirited dispute took place, and the governor flew into a violent passion at having his wishes thwarted. He was noted for these outbreaks of temper, which were fierce and uncontrollable while they lasted, and seemed to cause him to lose his reason. After he had been in one of these fits, an Indian said to an officer, "The governor is drunk." "No!" answered the officer; "he never drinks any strong liquor." The brave replied, "I do not mean he is drunk with rum. He was born drunk."

XVI

James Alexander

Alexander's Family in Scotland—His Mathematical Instruments and Library—The Official Position Occupied by James Alexander—Governor Burnet—His Godfather Prince William of Orange and the Christening-gift—Tastes and Occupations of the New Governor—His Silver-gilt Tea Equipage—The Marriage of the Governor to an American—Dr. Colden and His Family.

THE reigning sovereign of England, Anne, daughter of the deposed James II., died on July 31, 1714, and was succeeded, pursuant to the Act of Succession, by George I., son of Ernest Augustus, first Elector of Brunswick, and the Princess Sophia, granddaughter of James I. The Scotch had no love for the foreign prince now brought to occupy the throne of Great Britain, while the country was governed by a number of clever politicians who filled all the fat offices with their own relations, and left no places for the envious Scotchmen, who forthwith turned their eyes toward their exiled countryman, and invited the son of the deposed James II. to occupy the throne of Scotland.

The Earl of Mar proclaimed the pretender at Castledown, the Duke of Argyle collected his clans at Dumblain, and the rebellion spread to England, although with little success.

The pretender, who had been conveyed to Scotland by a French fleet, discovering that, although surrounded by a few interested noblemen, his army was not strong enough to overthrow the better equipped forces of England, was disheartened at the outlook, and returned to France after a series of adventures that have cast a glamour of romance over a not very worthy scion of a royal house.

A large number of young Scotchmen had cast in their fortunes with those of their prince, and they now found themselves in a precarious position. Among others was James Alexander, the great-grandson of John Alexander, of Gogar, who had joined the uprising in favor of the prince of his nation. The memoirs of James Alexander state that he thereby incurred the resentment of the government, and was forced to flee to America in order to save himself from imprisonment, but he must have done this in a very leisurely fashion, as he sailed from London, May 24, 1715, after an interview with his relative, Henry, the fifth Earl of Stirling, who was living on his English estates (which he had inherited from his great-grandfather William, the first earl) at Wakehurst, Devon. Lord Stirling commissioned his cousin to act as his representative in the American colony to which the young man was bound, and desired him, if possible, to secure some revenue from the great estates that had been seized by the

Duke of York and had never been paid for, and the earl fancied that he would now be able to regain possession of the whole of his property, owing to the change of the succession to the English throne.

James Alexander was well qualified for a colonist. He had been carefully educated, and was clever at adapting himself to the exigencies of a situation. He received from his Scotch and English relations numerous letters of introduction to persons who had preceded him to the colony of New York, and, among others, to Robert Livingston, Cadwalader Colden, and the family of John Spratt, and these at once admitted the young and clever Scotchman into the best circles of the colony, and even opened the doors of the exclusive Dutch families, who usually held aloof from all foreigners, although more inclined to those from Scotland than to those from any other part of Great Britain.

James Alexander was accompanied on his voyage by a friend and life-long comrade, William Smith, a young Englishman who had been disgusted by the prospect of a Hanoverian ruler on the throne of England, and who had determined to emigrate in the hope of making his fortune in the New World. William Smith was born in London in 1697, and was therefore about the same age as Alexander, and both young men were destined to become law-givers to their adopted country and occupy some of its highest official positions, while Smith has left us, in addition, a most valuable and accurate history of his times.

James Alexander

James Alexander left his father and mother living in their old home at Mustrie, surrounded by their numerous family. These were: Janet, who married John McClish; William, the husband of Elizabeth Lumsden; Christina, the wife of Thomas Camm, and Elizabeth, who afterward married David Drummond, of Crief.

James Alexander took leave of his family, determined never to return to his native land until he had made his fortune, and he carried with him a valuable outfit of mathematical instruments, in which he had invested the money given him by his father. Such instruments were rare in those days, and some of them were made especially for his use, and from his own designs, by one of the best mathematical instrument-makers of London, and this outfit was as remarkable as the library that he carried with him across the ocean. One of these books is still in the library of a descendant, and was a present to James Alexander from Robert Sandilands, sixth Lord of Torpichan, who had married Catherine Alexander, granddaughter of the first Earl of Stirling. There are other books that were imported at the same time, some in the libraries of James Alexander's descendants and others in the Society Library of New York, all of which were marked with an ex-libris, displaying the coat of arms of the family of the Alexanders of Gogar.

The profession for which Alexander had qualified himself was that of a civil engineer, and he found no trouble in getting employment on his arrival in New

York, August 17, 1715. His education and abilities caused him to be offered the position of deputy clerk of the council in 1719, only four years after his arrival in the colony. Alexander almost immediately took up the study of law, seeing in that profession an opening for a man of his ability, and he combined his newly acquired profession with that of engineering, and rapidly rose to eminence in everything that he undertook. The scientific studies that had been begun at home were not abandoned, and Alexander became a valued correspondent of many of the scientific and philosophical societies of Europe, and finally founded the American Philosophical Society. He was also appointed surveyor-general of West Jersey, an office which he held for the remainder of his life; became the receiver-general and collector of quit rents for the province of New Jersey, and was commissioned a member of the king's council for the province of New York, and also for that of New Jersey, which was an unwonted honor, and was a position that was never occupied except by James Alexander and subsequently by his son.

James Alexander also filled the offices of attorney-general for New York, was a member of the assembly for the city of New York, was one of the representatives of New Jersey to try pirates, commissioner for New Jersey to survey the boundary line between that province and New York, and received the freedom of the city of New York in 1731, having been naval officer of the port in 1723 and 1728.

James Alexander

On the arrival of William Smith and James Alexander in the colony of New York they found matters in a prosperous condition. Governor Hunter had been a welcome ruler, as he was wise and gentle in the management of the tangled affairs inherited from the abuses of the deposed governor. Mrs. Hunter entered into the social life of the place with her husband without any of the condescension that had marked the behavior of former governors and their wives, who acted as if their official position elevated them almost to the status of royalty, and behaved as if they considered themselves much superior to the colonists, although often of very inferior birth, talents, and education. Governor Hunter was cordial and easy in his manners and accepted all the invitations to the suppers, assemblies, and fêtes which were given in his honor by the townspeople and the country gentry who lived within the confines of his rule. To the great grief of all who had the honor of knowing her, Mrs. Hunter died in the summer of 1716. Her husband never recovered his cheerfulness, and, finding his surroundings too painful, he begged the home government to recall him to England.

No governor ever left New York more heartily regretted than did Robert Hunter. He sailed from the port, July, 1719, leaving the command of the colony to Peter Schuyler, the senior member of the king's council, who filled the office for thirteen months and then resigned it to the newly appointed official, William

Burnet, who reached New York, September 17, 1720, and was welcomed by the council and citizens in the most hearty way. When the news reached the city of the arrival of the ship in the lower bay, bearing the governor's pennant, the chief men of the colony embarked in their yachts, a necessary conveyance that nearly everyone owned, as the simplest means of transportation from the busy island to its neighbors beyond the rivers that surrounded them. The English war-vessel was boarded by men of all degrees, bearing addresses of welcome to the governor, and they escorted him to the city with due honors and appropriate ceremonies, first to the government house, White Hall, and then through the streets to the City Hall, in Wall Street, to take the oath of office.

William Burnet was the son of the historian, Bishop Burnet, by a Dutch lady to whom he had been married when living in exile in Holland. The worthy divine had ingratiated himself with Prince William of Orange, and the future governor of New York had received the name of that prince, who had also condescended to act as his godfather, and had presented the infant with a silver fork and knife, the handles of which were richly embossed with scriptural scenes, in which the dresses and even the faces of the subjects were so cleverly designed and executed that they are charmingly characteristic and life-like. This christening-gift is now owned by one of his descendants, William d'Hertborne Washington.

James Alexander

Governor Burnet was a portly man, with a fine presence and courtly manners. The interest of his father had obtained for him the preferment to this elevated position of governor of the province of New York and New Jersey, and he was the more eager to obtain it as he had but lately lost his wife, and he hoped to forget his sorrows by surrounding himself with new scenes and occupations; and as his greatest extravagance was the desire of accumulating a large library, the colonists soon found that they had nothing to fear from him, and need not dread constant demands for money to gratify expensive habits. His companions and friends in Europe had been men of literary attainments and tastes, and he soon selected men of similar likings as his associates in the colony.

The new governor was a man of impulse, who said of himself: "I act first and think afterward," and one of the leading men of the colony, Dr. Colden, said of him: "Governor Burnet had a very extraordinary memory, and no man was freer from avarice. He expended considerable sums in charity, which he managed so that none knew of it."

When arranging his plans to make the voyage to America, Burnet determined not to be parted from his beloved books, and he had them all packed and conveyed to the colony, where they proved most welcome to the gentlemen to whom the governor was always generous enough to lend them. Bishop Burnet had been a great favorite of the Princess Sophia's and she had given her esteemed pastor a very handsome "tea equipage," which he gave to his son. This service was of silver gilt, and the governor was so proud of it that he arranged for a series of weekly tea-parties at White Hall, to which all the ladies of the colony were invited. The warm-hearted, affectionate disposition of the governor made for him many friends, the principal ones being Chief-Justice Morris, who was his director and confidant; Dr. Colden, to whom he was attracted by the similarity of their tastes, and James Alexander. A contemporary historian says of these friendships, that "he showed his wisdom in his selection, for they were all men of learning, good morals, and solid parts. James Alexander had been bred to the law, and though no speaker, was at the head of his profession for sagacity and penetration, and in application to business no man could surpass him; nor was he unacquainted with the affairs of the public, having served in the Secretary's office, the best school in the province for instructions in matters of government, and Mr. Burnet soon raised him to the Council Board."

The old government house still looked very much as it had done when first built by Governor Stuyvesant, when it had received the name of White Hall from its color, and this name, first given it as a joke, was seriously adopted by the citizens. The great entrance to the enclosure fronted to the west, but the principal rooms looked to the south and over the harbor of New York. The large enclosed space on the roof was a favorite lounging-place, as from it there was a beautiful view; and it was there that he would welcome his friends and brew them a cup of tea in his famous teapot, and everyone loved to gather on this cool spot that was swept by ocean breezes.

His excellency was not long in making the acquaintance of Mrs. Provoost, and was soon admitted to her hospitable tea-table in return for the civilities received from him. And it was there that the governor was presented to the eldest daughter of Mrs. Provoost's half-sister, Maria Provoost, who had married, in 1700, Abraham Van Horne. Mary Van Horne was barely twenty years of age, and was already one of the belles of the town, so it was no wonder that his excellency was captivated by her beauty, and soon paid his addresses in form. The worthy citizens of New York were much elated at this compliment to native charms and beauty, and accepted it as if bestowed on themselves rather than on the bride; and the wedding that soon took place was marked by imposing ceremonies, which were attended by everyone, whether of high or low degree. Even the remnants of the tribe of Indians, that had once been so powerful on Mana-ha-ta, presented the bride with some very valuable beaver pelts, and the governor, in return, ordered several barrels of beer to be given to "his brethren to rejoice and dance over." The honeymoon was spent at the Livingston manor-house, which was put at the disposal of the governor, and the bridal party went up the river in their yacht, but on their return they drove down the banks of the Hudson in their own chaise, making the long journey leisurely and stopping at the houses of their friends, so that they did not return to the city until long after the "month of honey" had elapsed.

Three children were the fruit of this marriage—William, Mary, and Thomas. Mary married William Browne, of Beverly, Massachusetts.

Abraham Van Horne was immediately raised to a seat in the council by his son-in-law, and Governor Burnet began his rule in the colony with more friends and adherents than any English governor had ever obtained. There were three causes for this: firstly, the alliance with one of the leading Dutch families; secondly, his friendship with Dr. Colden, Robert Livingston, and James Alexander, which cemented the bond between him and the Scotch emigrants who were then flocking to the colony and becoming the stanchest upholders of its government; and, thirdly, the kindly manners of the governor had ingratiated him with the French Huguenot families, who were already well represented at the council board and in the assembly by the de Lanceys, the Bayards, etc.

Weekly evening clubs were now established by the gentlemen of the town, and several of the ladies who were fond of music arranged to give a series of concerts at which glees were sung.

An eminent Scotchman had settled in the New York colony a few years before the advent of Governor

James Alexander

Burnet, who requires more than a passing notice, as he became one of the principal members of the government and subsequently occupied the governor's chair. This was Dr. Cadwalader Colden, a man of good birth, with talents of no common order, who had married in his own country the daughter of a clergyman, Miss Alice Christy by name, and was now happily settled in the New World, contentedly bringing up a large family of children. Although Dr. Colden was living in a country that was only partly inhabited by educated persons, he lost no opportunity of self-cultivation by study, and by correspondence with the principal savants of Europe. With uncommon perspicuity he turned his attention in particular to his novel surroundings, and made searching inquiries into the language, customs, and habits of the Wilden, who were still the principal occupants of the forests that surrounded the scattered settlements of the white people.

Dr. Colden had graduated at one of the best medical colleges of Europe, and with the keenness of a man of his profession and the acumen of one not above learning even from simple savages, he applied himself to the study of the flora of the country, and under the tuition of his Indian friends acquired a knowledge of the herbs and simples which they had used to cure their ailments from time immemorial, and his use of this knowledge was so intelligent that he gained great popularity as a medical man. Through pursuing these studies Dr. Colden became the correspondent of the celebrated Swedish naturalist Linnæus, who taught him the newly invented classification of plants, and through this intimacy between Dr. Colden and the noted Swede much of the flora of North America was grouped and divided into the proper classes and species.

Dr. Colden had five sons and five daughters, and nearly every one of them became as distinguished as their celebrated father. The second daughter was Jane Colden. She was born in New York, March 27, 1724. A notice of her in the "Genealogical Record" says:

"She early developed a fondness for the study of natural history, and under the direction of her father she became at an early age the first botanist of her sex in this country. Soon after Linnæus originated and gave the scientific world his system of dividing plants and herbs into classes Dr. Colden taught it to his daughter, putting it in an English form, and freeing it from technical terms, for her use, and showed her how to take impressions on paper with printer's ink. She took the impression of three or four hundred growing in the vicinity of Coldenham (her father's place near Montgomery County, New York), which were sent to a number of eminent naturalists in Europe. Her style of description and the skill displayed in taking impressions of the leaves gave her great reputation among the scientific men under whose observation they were brought. John Ellis, the London naturalist, writes to Linnæus, April, 1758, thus: 'This young lady merits your esteem and does honor to your system. She has drawn and described four hundred plants in your method. Her father has a plant called after him, "Coldenia." Suppose you should call this (referring to a new genus) "Coldenella," or any other name that might distinguish her in your genera.' Peter Collinson also wrote to Linnæus: 'I have lately heard from Mr. Colden. He is well, but what is marvellous—his daughter is perhaps the first lady that has perfectly studied your system. She deserves to be celebrated.'"

This young lady married a widower, Dr. William Farquhar, in March, 1759, and died in childbirth, March 10, 1766. Dr. Farquhar was one of the best-known and accomplished medical men in the colony at that time. We may quote from "Family Records and Events" the following letter, written some years later by Walter Rutherfurd, a young Scotchman who married one of the daughters of James Alexander, as it gives a glimpse of Dr. Colden and his truly remarkable family:

"Our voyage to Albany was purely a party of Pleasure. At one of our landings we made an excursion to Coldenham, the abode of the venerable philosopher, Colden. He is as gay and facetious in his conversation as he is serious and solid in his writings. From the middle of the Woods this Family corresponds with all the learned Societies in Europe. Himself on the principles of Matter and Motion, his son on electricity and experiments. He has made several useful discoveries and is a tolerable proficient in music. His daughter Jenny is a Florist, and a Botanist. She has discovered a great number of plants never before described, and has given them Properties and Virtues, many of which are found useful in Medicine and she draws and colors them with great beauty. N. B.—She makes the best cheese I ever ate in America."

XVII

My Lady of "Petticoat Lane"

The Assemblies—Prominent Families—James Alexander Weds the Widow Provoost—Petes and Gossips—Emigration of Mr. Alexander's Nephew — Petticoat Lane — Tea-parties — Supper-parties — Bogart's Biscuits—Death of David Provoost—Death of Madame de Peyster, and Her Will—Birth of William Alexander—Death of Governor and Mrs. Burnet—Colonel Montgomerie—The First Public Library—Trinity Church and St. Paul's Chapel.

FEW months elapsed after his arrival in New York before James Alexander found himself a welcome visitor in the home of Mrs. Provoost, who at that time was just twenty-one, a matron of less than four years' standing, and one of the most beautiful women of the colony.

The assemblies at this time were particularly fashionable, and were held at one of the taverns, near White Hall. Admission to them was only by inheritance or by special favor from the ladies who managed them, and the list was such a long one that the managers were forced to have the ball-room enlarged, in order to accommodate all those who wished to attend.

Among the families who were then prominent members of the assemblies were the Van Cortlandts, Bayards, Van Rensselaers, Van Schaicks, de Lanceys, de

My Lady of "Petticoat Lane"

Peysters, Staats, Beekmans, Bleeckers, Schuylers, Coldens, Van Hornes, Clarksons, and many more too numerous to mention.

At all these merry-makings young James Alexander was a welcome guest, and when death entered the home of Mrs. Provoost and carried off her husband, Mr. Alexander was still permitted to visit at the house of the widow on terms of easy intimacy, and he soon followed up his advantage by persuading her to accept his addresses, and on June 5, 1721, when the "Pinxter bloem" were hardly in blossom, pretty Polly laid aside her heavy widow's weeds and became Mrs. James Alexander.

The interests of the bride were again carefully attended to by her uncles, who caused elaborate settlements to be drawn up. Mrs. Alexander continued to pursue her own business affairs, side by side with the offices that she had arranged for her husband. Never was there a more congenial and happy couple than Mr. and Mrs. Alexander. Their tastes were similar, and her vivacity met its match in his keen Scotch wit and ready repartee. John and David Provoost found a kind and loving friend in their young step-father, and the only clouds that came to mar the happiness of the newly married pair were the constant excitements and embroilments in which Mr. Alexander became entangled, owing to the hearty interest and concern that he developed for the health and prosperity of the colony, with which he became thoroughly identified.

The Goede Vrouw of Mana-ha-ta

There is a letter still extant, written October 21, 1721, by Mr. Alexander to his brother, William Alexander, in Scotland, in which he enlarges on his comfortable home, charming wife, prosperity and happiness, and also announces the birth of his eldest daughter Mary, who had been born on the 16th of that month, and who was honored by having for godparents his excellency the governor of the province, William Burnet, the governor's lady, and her cousin Elizabeth, wife of Colonel John Hamilton, who was the daughter of Abraham de Peyster and a cousin of Mrs. Alexander's. These ladies were called "Petes," a word that is synonymous with sponsor, witness, or godmother.

William Alexander, the elder brother of James, died soon after this date, leaving a son William and a daughter Kitty, who had married a Mr. Stapleton, but who was then a widow; and these relatives of Mr. Alexander joined their uncle in the colony and took up their residence at Jamaica, Long Island, where Dr. William Alexander practised as a surgeon.

In a pretty little tale called "A Day in New York," written by William Alexander Duer, LL.D., judge of the Supreme Court of New York, president of Columbia College, a grandson of Mrs. Alexander's, is the following account of the home of Mrs. Alexander:

"It contained apartments innumerable, sumptuously furnished in all the pomp of that period. There was the great dining room and the lesser dining room, the room hung with blue and gold leather, the green and gold room, and the little front parlor and the little back parlor, and the great tapestry room up-stairs, besides red rooms and green rooms and chintz rooms up-stairs and down, furnished with damask hangings, costly carpets, and buffets furnished with costly plate. Adjoining this dwelling there was a large garden running back for a considerable distance and extending on one side to Jew's Alley, now Mill Street. And here in their proper seasons might be seen in great profusion the favorite flowers of our ancestors—paus bloemies of all hues, 'laylocks' and tall May roses, and snowballs intermixed with choice vegetables and herbs for pharmacy, all bounded and hemmed in by huge rows of neatly clipped box edging."

The house stood on Broad Street, nearly facing Marketfield Street, and the worthies of the place dubbed the latter "Petticoat Lane," as it led to the home of Mrs. Alexander, who was the acknowledged controller of the social affairs of the place, as well as having great influence over its commercial interests, and supposed to have something to say in all important political events, as her mother and grandmother had had before her. The gardens stretched on either side of the house, and in front of them Mrs. Alexander had built her counting-house and the law-offices of her husband. The site of the house is now covered by the stores Nos. 67 and 69 Broad Street. In front of them lay the famous pavement.

The first years of Mrs. Alexander's married life were

tranquil and passed happily. Her husband's law-practice was extensive and profitable. He was the most accomplished surveyor of the province, and held such a high position under the government that his salary, together with her private fortune and the proceeds of her mercantile enterprises, placed the couple in unusually comfortable circumstances for such a young pair.

It was about this time that Mrs. Alexander's uncle, der Heer Abraham de Peyster, resigned his office as treasurer of the province, a position that he had held for fourteen years, and he was succeeded by his son and namesake, Abraham "de Jonge," who had married Miss Margaret Van Cortlandt. It was little wonder that Mrs. Alexander, who had always had much influence in her family, had some voice in public ones also (although it was not openly wielded), owing to the fact that almost every male member of her family held some prominent position under the government; and as they were accustomed to discuss matters with her in an informal way and allow her opinion to have great weight with them, it really seemed as if "Mrs. Alexander held matters in the hollow of her hand," as her friends declared she did, and that "Petticoat Lane," which led from her door to the government-house and fort, was no undeserved name. By reason of her descent and first marriage, there was hardly a family in the province to which Mrs. Alexander was not closely related, and in a small community where everyone knew everybody else from childhood, the bonds of friendship were nearly as close as those of family, and as Polly Spratt had been a favorite from her birth, her house naturally became the centre of hospitality, and her parlors in the evenings were always sure to be filled with all the gayest and brightest people in the city; but politics was eschewed at these gatherings, which were devoted to the discussion of the latest news of the literary world and the newest books, just dashed with a little tittle-tattle about the island and its inhabitants.

The daily habits of the people of New York of those days were simple and easy in the extreme, and those of all families were almost precisely alike. After an early breakfast, the ladies would devote themselves to their household duties, and at eleven o'clock would retire to their rooms and consecrate an hour to reading their Bibles and other religious works. This hour was never intruded on by servant, child, or visitor. The early dinner followed, after which all the matrons of the town would dress themselves for visiting or being visited in rustling silks, with neat white caps tied demurely under the chin, and large silk aprons (which at the time was part of the full dress of the English court). For the street, a large cloak called a "cardinal" was thrown over the shoulders and an enormous hood put on the head, which made the wearer look like a ship in full sail, and with the inevitable knitting-bag slung on the left arm, the ladies would start out ready to spend the afternoon at some friend's house, and "stop and take a dish of tea." Toward sundown, when the men came home from counting-house, the courts, or the council-chamber, the pleasantest and most hospitable meal of the day took place. No formal invitations were issued for it, but the table was generally filled with casual visitors, who were always made welcome. There were

> "Panado, caudle, many a cup;
> Choice figs and raisins of the sun;
> And cakes of every sort made up—
> Pound-cake, wig, waffle, cruller, bun;"

and the tables groaned under these and many sorts of home-made sweetmeats and confectionery, eggs served in different fashions, shortcakes, "Izer cookies, etc."

Mrs. Alexander's tea-table was particularly distinguished for a delicacy made after an old Dutch receipt of her grandmother's, Madame de Peyster. These biscuits were split when hot and butter placed inside them before they were sent to the table. They were great favorites with the children, and were always carried to picnics by the little "companies." General Shirley, an English officer, became so fond of them that he begged Mrs. Alexander to have a quantity made for him to carry with him on the expedition against the French and Indians, and these biscuits were found to keep fresh so long, and to be such an addition to the camp fare that the treasured family receipt was given to a public baker who had orders to supply the army with them, and they were given his name, and became known as "Bogart's biscuits."

My Lady of "Petticoat Lane"

Mrs. Alexander also organized a series of weekly supper-parties soon after her second marriage. These were very fashionable affairs, where the guests assembled at nine o'clock, and after chatting for about an hour, the younger ones would send for old Cæsar and his fiddle, and dance in one of the parlors, and the older ones would sit down to the then lately introduced game of whist, an amusement that had been originally confined to the servants' quarters, and was only just beginning to be recognized as scientific and worthy of adoption by the higher classes. Supper was always handed round by the servants, who entered the parlor about eleven o'clock, carrying great trays covered with goodies, such as jellies, in tall slender glasses, custards, syllabubs, cake, etc. Sometimes roasted oysters were served, but not when the light dishes just mentioned were offered, as "oyster supper-parties" were a thing by themselves and were usually given only when some very grave political situation was to be discussed, and served in the dining-room, and only attended by gentlemen, who discussed oysters, politics, and good rum punch, at one and the same time.

James Alexander's eldest son was born in 1723, and received his father's name, having for one of his sponsors his good-natured, fat uncle, John Spratt. The happiness of the young pair was hardly rippled the following year by the death of Mrs. Alexander's step-father-brother-in-law, David Provoost, as there had been more or less friction between them owing to his mismanagement of her mother's estate. The old gentleman was nearly eighty years of age and had become garrulous and tiresome to a degree, but the gayeties of the city were brought to a sudden stop, as so many of its inhabitants were related to him, and the governor's wife was forced to stop all the entertainments at White Hall and go into deep mourning for her grandfather. And the following year Mrs. Alexander was prostrated with grief over the death of her beloved grandmother, Madame Johannes de Peyster, who as Cornelia Lubbetse had been one of the pioneer women of Mana-ha-ta, had seen the birth-throes of the hamlet, witnessed its growth, and the sundering of its Dutch leading-strings, the rough nursing of its step-mother England, and the present state of prosperity, and she now died, in the ninety-first year of her age, surrounded by a large family who felt as if they had, indeed, lost everything when this last link with the past was broken and the kind old lady sank to her well-earned rest and was laid beside her husband in their family vault.

Madame de Peyster's will was dated April 23, 1692, and proved September 25, 1725. It begins in the usual way: "In the name of God. Amen." And after some provision with regard to the disposition of her slaves, it goes on to say:

I confirm the last Will and Testament made by my husband deceased Johannes de Peyster before the Notary Walwyn van der Veen, dated ye 8th day Aug. ANO. 1663.

3. I make and bequeath to my eldest Sonn Abraham de Pey-

ster, ye summe of Tenn pounds, for his privilege of first born to be delivered to him before any division is made of my Estate.

4. I make unto my youngest son Cornelius in case I come to die before he is married an outsetting equal as ye others had of bed furniture and household stuff and BYBEL.

5. I do make all my children by name Abraham Maria Isaac Johannes and Cornelia de Peyster my only universall and equal heirs, etc., etc.

In witness Whereof I have set my seal ye year day and month as above said.

Sealed and
delivered in   CORNELIA DE PEYSTER.
the presence of
P. D. la Noy.
Isaac Van Vlecq.
William Jackson.
A. de la Noy.

The baby-boy who came to comfort his mother in this hour of grief was christened January 4, 1725-26, William Alexander, after his wise and great relative, William Alexander, first Earl of Stirling. Mrs. Alexander's other children were Elizabeth, Catharine, Susanna, and Anne. The last was born at a time when the small-pox was prevalent in New York, and there were five hundred deaths in the city in two months. Mrs. Alexander lost her oldest son, James Alexander, by this disease on September 28, 1731, and his death is recorded by his father in the old Bible, the record stating that this was the first burial in " my vault in the English [*i.e.*, Trinity Church] yard which was then made for my family." This vault is close to the southwest corner of the present church, and the coffin-plate of the little fellow was lately found in it. It is of pewter, and the inscription is almost entirely obliterated.

Again the hearts of the community were wrung by the death of the governor's lovely young wife, who left a little family to mourn her loss, as well as a sorrowing husband, relations, and friends. Governor Burnet was therefore resigned to leaving New York, and accepted the position of governor of the Massachusetts and New Hampshire colonies, and he moved to his new home in 1728 to enter his new duties as a widower again. But this much loved governor died within eighteen months after leaving New York, regretted by all who knew him; and his career still stands out in bold relief as that of an efficient and honest official among a long line of reprobates who were sent out by the English government to represent them in the new world. The succeeding occupant of the gubernatorial chair was a soldier, a courtier, and a diplomat, fresh from the Court of St. James, and owing his position to the especial favor of the king, whose gentleman-in-waiting he had been, and his majesty gave him his choice of several offices both in England and abroad. He chose the government of New York, as it was declared to be the most lucrative and attended with the least trouble, although he was for some time divided in his own mind whether he could make more out of the island of Jamaica or this colony. He finally decided that the old Dutch settlement on the Hudson River would afford him more advantages, and he therefore arrived here in the spring of 1728. Colonel John Montgomery was a fine-looking man, but he had none of the accomplishments of his predecessor, and the colonists therefore withdrew themselves from too much intercourse with White Hall and returned to their wonted exclusiveness.

The year 1729 was marked by the foundation of the first public library in New York. It was started by a donation of books from the S. P. G., or Society for the Propagation of the Gospel, and the works were chiefly of a religious character. This was no drawback in the eyes of a community whose discussions were usually on religious topics, local politics, and gossip. Philosophy and law-books were interesting only to professional men; light literature, magazines, novels, etc., were unheard of. A daily newspaper was issued for the first time this year. The colonists had no books except those imported from Europe, which were in private libraries, and the foundation of a public library, where authorities on religious subjects could be easily consulted, was a boon to the inhabitants.

Social life in New York was marked by a strong dividing line on the accession of the English, as the Dutch settlers held themselves aloof from intercourse with them. These barriers gradually melted as the children of the pioneers grew to manhood and found that the Scotch, French, and English emigrants were intelligent and pleasant companions. The social line, which had been a national and political, then became a religious one, and the towns-people were broken into three sets, the English set, or those who worshipped at Trinity Church, being the foremost in everything and the most prominent in entertaining. This set was composed of the governor *ex-officio*, his council, and many of the members of that congregation. It was by far the most fashionable and lively set of the town, and Mrs. Alexander was its recognized leader, as she had deserted the Lutheran Dutch congregation when she left her grandmother's home to marry, and as Mr. Alexander had met her half-way by abandoning Presbyterianism, they both became members of the English Church.

There was always a fashionable gathering at Trinity Church on Sunday morning. The latest arrivals from England made their first appearance there. Visitors from the manors, and the country-people in general, announced their arrival in town by attending the services, although they might belong to another denomination. Families ranked in the social scale according to the pew that they occupied. Everybody knew everyone else.

It was the custom for all the children of the family to attend the long morning services, even though they had hardly passed infancy. The youngest one was seated next to the mother, where it could cuddle to her side and sleep quietly during the sermon, while the rest of the family were ranged around the great square pew, the father next to the door and the others with their backs to the chancel, a position that gave them a fine opportunity to overlook the congregation, and, when the parental eye was not on them, to exchange glances with their young neighbors.

The pews were fitted with cushions and hassocks, which were considered great luxuries, and the edifice was warmed in winter, so that the ladies were not obliged to carry with them the little tin foot-stoves that were heated with a hot stone and were carried on the arm to all the other churches. All around the pews were hung, from a slender brass railing about a foot high, little green moreen curtains, and these shielded the family from observation during prayers, but were drawn back when Dr. Vesey or his successor ascended the pulpit and gave out the text. After service the congregation gathered in the church-yard to exchange kindly greetings, and the youth and maidens found it a pleasant opportunity to indulge in quiet flirtations. Belles made engagements for the walk home from church very much as those of to-day arrange for partners for the cotillions, and the damsel who was left to walk demurely by the side of her parents was a marked person.

Those who attended the Dutch church formed another and distinct set. They held themselves aloof from and superior to the Trinity congregation, whom they considered frivolous and foreign in their ways, while they alone were representative of the true Dutch element, and upheld its staid, hospitable customs. The Beekmans, De Peysters, and Van Cortlandts, etc., were the leaders of this set.

The third congregation that became of importance was that of the Presbyterian church, and of this the Livingstons were the chief supporters. In such a small place it was impossible for older members of families to prevent intimacies among the younger folks, and constant intermarriages led to strange mingling of creeds and sets; but the impalpable line drawn by the original Dutch families was still strong enough to be noticeable until long after the Revolutionary War, and indeed until about 1870, when the city of New York increased to such a size that all such distinctions were obliterated. Since religion was, in fact, the dividing line in the town, nothing was more natural than that the different creeds and beliefs should be the main subject of discussion, and the good folks were glad to have such a valuable library as the one that had been presented to them so that references might be made and authorities quoted. The books having been the gift of the Established Church of England, the tendency was, of course, Episcopal. As the community was constantly increased by members of the government, English army and naval officers and their families, Trinity Church became more and more crowded, until its congregation overflowed into St. Paul's Chapel, which was a small church that was erected in 1766 on the outskirts of the town, up Broadway, overlooking "the fields," or old cow-pasture.

The chapel was built facing the Hudson River, and from its portico commanded a fine view. The chancel was placed on the eastern side of the chapel, in accordance with a growing predilection for the exact observance of the ritual, and this excited great discussion and much grave debate; but the church was built in this way notwithstanding the pros and cons, and turns its back to-day on the busy street on which it stands, much to the wonder of inquiring strangers, while St. Paul stands in his niche over the portico, sword in hand, and faces the busy mart, and looks down with calm indifference on the shifting crowd of Jews and Gentiles bustling about in the streets, as he has done for many decades.

XVIII

Petticoats and Politics

James Alexander made "Freeman of the City"—Van Dam, Governor—His Successor, Colonel Cosby—His Bad Character Precedes Him—He Insults Colonel Morris—Disputes with Van Dam—Mrs. Cosby—The Governor's Ball—Lawsuit Against Van Dam—Miss Euphemia Morris—The Family Coach—Miss Cosby's Elopement—Colonel Morris Leaves for England.

WHILE the home-life of Mr. and Mrs. Alexander was passing happily and quietly, the public life of the great lawyer was becoming more and more noteworthy. At a meeting of the common council, held February 11, 1730–31, the following resolution was entered on the minutes:

"This day the Corporation received from the hands of Governor Montgomerie, the new Charter of the City, which was published at the entrance of the City Hall, with the usual formality of ringing three bells, and making proclamation for silence, they then returned to the Comon Council Chamber.

"Robert Lurting. MAYOR, Francis Harison Esqr. RECORDER, Frederick Phillipse Esqr., Gerardus Stuyvesant Esqr. and James Roosevelt Esqr. Samuel Kip, Mr. Isaac de Peyster and Mr. John Moore, (all members of this Court) were sworn Freemen of this Corporation and ordered to be registered accordingly. Ordered this Corporation do compliment, James de Lancey, Esqr., Peter Warren Esqr. Commander of His Majesty's Ship Solebay, James Alexander Esqr., William Jaimeson, and William Smith Gent. Attorneys at Law, and John Avery Gent. each with the Freedom of this Corporation."

James Alexander had been a member of his British majesty's council and one of the rulers of the province of New York, for several years, and when Colonel Montgomerie died suddenly, after a brief and uneventful reign, the oaths of office were administered to the president of the council, Rip Van Dam, in the presence of his colleagues, and with the usual imposing ceremonies, by Mr. Alexander, as the next oldest member of the council.

It would have been well if the Lords of Trade had ratified Mr. Van Dam's succession as governor, and had permitted the colony to be ruled by one of its inhabitants who was thoroughly conversant with its peculiar temperament, its diverse interests, and its cosmopolitan population. New York was a loyal and peace-loving colony in those days, and under the capable management of those men who then composed the cabinet it would have thriven, and would probably never have thrown off its allegiance to England.

But with the blundering, persistent ignorance that marked the policy of England toward this American colony, another governor was accredited to New York who had a record that in these days would have sent him to jail for life as a common swindler and thief, but at that time family influence was all-powerful, and Colonel William Cosby was elevated to one of the highest colonial offices that it was in the power of the government to bestow and put in a position to enrich himself at the expense of innocent victims, and thereby relieved his relations and friends of the burden of supporting him. William Cosby had first been sent to Minorca as its governor. The inhabitants of the island soon petitioned the home government to remove him, and openly accused him of stealing.

These statements were followed up with such undoubted proofs of the governor's dishonesty, that the Lords of Trade had no alternative, and for very shame were obliged to recall him to England. It was then determined that his field of action should be changed and that he should be promoted to what was the most valuable gift in the hands of the government, and Cosby was appointed to the post of governor of New York.

A knowledge of the character of Cosby preceded him to the colony, and its inhabitants prepared themselves with foreboding hearts to struggle for their rights, although they fortunately did not foresee what a bitter fight it would prove to be.

Methods of conciliation were at first tried, as it was intimated that the governor was not wealthy, and that a gift on his arrival which would cover his expenses of moving would be acceptable. This hint was thrown out in such a way that it could not be disregarded, although the public wondered to what great expense his excellency had been put, as he had had free transportation to the colony for himself, his family, and retinue, in one of the English men-of-war. But the assembly deemed it best to consider the demand as a worthy one, and voted the governor £750, a gift which was announced to him on his arrival in New York, in the most formal and courteous terms, by the stately chief-justice, Lewis Morris, who was vastly astounded by the colonel's reception of the announcement, as he cursed his new subjects for the meagreness of the sum, and behaved in such an insolent way to the chief-justice that Mr. Morris bluntly told the governor that for the future he would not acknowledge his acquaintance and should refuse to meet him except on official business.

The news of this insolent treatment of Mr. Morris by the governor soon spread over the colony, but before it became generally known it was reported and commented upon at Mrs. Alexander's tea-table on the very evening of the day that it had occurred, by Mr. Morris himself; and she watched anxiously the cloud that gathered over her husband's face at such intelligence. After tea a little knot of friends gathered in Mrs. Alexander's small back parlor, which was her own particular sitting-room and into which the usual evening visitors were never ushered, and the friends were assured of absolute privacy; it was even possible for them to leave by a back door and a small gate that opened from the garden into a back alley, and persons entering and leaving the house in this way were almost sure to escape observation. The gentlemen who were gathered in this anxious consultation with Mr. and Mrs. Alexander were Colonel Morris and Mr. William Smith. The latter had been Mr. Alexander's fellow-emigrant, and he and Colonel Morris were among the foremost men of the province, and were now among the richest and most influential men of the place; and all agreed that a governor without the instincts of a gentleman and with the reputation for dishonesty that had preceded Colonel Cosby from his previous situation, was not the person to hold the reins of government. For they foresaw that business would languish, owners of property would not feel secure, emigration would cease, and many calamities would follow in the train, if public confidence were shaken in the government, as it was bound to be under a dishonest and unscrupulous ruler.

Such were among the prognostications of the friends, who saw many troubles before them. And, indeed, sad times were upon them. Cosby at once demanded that Governor Van Dam should pay over to him the salary received by Van Dam for thirteen months' service as acting-governor, while Cosby had remained in England after he had received orders to proceed to America to take charge of the colony. The sturdy Dutchman pointed out that Cosby had already received in England, for pretended services to the New York colony, over £2,000, and Van Dam very positively refused to give up his hard-earned wages, and in this refusal to permit himself to be robbed he was strenuously supported by his friends in the government, chief among them being Colonel Morris, Mr. Alexander, and Mr. Smith; and this episode caused the first rupture between the governor and his council.

The wife of the governor was the sister of the Earl of Halifax, the president of the Board of Trade, and she and her young daughters thought that life in New York was an exile almost too great to be borne. They would not return the visits of courtesy that were paid them by the ladies of the colony, and my lady, with a toss of her head, refused to permit any of the native young men to be presented to her or to her daughters. The only beaux that she allowed to enter White Hall were the young English officers who were stationed with their regiments in the colony, or those on board of his majesty's ships that were lying in the harbor.

In spite of the bad reputation and the arrogance of the governor some of the gentlemen of the place still hoped for the best, and his majesty's representative was entertained as was customary, although in a perfunctory way. It was after much discussion and a spirited debate that the governor "was admitted and received as a member of that ancient and truly honorable association, the Humdrum Club," and according to the notice in the New York "Gazette" of January 24, 1733 "The Honorable William Cosby attended a meeting on the previous evening, when he was admitted as a member of the club, over many bowls of punch made from peculiar and valuable receipts that were known only to members of the club, that was potent in its effects even over a well-seasoned veteran like the late governor of Minorca."

It was the duty of the governor to celebrate the birthday of the consort of his sovereign by marking it in some particular way, and as he was also obliged to return some of the hospitalities that had been shown to him by the citizens of New York, he determined to combine the two duties and give a grand ball to the people of the place. This was much against the wishes of Mrs. Cosby, who was not anxious to spend any money in entertaining, but she was overruled.

The issue of the New York "Gazette" for March 10, 1733, contained the following notice:

"Last Friday, being the anniversary of her Majesty's birthday, the same was celebrated in this city with the utmost Demonstrations of Loyalty and Affection. At Twelve o'clock the Magistrates and chief officers with a great Company of other Gentlemen waited upon his Excellency our Gouvernour to drink the Public Healths, while at the same time the guns upon the Ramparts were discharged. In the Evening there was a Ball at the Fort, and a very Rich and Splendid Entertainment for a vast Concourse of the best Gentlemen and Ladies in the Place who were then Assembled upon this occasion, and concluded the night with universal Mirth and Satisfaction, his Excellency and his Lady having to the utmost of their Power Contributed Thereunto."

The dispute between the two governors, Cosby and Van Dam, culminated in a lawsuit, and William Smith and James Alexander were retained as counsel for the latter. After much debate Chief-Justice Morris delivered an opinion in favor of Governor Van Dam, and in order that the whole subject should be understood by the colonists and not perverted by the misrepresentations of Governor Cosby, the chief-justice published his "opinion" in the papers. The sentiments expressed in this publication were so clear, and pointed out so forcibly the dishonesty of the claim, that the governor became enraged, and as the chief-justice also took public occasion to announce that he would not speak to the governor, owing to his ungentlemanly behavior when they had been brought in contact while transacting public business, it was most justly considered that the governor had insulted the whole of the colonists in the person of one of their chief representatives. The governor was furious that the chief-justice should have made the lawsuit so public, as he wished to give his own coloring to the affair, and he took secret steps to revenge himself on all the opponents that he found arrayed against him to prevent his encroachments on the rights and purses of the colonists.

The names of Van Dam, Morris, Smith, and Alexander, of course, headed the list, and this was not unknown to the gentlemen, who found that their every movement was watched by creatures of the governor and reported to him. Matters went from bad to worse, and the governor, finding that his wishes were daily being thwarted by his council, resolved to have them removed by the home government, and wrote despatches to the Board of Trade abusing his councillors and giving them characters that were so directly contrary to the description given by former governors, of the same men, that the Lords of Trade might have been vastly confused by the contradictory statements, if they had taken the trouble to compare or weigh them. It was more than shrewdly suspected that all despatches to England were opened, read, and suppressed when unfavorable to the governor, and it was therefore resolved, at a secret meeting held at Mrs. Alexander's house, under the pretence of the usual informal gathering around her tea-board, that Colonel Morris should at once proceed to England to lay the grievances of the colonists before the Lords of Trade, and beg for the removal of the present governor.

The simple-minded gentlemen imagined that it was only necessary for them to tell the lords in power how untrustworthy their representative was to have him removed at once. They were to find, on the contrary, that such trifles as dishonesty, untruthfulness, and other vices were deemed worthy of reward when perpetrated by a member of the English aristocracy who was fortunate enough to have influential friends in the government.

Cosby suspected and dreaded that some such step would be taken, as it had already been done in Minorca when its inhabitants had found it desirable to get rid of him, and he required that the passenger-lists of all outgoing vessels should be brought to him; and when such an extraordinary step on the part of the governor caused some comment, he alleged some frivolous excuse. He also ordered that all ships dropping down the river should be closely inspected, and no one allowed to sail on them without a written permit issued by himself. "The Documents of the Colonial History of New York" and William Smith's "History of New York" give vivid and detailed accounts of these occurrences.

As arranged in Mrs. Alexander's parlor, Colonel Morris asked for leave of absence at the next meeting of the assembly, in order, as he phrased it, "to go home." The permission was readily granted, as it was supposed that he intended to go to his country-seat, Tinton, at Shrewsbury, to attend to private business.

In order to divert the suspicions of the governor, it was further arranged that Messrs. Alexander, Smith, and Morris should not meet at all, but that all communications should be carried on through the ladies of the families.

Accordingly, Colonel Morris sent his oldest daughter, Euphemia, from their home at Morrisania under pretence of visiting Mrs. Alexander in New York. The journey in those days was long and tiresome, the Harlem River having to be crossed in a scow, poled by two negroes, from the mainland to a point on Mana-ha-ta, where the horses and coach were kept. The latter was a heavy, cumbersome affair, hung on great straps, with a hammer-cloth covering the coachman's seat; the doors were emblazoned with the family coat of arms and the crest of a flaming castle, with the motto, "Tandem Vincetur." The horses were the strong, ugly geldings of Holland blood that were necessary in order to drag such a cumbersome affair through the mire and over the stones on the Boston highway, that ran from the village of Harlem, past Governor Stuyvesant's Bouwerie, the Collect, and the gallows-field into Broadway.

A negro coachman dressed in a livery of pale blue cloth laced with silver, and wearing a triangular cocked hat trimmed with broad silver lace, sat on the box and skilfully drove his clumsy horses, and a negro boy hung by the tassels behind, wearing the same livery, with the exception that a jockey-cap of Turkey leather, with silver seams and band, took the place of the coachman's cocked hat.

Like all the ladies of the day, Miss Morris wore a black velvet riding-mask, and was dressed in a sack of flowered chintz, over which was thrown a taffeta scarf. After a long and tiresome drive of many hours' duration, Miss Morris was glad to stop before Mrs. Alexander's house and send her footman to rap at the door. She was immediately shown into Mrs. Alexander's parlor, where she found a knot of ladies busily discussing the latest tit-bit of scandal, which was the elopement of the governor's daughter, Elinor, a girl barely eighteen, with the Hon. Augustus Fitzroy, the son of the Duke of Grafton.

It was said that the governor was cognizant of the

love affair, which had been planned and promoted by his scheming wife, but as the Duke of Grafton was at the time at the head of the government, his excellency feared to incur the displeasure of his superior, and consequently pretended to know nothing about the affair.

The young lady was conducted by her mother to the garden gate, where the groom and his friends were in waiting, and the couple were speedily married by the governor's chaplain. In order that there should be no interruption to the elopement, Mrs. Cosby locked the servants in their quarters, and herself threw a great red cardinal-cloak over the bride's dress, the better to disguise her. The governor made himself very conspicuous that evening at the Humdrum Club, and he finally became so uproariously drunk that he was carried home in the early hours of the morning by two burly negroes.

All these details were being eagerly discussed by the ladies in Mrs. Alexander's salon, and the gossips were so busily engaged talking it over that they hardly noted Miss Morris's arrival or her exit after a few moments' chat with her hostess, by whose permission she went in search of Mr. Alexander, who was in his private office. On giving her host a letter from Colonel Morris, she was handed a bundle of papers containing the proofs of the governor's repeated attempt to defraud his subjects, which had been prepared by Messrs. Alexander and Smith, and which the gentlemen hoped would prove so overwhelming that the Lords of Trade would have no option but would be forced at once to find another place for their dishonest representative.

Miss Morris carefully concealed the package in a capacious pocket, and at once took leave of Mr. Alexander, who escorted her to her coach, with many whispered messages to her father. The young lady then went to the house of Governor Van Dam, where she met her father, who took a seat beside her, and at once started on their return journey to Morrisania.

As they were passing over the high hill that is now about Ninetieth Street, on Second Avenue, Miss Mòrris called her father's attention to an English man-of-war which could be seen passing through Hell Gate, and they recognized it as the Tartar, a frigate commanded by Captain Norris. The young lady was engaged to marry that officer, and had used her influence with him to obtain for her father a passage to England. By taking the vessel through Long Island Sound the captain avoided the spies set by the governor at the Narrows, who had strict orders to allow no passengers to sail from thence without a pass signed by himself. As had been previously arranged, the ship was to anchor off Morrisania that evening, so that the lovers could have a quiet opportunity of saying farewell, and Colonel Morris could embark from in front of his own home and set sail for England with his precious documents.

Colonel Morris and his daughter landed at their dock at the same time that Captain Norris, in full uniform, sprang on shore from the ship's pinnace. While the lovers took a hasty leave of each other, Mrs. Morris and her other children were bidding farewell to the husband and father, who tore himself from their embraces, and calling to Captain Norris to hasten his good-byes, the two gentlemen embarked and were soon under way, and were on the ocean before Governor Cosby realized that his deeply laid plans were frustrated.

The following verses were published in the New York "Weekly Journal," December 30, 1774, much to the wrath of the governor :

> " Neptune, be kind and calm the raging sea ;
> Let no rough wave retard the patriot's way.
> Protect him—oh ! protect him safely on
> Thy vast dominions to the British shore."

XIX

New York in 1732

Trouble Between the Governor and His Council—The Anonymous Letter—The Prosecution of Zenger—"The Ladies, God Bless Them"—The "Weekly Journal" Ordered Burned—The Attorneys Disbarred—Mrs. Alexander's Common-sense—Her Trip to Philadelphia—The Zenger Trial—Andrew Hamilton—Balls and Dinners—Death of Cosby—The Successor—The Attorneys Restored to the Bar—The Servant Question—Horace Walpole on the Slave Trade.

CHIEF-JUSTICE SMITH, in his "History of New York," gives the following account of the habits of its denizens about the year 1732:

"The men collect weekly at their clubs in the evenings, and the ladies in winter frequently entertain either at concerts of music or assemblies, and make a very good appearance. They are comely and dress well, and scarce any of them have distorted shapes. Tinctured with a Dutch education (which was at variance with the custom of the thriftless English), they manage their families with becoming parsimony, good providence, and singular neatness. The practice of extravagant gaming, common to the fashionable part of the fair sex in some places, is a vice with which my countrywomen (of New York) cannot justly be charged. They are modest, temperate, and charitable, naturally sprightly, sensible, and good humored.

"The richer sort keep very plentiful tables, abounding with great varieties of fish, flesh, and fowl, and all kinds of vegetables. The common drinks are beer, cider, weak punch, and madeira wine. For dessert we have fruits in vast plenty of different kinds and various species."

The people were friendly and fond of entertaining, but under the new era all old barriers were swept away, new alliances formed, old political dissensions forgotten, and an entirely new order of things prevailed. Even the ties of relationship, which in the Dutch families were so strong, seemed weakened, and those of the childish companies were broken by the fierce political discussions that now broke out with an unprecedented virulence. The De Lanceys (headed by the chief-justice) were on the side of the "court," with Francis Harison (an Englishman who had not been long in the colony, but who had been raised to a position in the council), and many others who were devoted to the same interests, while Colonel Morris, William Smith, James Alexander, and some of the Livingston family, were the leaders of the opposition.

New Year, 1734, was celebrated in the city of New York with particularly marked festivities among the leading representatives of the Dutch families. The ladies were determined to emphasize their connection with the early rulers of the province, and by so doing to show the distinction between their adherents and those of the English faction; and it was for this reason that the "Nieu Jaar" was marked by a strict observance of all the Dutch customs, which had been allowed to become somewhat slack after the death of Madame de Peyster and her contemporaries. Mrs. Alexander's reception was particularly well attended, and she was kept busy from morning to night in receiving and returning the hearty greetings that every man of note in the colony who could boast of the slightest acquaintance with "the wife of his majesty's councillor, James Alexander," was eager to bestow on her. The servants were occupied all day handing to the guests on their arrival huge silver salvers on which were decanters of old madeira and crusty port, accompanied with the cakes for which the Dutch were famous, "oly koecks, crullers, and Nieu Jaar kookies." Old Peter stood at the door and welcomed all comers in his hearty negro fashion, with broad grins and pleasant wishes for "A happy New Year!" A great stickler for etiquette was the old darkey, who had been born and brought up in the family, and considered himself no insignificant part of it. He had been given to Mrs. Alexander as her own property when a mere boy, and had followed her to her home as her "major domo" when she married and began to keep house for herself, and the aid of such a well-trained and experienced servant (as anyone who had been brought up under the eyes of Madame de Peyster was sure to be) was an invaluable adjutant to a young house-keeper, as Polly Spratt was when she first married. Everyone knew the old servant, who was also perfectly informed about everyone's affairs in the city, not only through the "back-stairs agency," which always knows as much of the affairs of the "parlor-people" as they do themselves, but also from the bits of gossip and sly jokes that he overheard from his station behind his mistress's chair. Peter was vigilance itself to all such gossip, and as he never left his post he had excellent opportunities for knowing all that was going on in the colony. He stood there armed with a huge peacock-tail brush, with which he ostensibly brushed the flies from the table, but in reality he was an interested but silent participant in all that was going on.

There were some guests who presented themselves at the Nieu Jaar reception whose presence old Peter bitterly resented as a piece of unwarranted presumption on their part. He did not hesitate to express his opinion on the subject to his mistress the following day, and she was forced to point out to him the political condition of affairs and the necessity for her conciliating certain men of mark although they were not socially accredited, before she could assuage the old servant's wrath at what he was pleased to consider an indignity that had been offered to his beloved mistress. The position of slave and mistress in the colony at that time was a peculiar one, and it was only among the Dutch families that the servants were treated with a consideration which made them consider themselves integral parts of the family; and troubles were brewing for the colonists because the new rulers and their adherents were misusing the negroes whom the English government were sending to the colonies in such numbers, not openly, it is true, but still with the connivance and assistance of those in authority.

As time went on the disputes between the governor and his council became more and more violent. While some of the members openly sided with his excellency others did not dare to oppose him, though detesting his views and methods, and James Alexander seemed to stand alone in the council-chamber as the firm supporter of the rights of the colonists, one who never swerved in his freely spoken allegiance. The governor now demeaned himself by conniving at a clumsy plot which he hoped would drive his opponents, both secret and open, from the council board and leave him in full possession of the field. The first part of it was to frighten his enemies by secret threats and intimidations; the second was to malign them, not only in the "presence-chamber," the clubs, and assembly, but also by anonymous letters secretly conveyed to those who, it was thought, would be most easily influenced by such measures.

Mr. Smith, in his "History of New York," says: "At the parting of some company from Mr. Alexander's, late in the evening of February 1, 1734, an incendiary letter was picked up in the hall. It had been shoved under the outer door, and was instantly pronounced by Mr.

Alexander to be the handwriting of Mr. Harison, then a member of the council. It was in these words:

"To Mr. Alexander:

"I am one who was formerly accounted a gentleman, but am now reduced to poverty, and have no victuals to eat; and knowing you to be of a generous temper, desire you would comply with my request, which is, to let me have ten pistoles (thirty dollars) to supply my necessities and carry me to my native country. This is a bold request, but I desire you will comply with it, or you and your family shall feel the effects of my displeasure. Unless you let me have them I'll destroy you and your family by a stratagem which I have contrived. If that don't take the desired effect, I swear, by God to poison all your tribe so surely that you sha'n't know the perpetrator of the tragedy. I beg, for God's sake, that you would let me have the money, and hinder me from committing such a black deed. I know you can spare it, so desire you would let me have it Saturday night about seven o'clock. Leave it by the Cellar door, wrapped in a rag, and about an hour after I will come and take it. Put it on the ground just where I put the stick. If you don't leave it I advise you not to drink your beer, nor eat your bread, if you value your lives and healths, for, by my soul, I will do what I have mentioned. If I find any watch to guard me from taking it, I'll desist and not take it, but follow my intended scheme, and hinder you from acting any more on the scene of life. If you comply I'll never molest you more; but if not I'll hazard my life in destroying yours, and continue what I am."

Smith, in his "History of New York," says: "From the neglect to disguise the hand, which Mr. Smith, Mr. Hamilton, and Mr. Lurting, the mayor, all pronounced to be Mr. Harison's, it was conjectured that his design was to provoke a criminal prosecution, establish the precedent of convicting on the proof of similitude of hands, and then by counterfeiting the writing of one of the demagogues of the day, to bring him to the gallows, while the governor's friends were to escape by pardon."

When the case was laid before the grand jury, Mr. Alexander, as well as his friends, who had penetrated the plot, contended against the grand jury finding an indictment against Mr. Harison, on such evidence only as the similarity of the writing in the anonymous letter with that of Mr. Harison's. As Mr. Alexander declared that he cared nothing for discovering and punishing the culprit, at the expense of future entanglements such as he foresaw that a commitment on such evidence might lead to, it was therefore in compliance with his wishes that the jurors contented themselves with an address to the governor, in which they declared that they could not discover the author of the letter on the evidence submitted to them, as they did not consider that the similarity of the handwriting in the letter with that of Mr. Harison was sufficient to convict the latter of such a dastardly deed, and they refused to indite him as they feared that they might ensnare an innocent person in a trap. The matter was, of course, laid before the council by the governor, and as Mr. Harison and Mr. Alexander were both members of it, the matter rested there, although Harison was universally suspected of the authorship of the letter, and was shunned by most of the respectable members of the colony, many of whom openly accused him of writing it at the dictation of the governor. In order to defend himself, Mr. Harison publicly declared "that Mr. Alexander and Mr. Smith had forged the letter, to ruin him." These gentlemen immediately published a refutation of the scandal, which by assigning proofs of Harison's enmity to them, strengthened the general suspicions that were then prevalent against him. "The cause of Harison's enmity had been a discovery of his design to rob the colony," says Mr. Smith, "during Governor Montgomerie's rule, a plot that had been unearthed and frustrated by Messrs. Smith and Alexander. Added to this, Harison was under a prosecution tending to overwhelm him with disgrace, which terminated against him, and eventually caused him to flee the colony."

Mr. Smith says: "Whether the governor was let into the design of the author of the letter was never discovered, though some stress was laid upon words dropped by a man intimate in the family, who, coming home in his cups late one evening, shortly before the letter was found, said, 'A scheme was executed to hang Alexander and Smith.' And Mrs. Cosby, frequently and without reserve, had declared that 'it was her highest wish to see them on a gallows at the fort gate.'"

This virulent enmity on the part of the governor and his faction, against law, decency, and order, as represented by Messrs. Smith and Alexander, showed itself in a new way before the summer was over. Cosby retreated to the governor's house at Perth Amboy after his suit against Governor Van Dam had terminated adversely to him, and in this quiet retreat the worthy representative of King George concocted a plan that some members of the council were only too willing to aid him in, in the hopes of ridding themselves of their opponents; and under their able mismanagement the famous prosecution of Zenger, the printer of one of the papers devoted to the interests of the colonists, was planned. This paper, called the "Weekly Journal," had lately been started. Its leading articles, contributed by some of the ablest writers of the day, consisted of attacks on the governor and his party, who determined to put a stop to this wholesale exposure of their nefarious actions, and concocted a plot that resulted in the complete discomfiture of the governor and his party instead of that of their enemies, as had been intended, and in the establishment of the "liberties of the press," which was one of the first steps toward overthrowing the English rule in the American colonies and hastened the exposure of the governor's malpractices.

In 1734 Peter Zenger, a German emigrant who had been brought to the New York colony by his parents while a mere infant, and who was in humble circumstances, left the master under whom he had learned his trade as a printer and started a newspaper of his own in New York, and called it the "Weekly Journal." It was openly said that the funds to start the sheet were advanced by prominent members of the opposition party who needed such a vehicle in order to communicate with the public, and that the printer, Zenger, was merely the mouth-piece of other and more able persons, who secretly supplied him with matter that he merely printed and distributed. The "Weekly Journal" was filled with criticisms on the governor's "policy, his life, and his habits," and they gave evidence that the articles were penned by no unpractised hand. The squibs, lampoons, and witticisms are almost incomprehensible at the present day, but it is evident that "every bullet had its billet," and that the public delighted in these open attacks on the governor, and that he was galled to madness by them. That these articles were written by someone behind the scenes was proved by their evident acquaintance with the inward workings of the council, and everyone pointed to Messrs. Smith and Alexander as the authors. But although universally credited with the production of these attacks on the governor and his party, nothing could be proved as to their authorship, as the secret was well kept. A watch was put on the movements of both gentlemen, but they could not be detected visiting or communicating with the printer Zenger in any way. The governor then offered a reward of £200 to anyone who would reveal the secret, but he was as unsuccessful in this effort as he had been with his spies. The secret was probably known to very few persons, and all had too much at stake to reveal it; but in after years both gentlemen acknowledged their share in the preparation of the articles in question, in which they had been assisted by Colonel Lewis Morris, his son, and Governor Van Dam.

Cosby fancied that he was very clever when he set his spies to follow the movements of his councillors, but he never imagined for a moment that they could outwit him, and that the ladies of their families were as much interested in the success of their schemes as they were themselves, and could aid them by being the means of conveying secret intelligence from one person to the other, and communication in this way was easily kept up. Mrs. Alexander's evening receptions were also used as a means of exchanging secret intelligence, and into the privacy of Mrs. Alexander's parlors the governor could not penetrate, although family tradition declares that he attempted to suborn old Peter and make him a spy on his master and mistress and their guests, and offered him large rewards if he would betray them. The governor by this means converted the old servant into a very active foe, and one who proved no despicable one.

The attacks on the governor continued in spite of all his efforts to stop them, and his excellency now carried into effect the plan he had formed in his rural retreat, which was to throw the printer into prison as a means of putting an end to them. This was unavailing, as a particularly virulent article at once appeared. The number in which it was issued was ordered to be "burnt by the common hangman November 2, 1734," and the mayor of the city, Robert Lurting, and the common council were commanded to attend the cremation. But the mayor and the aldermen protested that this was not part of their duty, and that the governor had no right to demand it of them. The governor and Harison insisted on their compliance, but they rebelled and refused in the most positive terms to obey the governor, and they proceeded still further, as they commanded the city hangman not to execute the commission, and the paper was therefore burned by a slave in the presence of Harison and some of the governor's adherents, which proved to be a very flat and laughable termination of the affair. Zenger was in prison, but he was allowed to receive daily visits from his wife, and through her he issued his directions, and Mrs. Zenger contrived to have the paper issued regularly and distributed to the subscribers.

Messrs. Alexander and Smith were retained as counsel for Zenger, and they appeared in court fully prepared to defend him; but de Lancey, the chief-justice, was of the governor's party, and keen to take advantage of the position and the power that it gave him. He was aware that the stand taken by the governor was unpopular and unconstitutional, and he knew that with the two most capable lawyers of the colony prepared to defend the prisoner, it would be almost impossible to obtain a verdict against him from the jurors, who were necessarily drawn from the freeholders qualified for the position, and were less than a thousand in number. He knew also that these freeholders were deeply and personally interested in the result, and probably felt that on the acquittal of the prisoner much of their own independence in the future depended. Chief-Justice de Lancey listened with undisguised impatience to the opening address by Mr. Smith, and interrupted him abruptly, and ordered that his name, and that of his partner, Mr. Alexander, "should be stricken from the roll of attorneys-at-law of the province of New York."

This high-handed act of de Lancey's caused the trial to come to an abrupt termination, and nearly caused a panic in the community when it became publicly known. Everyone felt that the safeguards of law and order were overthrown when the chief-justice could defy them with impunity, and many people felt that property, and even life itself, was not safe when controlled by the governor and his minions. Many of the inhabitants now determined to sell their possessions at a sacrifice, if necessary, and leave the province for that of Pennsylvania, where they believed that they would be more secure, as that colony possessed an independent charter given it by the king, and was empowered to select its own rulers. Under this charter the province of Pennsylvania had a comparatively stable government, which was not liable to sudden alterations, and it was rapidly rising in importance and rivalling in wealth and prosperity the older colony.

It was now that the clear common-sense of Mrs. Alexander came to the rescue of the disheartened partners and their dismayed friends. Mr. Smith was firmly resolved on moving his family at once, and Mr. Alexander was so thoroughly disgusted with the corruption of the political affairs in New York, that he was more than half inclined to follow his partner to another sphere of action. With their law-practice wrested from them, and many of the chief colonists so blind to their own best interests that they were willing to be the tools of an unscrupulous governor, both men thought that the province was doomed to anarchy, and they dreaded sharing its fate. Now it was that Mrs. Alexander took prompt and effective action. She pointed out that it would be the height of folly to abandon their homes, for wherever they settled some unforeseen turn of affairs might again wrest their property from them, and she implored her husband to meet bravely the present aggravations, withstand them with a spirited opposition, and remain steadfast in his present position. With some of the quiet mother-wit for which she was noted, Mrs. Alexander asked if Messrs. Alexander and Smith were the only clever men in the colony who were able and competent to defend the unfortunate Zenger. The spirited words of Mrs. Alexander put the gentlemen on their mettle, and they consented to make a determined stand against the governor and his party; but they despaired of success, and even Mrs. Alexander was forced to acknowledge that there were few men in New York who were capable of taking their places, as well as willing to risk the governor's displeasure in defending the printer and his publications.

For any lawyer of the place ran the risk of being disbarred by the chief-justice merely for undertaking the position that he had already prevented Messrs. Alexander and Smith from occupying, and with no more excuse than he had had in their case, and there were few men who would consent to place themselves in this predicament.

In this dilemma Mrs. Alexander suddenly bethought herself of a talented lawyer who at the time lived in Philadelphia, and who was in constant correspondence with her husband. This was Andrew Hamilton, a man who was highly esteemed by his fellow-citizens. Mr. Hamilton had been educated for the bar in England, was noted for his eloquence, and was abundantly capable of defending the case with success; and as he had nothing at stake in the New York colony, he could defy the governor, the chief-justice, and their friends with an impunity that would strengthen his hands. This happy thought was applauded on all sides, and Mr. Hamilton was communicated with as secretly as possible, as it was deemed most important that the government party should imagine that no steps were to be taken to defend Zenger when the case again came up for trial, which would throw them off their guard, and they would not have time to concoct new measures to defeat the ends of justice.

In this crisis Mrs. Alexander undertook to pay a visit to Philadelphia and have a personal interview with Mr. Hamilton and lay all the facts of the case before the great lawyer, and entreat him to come to New York when the time came for the trial, prepared to defend the unfortunate printer. For this purpose Mrs. Alexander announced to her friends that she was going to Perth Amboy for a short time in order to look after some property there, and she publicly took leave of her husband and friends at the White Hall landing and sailed for "the Jersies" in her own yacht. On reaching that place, Mrs. Alexander quietly hired a wagon and went on to Philadelphia and had an interview with Mr. Hamilton, who, after hearing her story, undertook Zenger's defence with pleasure, and promised to be in New York when the time came for the trial as if he were there to attend to other business, and declare his errand only when the proper time came. Mrs. Alexander was thoroughly conversant with every point, and was in a position to state it clearly to Mr. Hamilton, and also the opinions of Messrs. Smith and Alexander as to the line of argument to be used, and he was also supplied with all the necessary papers, which tradition states were carried to Philadelphia quilted into Mrs. Alexander's best silk petticoat. After this hurried journey, Mrs. Alexander returned to New York and rejoined her family without anyone having suspected or discovered her mission, and her friend Mr. Smith (who was the historian from whom part of this account has been taken) has been discreetly silent on the share of the lady in this important flank movement against the common enemy.

The Goede Vrouw of Mana-ha-ta

The trial of Zenger came up in ~~July~~ Aug, and Chief-Justice de Lancey and Governor Cosby were dismayed when they saw Mr. Hamilton appear in court and announce that he had been retained as counsel for the defendant. Mr. Hamilton's argument was clever, and was listened to with the deepest attention by a crowd of interested citizens. It was based on the law of libel, and a covert attack was made on the governor and his friends, together with their methods, which was so scathing and yet so true in every particular, that it made his excellency wince, while he was in no position to retaliate or justify himself. The trial was a long and stormy one, but it ended in a verdict of "Not guilty," as it was held that "truth was no libel." The verdict was met with storms of applause from the spectators, and echoed by the concourse of people who were gathered outside of the court-house anxiously awaiting the result of the trial, which all parties had now begun to realize was not merely that of an unfortunate printer, but involved the maintenance of law and order in the colony against anarchy and ruin; and when the verdict was rendered for the defendant, it was received with a deep sense of relief, as in it the colonists saw hopes of liberty, stability, and prosperity in the future, instead of the anarchy that had threatened to engulf them.

The verdict was canvassed and discussed in all parts of the town and by all classes of society, and as it gradually dawned on the minds of those not versed in the law that it had been won from the jury by the specious pleading of a master-mind, and was rendered more in accordance with sentiment than under the law, the admiration of the public for Mr. Hamilton was increased, and "Smart as a Philadelphia lawyer," or "It takes a Philadelphia lawyer to win," became proverbs in the city of New York.

But the first news that the public had of the verdict was from the bursts of applause that filled the court-house the instant it was known. The spectators filled the room with their shouts and acclamations, which enraged the judge, who threatened to stop the commotion by imprisoning any person who took part in it. Upon this, Captain Norris of the English frigate Tartar jumped on a bench and addressed the court, and declared that "huzzahs were common in Westminster Hall, and were very loud on the acquittal of the Seven Bishops." The significance of this remark had a quieting effect on the judges, who had no time allowed them for reply, for the shouts were redoubled and all remonstrance silenced by the clamor that ensued. Such a public defence of the rights of the colonists against the representatives of government by the son of an admiral and the commander of one of his majesty's ships, had great weight, and his bold defiance on such an important occasion made a hero of the young fellow, particularly as it now became generally known that it was by his connivance that Colonel Morris had been able to make his escape from the colony and proceed to England in order to lay the abuses under which they were suffering before the home government. Captain Norris had only just returned from his voyage to England, and had at once been married to his fair fiancée, who was then with him on their bridal trip.

Mr. Hamilton was overwhelmed with the gratitude of the citizens, and he was tendered a public dinner, at which he was presented with the freedom of the city in a gold box, and the ladies of the town requested his presence at a ball given in his honor, and on his departure for Philadelphia he was escorted by the enthusiastic citizens to Mrs. Alexander's yacht, which was lying in waiting (to carry him to Perth Amboy, on the first stage of his journey home) at the landing at the White Hall steps, directly under the eyes of the incensed and mortified governor, who saw that all his schemes had been baffled.

The party of the opposition were triumphant and now felt that the first step toward justice and order had been taken, and they were willing to forgive those of their fellow-citizens who had been led by fright or expediency to join issue against them, if by so doing they could make common cause against the governor. The ladies of New York were particularly delighted at the cessation of hostilities, more because they were able to resume their social functions and ruptured friendships than for any clear understanding that they had of the matter, or the political interests at stake. Woman-like, they fancied that men must be always squabbling about politics, and they disliked nothing so much as to be drawn into these discussions and forced to take sides against their own friends, owing to the partisanship of the men of their family. Mrs. Alexander, as has been seen, took an active part in the late disturbances, but she, too, hailed with delight the olive-branch that was now being held out by all parties, and was glad to renew the ancient intercourse with the friends of her childhood, which had been interrupted by political events. While sympathizing with her husband in his struggle for the welfare of his adopted country, she viewed with regret his opposition to her friends and could hardly help feeling that the vortex into which she was plunged was antagonistic to the Dutch traditions in which she had been reared. She realized too that, although she ought to be on the side of the first settlers (owing to her birth), she was undoubtedly prejudiced by her husband and his partner, and was therefore placed in a disagreeable position, and she hailed with delight the prospect she now saw of release. Taking advantage, therefore, of the lull in hostilities, Mrs. Alexander organized a series of balls for the ensuing winter, which she hoped would prove as a flag of truce, and would draw together all the opposing families and make them forget past differences; but these balls were not thrown open for public subscription, and the list was carefully supervised by the managers, who would not include the family of the governor, alleging as an excuse that it was intended merely for the colonists and that no foreigner might subscribe.

The Goede Vrouw of Mana-ha-ta

The winter of 1736 was therefore an extremely gay one, and a particularly brilliant ball was given at the Black Horse Tavern, close under the shadow of White Hall, at which fête Lieut.-Governor Van Dam presided. The occasion of it was the birthday of the Prince of Wales, January 19, 1736, which was celebrated, says the New York "Weekly Journal," "in a most elegant and genteel manner," at which the bride, Mrs. Norris, "led up two new country dances, mounted for the occasion, the first of which was called the 'Prince of Wales,' and the second the 'Princess of Saxe Gotha,' in honour of the day."

But these hospitable entertainments were fruitless, and the truce was a hollow one and of no long standing. The contesting parties were not contented with the defeat on one side and signal success on the other, and both sides renewed hostilities. It would probably have been a long and bitter struggle on the part of the colonists against oppression and misrule, as the appeal made by Colonel Morris to the home government had been met by a quiet contempt and indifference, in spite of the overwhelming proofs that he was able to lay before the Lords of Trade of the corruption of their representative. Colonel Morris was informed that the lords were aware of all that he could tell them, and they were perfectly indifferent to all such complaints, and intended to support their governor in spite of everything; they also made the same reply to another representative of the colonists, who laid the grievances of his fellow-citizens before the government at the same time. The papers that were presented to the Lords of Trade by the two gentlemen have never been given to the public, but they are preserved in the families of their descendants, and if anything be wanting to complete the chain of evidence of the corruption of the English government of that period, indubitable proofs are not wanting. The colonists were relieved from their rapacious, unscrupulous ruler by the death of Governor Cosby, March 10, 1736. A few of his misdeeds have been mentioned, but in addition to these he was guilty of so many high-handed and culpable acts that his name has been handed down to posterity as one to be universally execrated. Forgery, malfeasance in office, etc., have been charged and proved, such as that Governor Cosby had asked to be permitted to study some title-deeds of property in Albany and the Jersies, and, as soon as they were in his possession, had thrown them in the fire, in the presence of witnesses. Some of the papers related to the patents of the Mohawk reservation, and this action of his was taken in order to destroy the evidence of ownership, after which he asserted, "That as there were no proofs of ownership forthcoming, the property in question reverted to himself." This procedure of the governor's soon became known, and the colonists were naturally indignant; no one felt secure lest his turn might come next, and even Chief-Justice de Lancey ventured to remonstrate on this and on other unconstitutional actions of Cosby's, only to receive the reply, "What do I care for these grumbling rustics." It is therefore little wonder that all members of the province of New York felt a sense of relief when they heard of the death of the governor.

Cosby was a man of low cunning and limited sagacity, but he knew well how far he might proceed in robbing the colonists of New York, protected as he was by the indifference (or worse) of the members of the home government, who were willing to throw a cloak over his misdeeds, as is proved by the documents on file, some of which have been printed in the "Documents Relating to the Colonial History." Mr. Smith relates of Governor Cosby that, on one occasion, it was suggested to him that a proceeding of his was contrary to law, and his reply was, "How, gentlemen, do you think I mind that? I have great interest in England."

Governor Cosby's rule had been a dishonest and law-breaking one:

"Stiff in opinion, always in the wrong,"

and the final act, when on his death-bed, was a fitting conclusion to his maladministration when in office. Finding that the disease from which he was suffering was likely to prove fatal, the governor called a secret meeting of the council, to which only the members who were attached to his interests were summoned, while Lieut.-Governor Van Dam, Mr. Alexander and their friends were not called; and at this hurried, secret, illegal meeting the dying governor deposed the president of the council, Lieutenant-Governor Van Dam, and substituted a creature of his own, by the name of Clarke, in the place of the old Dutchman, who had served his countrymen so long and faithfully.

The governor also directed his wife to take charge of all the despatches that should arrive from England and turn them over to Clarke, to whom he gave secret instructions. This unprecedented conduct was probably caused by the hope that his illegal practices might be concealed by his friend, Clarke, while they would certainly be revealed by Van Dam if he were allowed to assume the reins of office, as he would do, according to precedent, having acted as governor previous to Cosby's arrival, and being still senior member of the council, a position that he had held unmolested for a number of years.

The colonists were aware that Van Dam should take Cosby's place, and were rejoicing in the prospect of peace and prosperity that seemed opening out before them with this change in the administration; and the consternation of Van Dam, Alexander, and the public can be better imagined than described when on the death of the governor they learned the trick that had been played on them. The scene in the council-chamber was one of wild confusion, but in spite of the protests of the majority of the members, who then learned for the first time of the deposition of Van Dam and the secret succession of Clarke to the position, the oath of office was administered to the latter, and the council broke up in confusion, many of its members refusing to ratify the succession, and declaring their intention of appealing to the populace or to the home government for redress.

Mr. Alexander at once published a statement denouncing the illegal action of the late governor, and declaring that he was no party to the administration of the oath of office to Clarke, but that, on the contrary, he had in vain remonstrated against such precipitancy and had begged for delay until such time as deliberate action could be taken in the matter. This public statement was rendered necessary, as the friends of the new governor had pointed triumphantly to the fact that both Van Dam and Alexander had been present at the meeting of the council when the oath of office was administered to Clarke.

Mr. Alexander now refused to attend the meetings of the council, as he declared they were illegally summoned and conducted, and after publicly stating the position that he intended to adopt, he removed with his family to Perth Amboy, intending to pass the summer quietly amid rural scenes and devote his leisure to the philosophical pursuits that he delighted in, which had been for some time interrupted by the calls of his official position.

In the meantime Colonel Morris had reached England and had laid the remonstrances of the colonists against the illegal practices of Governor Cosby before the Lords of Trade, who, however, turned a deaf ear to all the statements, and disposed of Colonel Morris as quickly as possible by making him Governor of New Jersey, which they fancied would silence him, and that by accepting it he would be arrayed against his former friends, who would accuse him of having accepted it as a bribe. But Colonel Morris, although he accepted the office bestowed on him, was only half-satisfied, and returned to America, where his arrival was eagerly watched for. He was met on landing in New York, says Mr. Smith, "by a vast concourse, and escorted, with loud acclamations, to a meeting of the chiefs of the party. Having listened to the proceedings of the past few months, and to what extremes the contests were advanced, and being importuned for his advice, he replied, in a grave tone: 'If you don't hang them, they'll hang you.'"

Contentions continued until despatches arrived from England confirming Clarke in office, which for a time crushed the colonists, who believed that they were doomed to receive unjust treatment at the hands of the home government. Things were, however, mending, as Clarke was not the bare-faced villain that his predecessor had been, and he at once concluded that his easiest plan would be to conciliate his opponents, as he saw that there was nothing to be gained by inflaming them against him, when they had the powerful weapon of the public press, which he knew by bitter experience they would have no scruples about using.

Clarke was well aware that the bitter invectives, squibs, lampoons which had been hurled with impunity at Cosby had influenced public opinion against him in such a way as to hamper his best-laid plans, even if they did not succeed in defeating them completely; and the life of his predecessor had been tormented in a way that Clarke had no desire to inherit, so that he deemed it his best policy to disarm his antagonists by a seeming friendliness rather than by repelling their attacks by force.

The popular party on their side were heartily weary of the battle against oppression, which seemed to them almost fruitless, and Mr. Smith acknowledges that he was so thoroughly disgusted with the state of affairs in the province of New York that he at this time again seriously contemplated moving his family to Virginia. To the surprise and pleasure of Messrs. Smith and Alexander, the governor and one of his friends approached the partners and intimated to them that they should be reinstated at the bar if they so desired. Mrs. Smith and Mrs. Alexander were greatly relieved at this turn of affairs, and both wives used their influence with their husbands to persuade them to accept these offers of conciliation. They were brave women and had courageously borne all the miseries and worries of the past few years, but even they had quailed under the repeated attacks that had been made on the lives and reputations of their husbands.

After some punctilios, "*Honore Servando*," says Mr. Smith, "the judges cancelled the order of the chief-justice, and in the October term, on the 18th of the month, 1737, Mr. Alexander and Mr. Smith appeared again at the bar."

"It was quite an event," says Chief-Justice Daly, in his historical sketch of the "Judicial Tribunals of New York;" "Alexander was no speaker, but his breadth of learning, and depth of thought, and honesty of purpose commanded universal respect and admiration. He possessed the knack of throwing terrible significance into a few well-chosen words at certain times and was always a formidable antagonist. Smith was a born orator; speaking was no effort to him, his grandest orations were often impromptu. His voice was musical, which with an attractive face, fine presence, and great personal attractions were very effective with a jury."

The public were delighted that their favorite lawyers were reinstated in the position that they had been so unjustly deprived of, and Mr. Alexander was asked to accept the nomination as a member of the assembly, to represent the city of New York, an office to which he was immediately and unanimously elected. Lewis Morris, Jr., was speaker of the house, and their party was supported by gentlemen from each election district, which gave them an overwhelming majority.

It now seemed as if an era of peace and prosperity were dawning on the colony. Trade at once began to revive, industries started into life, and emigration, instead of being diverted to other colonies, as had been the case during the past few years, increased in a most gratifying way. To encourage and protect the infant industries Mr. Alexander introduced bills into the assembly to protect the manufacture of hemp and iron, for the prevention of frauds in products intended for exportation, and also for the encouragement of emigration. The last law was framed particularly to encourage persons to come to the colony who were willing to enter domestic service. The ladies had been in the habit of selecting children from the families of their poorer neighbors, and having them bound to them for a certain term of service, just as tradesmen received apprentices, but the demand fell far short of the supply. There were but few pauper families in the colony, and those were generally of mixed Indian and negro blood, and tainted with the worst vices of both nations. They were lazy and ignorant, and it was thought that if a better class of servants could be imported, the traffic in slaves would receive a check, as the subject of slavery was now beginning to be of paramount importance.

Negroes had been carried to New Amsterdam by English traders, and sold there, regardless of the remonstrances of the authorities, who were contemplating a stringent set of laws against this practice when the colony was delivered over to the English. There had been little abuse of the slaves under the rule of the worthy Dutchmen and their wives, who were mild and gentle, and the negroes found kind and lenient friends in their masters, and did not feel their bondage as a curse, but rather regarded themselves as important members of

New York in 1732

the family, and no punishment was worse than a threat to send them away or sell them to another person.

The colonial archives are full of records of the arrangements made by the English government to impose slaves on their colonies. Many members of the government had large interests in the slave-trade, and it was their policy to encourage the traffic. The instructions to Lord Cornbury in the "Colonial Documents" tell him to encourage the importation of slaves into the New York province, notwithstanding that the colonists tried to stop it, as they foresaw the misery that was sure to ensue and dreaded the consequences to themselves; but while it was upheld by the rulers in England, their efforts to stop the curse were unavailing, and the American colonies were left to groan helplessly under the bitter burden of slavery for two centuries, and after the yoke of England was thrown from their galled shoulders, and the country and its people were declared "free and independent," they had the mortification of being left with this canker-spot in their midst, and in addition were taunted by the English people for permitting a state of things that had been created by themselves.

That all the members of the English government were not equally corrupt, is proved by the following letter from Horace Walpole to his friend Horace Mann. In letter CCXI., of "Later Letters," he writes, "We have been sitting this fortnight on the African company, WE, the British Senate, the Temple of Liberty, and the Bulwark of Protestant Christianity, have this fortnight been pondering methods to make more effectual that horrid traffic of selling negroes. It has appeared to us that six-and-forty thousand of these wretches are sold every year to our plantations alone—it chills the blood. I would not have it to say that I voted in it for the Continent of America."

XX

Matches, Batches, and Despatches

Perth Amboy—The Hamlet of Greenwich—Death of the Fifth Earl of Stirling—William Alexander now Successor to the Title—Mary Alexander's Engagement to Peter Van Brugh Livingston—The Children's " Companies " Again—Birth of " Gentleman Phil "—Captain David Provoost—John Provoost's Marriage—The Negroes—" Major Drum "—Fires and Robberies—Father Ury—The GRAND Grand Jury—Cuffie and His Kind-hearted Mistress.

WEARIED by the contentions and discussions in which her husband had been embroiled, and anxious about his health, Mrs. Alexander determined to spend the summer of 1739 at Perth Amboy. It was particularly convenient for her to do this, as she had determined to build a country residence there, so that her husband could have his own home when attending to his duties as councillor of New Jersey. Mr. Alexander held office in both colonies, and the council sometimes sat at Perth Amboy during the summer months, where the governor had an official residence, the first one having been occupied there by Governor Burnet. The place had in consequence become a favorite summer-resort, and as it was on the high road to Philadelphia, it was gradually rising into one of considerable importance. In "A Day in New York," the author gives the following account of the village: "As there were no steamboats in those days, to annihilate both time and space, it may be as well to record how people reached the port of Amboy. Passages were obtained in the sloop Adventure, Peter Kearney master, and a short voyage of less than three days from New York brought them to the flourishing city of Perth."

Mrs. Alexander had purchased a beautiful spot that commanded a view of the bay of New York, and she hoped to engross her husband's attention in superintending the building of the house and laying out the grounds, and in this way distract his mind from the troubles that had agitated him for so many years. Small-pox was raging in New York, and the assembly was holding its meetings in Greenwich, that salubrious hamlet on Mana-ha-ta, which lay at least three miles beyond the city limits, and which was always the haven of refuge when yellow fever, cholera, small-pox, and other dreaded scourges visited New York, introduced there by sailors who carried these diseases from port to port. The centre of Greenwich was about on the spot that the Indians called Sapo-Kanican, which was the site of one of their villages. Minitie-water (or little brook) joined Bestevaar's Killitje or Grandfather (Van Cortlandt's) Creek, and ran through the place, and part of it had been the farm of Mme. Oloff Van Cortlandt, that she called "Bossen Bowerie," or Bush farm. The

Matches, Batches, and Despatches

English name was given to the place out of compliment to the palace of Greenwich (which was the haven of sailors, after it was no longer used by the king), when Admiral Sir Peter Warren, who was for many years stationed in these waters, bought the adjoining property.

In 1739 Mr. Alexander received the news of the death, at his family estates in England, of the great-grandson of the first Earl of Stirling, who was Henry, the fifth earl, who had died without male issue, leaving as heirs to the unentailed property the wives of William Philips Lee and Sir William Trumbull. According to the grant of the original title, it would now pass to the eldest male heir, through John of Gogar, the great-grandfather of James Alexander of New York. Letters and advices from England now reminded Mr. Alexander that "the heirs male bearing the arms and name of Alexander" were settled in America, and urging him to take steps to claim the title and the vast estates that went with it. The claim of the Duke of York to the American property, that he bought and omitted to pay for, had never been satisfactorily settled. The duke had become a king, and then a fugitive, and as the rents of the American estates were unpaid, the tenants began to believe they owned the land they occupied, although the titles of the property were in a most unsatisfactory condition.

The bustling affairs of the colony had left Mr. Alexander little time to arrange these matters, even if it had been in his power. Lord Stirling was unwilling to embroil himself with the English court by claiming estates that he saw little prospect of enjoying, and as he had no son to inherit them, he did not care to spend time and money in asserting his rights to property that could only be enjoyed by very distant members of his family, for whom he cared but little. John of Gogar's only son was David Alexander, whose eldest son, William, was dead, and his son, William Alexander, M.D., the nephew of James Alexander, was next in succession. He was a strong, handsome young fellow, a graduate of the Edinburgh School of Medicine, who was at the time living in America, at Jamaica, Long Island, where his widowed sister lived with and kept house for him, and the young man seemed likely to marry and raise a family of his own.

Mr. Alexander, on the receipt of the intelligence from England of the death of Lord Stirling, sent for his nephew and laid before him the prospects of his succession to the title; but the young doctor cared little for it, and his uncle could not persuade him to advance his claims. Although the matter was most seriously discussed between uncle and nephew, the latter refused to assert his rights to the honors and estates of the Earl of Stirling, presumably because, having strong Jacobite tendencies, he did not care to return to England while it was under the rule of the House of Brunswick; and he thought that when the Stuarts regained the throne of England, as he was always in hopes that they would do, he would have had an opportunity of fighting under their banner, and that he could then reclaim the ancient title and have it confirmed at the hands of the old masters of his house. The matter was therefore allowed to remain in abeyance, although Mr. Alexander wrote to his relations in Scotland to trace the family descent, and make sure that the succession was in his line, as he believed that the indifference of his nephew on this subject would soon pass when he had time to reflect on the matter.

A great happiness came to Mrs. Alexander during the summer months that she was spending so quietly with her family superintending the erection of their new house. The careful mother's eye had noticed that her eldest daughter Mary was nearly a woman, and Mrs. Alexander had pointed this out to her husband, and that the young girl seemed to have many admirers; but of all the beaux who followed her there was only one that she seemed to favor above all others, and Mrs. Alexander begged her husband to watch the young fellow, to see if he would be a proper husband for their daughter. Mr. Alexander, man-like, scoffed at the notion that his wife could discover a budding romance that his keen eyes had failed to detect, and declared that his little girl was still too young to think of such a thing.

Mary Alexander was at this time just eighteen, and, in truth, it seemed to both parents that it was but yesterday that Governor Burnet had stood godfather for her. But the young people did not agree with the revered councillor in believing that the maiden was too young to think of matrimony, and when her suitor presented himself in due form and asked for the hand of Miss Alexander in the stately and formal fashion of the day, Mr. Alexander had no choice but to give his consent with the best grace that he could summon up, and permit the engagement of the young couple. Indeed, there was every reason for all parties to be delighted with the match, for the lover was the second son of Mr. Alexander's old friend and neighbor, Philip Livingston, whose town house adjoined that of the Alexanders, although Mr. Livingston passed the greater part of the year at his manorial estates, of which he was the second lord.

Peter Van Brugh Livingston had been devoted to Mary Alexander since early childhood. He was a member of the same "company," and was the comrade and intimate friend of William Alexander, his fiancée's only brother, and now that Van Brugh Livingston had begun to think of matrimony, the young men were arranging for a business partnership.

Mrs. Alexander's large house had always been the rallying-place for the Saturday meetings of the little "companies" to which her children belonged. The garden had a play-house especially arranged for their use, and on rainy days the whole house would be invaded by a swarm of young ones, who played merry games of "I spy," "Hide and go seek," and "Follow my leader," all through the big rooms, and into the musty, sloping-roofed garret, the whole happy troop racing from cellar to attic, over and under the huge four-post bedsteads, and sliding down the broad banisters of the great staircase. The two boys by the first husband, John and David Provoost, had their group of friends, among whom were Eva, Elsie, and Catharine Rutgers, the children of the Alexanders' neighbor, Harmanus Rutgers, with some of the de Peysters, children of Der Heer Abraham de Peyster, who were cousins, and many of the large family of Provoosts. In the next "company" were Mrs. Alexander's children by her second marriage, Mary (Polly), Elizabeth (Betsey), and William (Bill), and their friends and associates were the younger members of the aforementioned families and many others. The third "company" in Mrs. Alexander's household was composed of the younger children, Kitty, and the delicate little Anna, and lastly Suky, the baby, the pet and plaything of them all.

As Mrs. Grant mentions in her "Reminiscences of an American Lady," "the consequence of these exclusive and early intimacies was that when the members of the company grew up it was reckoned a sort of apostasy to marry out of 'one's company,' and, indeed, it did not often happen." Mrs. Alexander had herself selected her first husband from the ranks of her own company, and it was little surprise to her to find her own daughter following the example that had been set her; nor did the careful mother regret the choice that the girl had made, and there was a merry marriage-feast on November 3, 1739, soon after the family returned to the town house after their summer spent at Perth Amboy.

Peter Van Brugh Livingston took his bride immediately to a handsome house that he had built for her in Prince Street. The young couple also had a country house at Dobb's Ferry, a few miles up the Hudson River. Van Brugh Livingston was a stalwart patriot and followed in the footsteps of his father, and Mr. Alexander, and when called upon to defend the rights of his country and free the colony from the oppressive English yolk, he joined his brother-in-law, William Alexander, first in a partnership for providing the commissariat department, then became one of the celebrated "Committee of 100," chosen by the citizens of New York to protect their interests, was president of the first Provincial Congress, in 1775; deputy to the Second Provincial Congress, 1776; treasurer of the State of New York, etc., etc.

The happiness of Mrs. Alexander seemed complete when a little grandson was born on November 3d of the following year. The child was christened Philip, after his grandfather, Philip Livingston. This was a favorite name in the Livingston family, and in order to distinguish one boy from the other, they were given nicknames that stuck to them through life, and by which they are known even to their descendants. This eldest son of Mary Alexander and Van Brugh Livingston was dubbed "Gentleman Phil," from his charming and courteous manners.

Matches, Batches, and Despatches

Mrs. Alexander's influence had been exerted in order to get for her son, David Provoost, a commission in the English army. The young man fancied the roving and adventurous life more than that of a mercantile house. It was an unusual step for one of Dutch descent to take, as the men of that blood seldom allied themselves in any way with what they considered the hated usurpers, but David Provoost longed for the life of a soldier, and there was no other opening for him. It was with a foreboding heart that Mrs. Alexander saw him depart in the autumn of 1740, when his regiment was ordered to Jamaica. This was the first real flight of the nestlings from the paternal roof, and the fond mother saw him sail with his regiment with an intense sorrow that she tried in vain to conceal. And, indeed, her worst fears were fulfilled, as she never saw her son again.

In 1741 Mrs. Alexander's eldest son, John Provoost, married one of his "company." This was Eva Rutgers, the daughter of Harmanus, by his wife Catharine Meyers, a match that gave universal satisfaction. Five children were born of this union, the eldest son being the famous Samuel Provoost, a graduate of the first class of King's College, rector of Trinity Church, chaplain to Congress, and bishop of New York, 1786.

All these family events had happily absorbed the attention of Mrs. Alexander and her friends, who believed that they were now to be allowed to lead a quiet, contented home life, free from political discussions or public embroilments. But the upper classes were never free from the fear of a negro outbreak, for which, as it proved, there was little reason, as the negro race were incapable of organization, or of making a concentrated plan of action. That fact was not grasped by the colonists at the time; so that it was with a terror that now seems almost incomprehensible that the denizens of New York learned on February 28, 1741, that a robbery had been committed at Mr. Robert Hogg's, a worthy middle-class tradesman, who lived in a small house near Mrs. Alexander's, on Broad Street, with a side-door opening on Jew's Alley. Mr. Hogg missed pieces of silverware, coins, linen, and other articles, and his neighbors were alarmed beyond measure when suspicion fell on some negroes, one of whom had been in Mr. Hogg's employ, and who was proved to have been in the habit of meeting a number of others of the same color at a tavern on the North River. This fact was in itself suspicious, as there were stringent laws against negroes meeting, or being seen on the streets after specified hours, when it was supposed that all those in the town were shut up in their quarters; and that they were thus able to elude their masters and the city watch, was in itself deemed an alarming state of affairs. Some of the stolen goods were found in the pig-pen behind the tavern, which led to a close watch being set on the premises.

The keeper of the tavern was a man by the name of Hughson. His wife had a white servant, Mary Burton, a girl of only sixteen years of age, who had been transported from England for some infraction of the laws, as, according to the custom of England, all the most worthless of her population, her criminals, and outlaws were sent to America as the simplest and easiest plan of getting rid of them. Mary Burton had come to the colony with such a bad record that no respectable family would admit her, and the tavern-keeper, therefore, had her bound, or in fact sold to him, for a number of years, and while in his service the career of vice, on which she had entered in her native land, was licensed and carried on to the advantage of her master.

Mary Burton was at once suspected of being an accomplice of the negroes, and was, therefore, arrested. In order to screen herself, she made statements implicating her master, his wife, his daughter Mary, some of the negroes who had been seen in the tavern, and several other persons. The girl was mischievous, and endowed with a sort of low cunning, and when she discovered the notoriety that she had gained by her treachery, she proceeded to invent a tissue of lies that threatened to inculpate all the citizens of the town, although at first her victims were only of the lowest class. Seeing that she had terrified the inhabitants by the idea that a negro uprising was contemplated, she encouraged this notion to the best of her ability until the whole country took alarm.

One of the first negroes to be pointed out and identified as a thief was a slave who belonged to John Varick, a baker, in whose bake-house some of the stolen goods were found. It was the custom then for the negroes to assume the surnames of their masters, and this fellow was known by the name of Cæsar Varick, and it was proved by witnesses who had watched his movements that he had concealed the property that was found on the premises, and he was immediately thrown into prison. Mary Burton continued to make disclosures, and next implicated a woman of bad character called Peggy Carey, who lived next to Varick's bakery.

Rumors were now spread that the negroes intended to make an organized attack on their masters and fire the town, hoping by so doing to rid themselves of their bondage, and when in the following month, on March 18th, a fire broke out in the "King's House," inside of the fort, in which Governor Clarke was at the time residing, the terror of the inhabitants was excited to the highest pitch. No one felt safe, and bands of citizens were secretly formed to patrol the city and protect the citizens. The fire in the fort was a most unfortunate affair, as the old chapel, the barracks, and the stables, together with the great gate, over which was the room that was used by the secretary as an office, were all burned to the ground. The amateur firemen were afraid to approach too near the fort, where a quantity of gunpowder was stored, and its explosion added greatly to the injury of the buildings that were spared by the flames. Among the young men who had been most active in organizing for the protection of the town was one of the Van Hornes, and, unfortunately for himself, he had been loud in his assertions of what he would do to rout the secret foe when the time for action came. He was in a constant state of fright, and furnished himself with a large drum, on which he sounded an alarm whenever he fancied that there was any reason for it. These signals became so frequent, and always proved so unnecessary, that the neighbors nicknamed him "Major Drum." It was the "Major" who beat his big drum when the fort-house caught fire. The citizens did not turn out as quickly as they might have done, thinking it one of his false alarms; and his fright at this fire and terror at the dread of the explosion of the magazine, which fortunately did not create any havoc outside of the fort, only furnished the "tea-table" of the ladies with funny stories for many a day.

In "Family Records and Events" we find the following letter from James Alexander and his wife to her son, David Provoost, describing these fires and the terror of the citizens:

"NEW YORK, Apl. 22, 1741.

"DEAR DAVID,

"We have had sundry letters from you which gave us great satisfaction to hear of your Health when many have been cut off by sickness. Your brother John has been in Georgia since you left where he has had pretty good success. Within these few weeks we have had above a dozen alarming fires in this City. By the first of them the Post, I mean the Governor's House, Barracks, and Secretary's Office in the Fort were almost in an hour reduced to ashes during the time of a high wind which much indangered the City. The other fires have some of them been during high winds and very threatening to the city, but thank GOD, there has not been any great damage by them. Five of these fires happening in one day, with many other strange cases of suspicion, render it likely that all or most of them have been on purpose. Diligent inquiry has been made, but no discovery is yet got, tho' a proclamation of pardon and reward is published for any of the accomplices who will disclose. Half of the company of Militia is in arms every night to patrol and watch the city. The Assembly sits and it is hoped that they will make sufficient provision for what may be wanting to put the City and Province in a sufficient posture of defence, it being highly recommended by the Governor.

"Your most Affectionate Father and Mother,
"JAMES and MARY ALEXANDER."

Mrs. Alexander had had cause for alarm, as her house was so close to the fort, and all her windows had been broken by the force of the explosion of the magazine. Her friends had gathered around her, prepared to carry off her furniture and pictures in case the fire spread in the direction of her home, which, owing to the wind, seemed to be likely. Fortunately the wind changed at a most critical moment, and the flames were driven toward the Hudson River instead of over the houses of the little town, and the firemen were able to subdue and confine them inside of the walls surrounding the fort. But of course there were many outlaws who were ready to take advantage of these scenes of confusion, and plunder any unprotected dwellings that they could find. The vigilance of old Peter and some of the other house-

Matches, Batches, and Despatches

servants prevented a robbery at Mrs. Alexander's during the height of the confusion; but Mrs. Alexander was greatly annoyed, as suspicion fell at the time on one of her own slaves as a ringleader among the thieves. As she lost nothing, she refused to prosecute the men who were arrested, but it made her suspicious and cautious, and a watch was set on the culprit.

There were at the time over two thousand slaves in the city, which only numbered some ten thousand inhabitants. A large cargo of negroes had lately arrived from one of the Spanish colonies, and they were called "the Spanish negroes," and were believed to be particularly desperate characters. The poor creatures were, indeed, desperate. They had been free negroes, and had been captured and were sold into slavery. They complained of the outrageous treatment they had received, and were turbulent and fractious under their new masters. A hint that they intended to rebel was quite sufficient to rouse the whites and add to their alarm.

The town was rife with rumors, which the governor tried in vain to disperse, and to allay the fears of the public, he sent a communication to the legislature, in which he stated that the fire in the fort had been of a purely accidental origin, and had been started by a plumber who was repairing the roof of one of the buildings, and had left his stove on it between the house and the chapel. The governor's statement would have had a calming effect on the minds of the public had not other fires followed in quick succession. One was caused by a smoker's pipe, another by a foul chimney; but the citizens were thoroughly demoralized, and traced everything to the unfortunate negroes.

The winter of 1741 was intensely cold, and was called "the hard winter." It began in November and lasted until the end of March. Snow fell constantly, and lay six feet on the ground, except where the drifts raised it to nearly fifteen. It was necessary to keep up enormous fires in the houses day and night, which made the soot accumulate in the chimneys, with no possibility of their being cleaned, as the sweeps could not reach the roofs. This, of course, added to the danger of fire, as much pine wood was used, the smoke of which forms stalagmites of tar, that break and drop on the hot coals, causing them to flare dangerously; or else they catch fire inside of the chimneys and set the interior in a blaze.

To add to the terror of the thoroughly demoralized citizens, a rumor was circulated that the Jesuit priests in Canada were inciting the Indians on the northern borders of the province to revolt, and that in this they were to be aided and abetted by a negro revolt in all the towns, the ulterior object being the subjection of the colony and its capitulation to the French. An unfortunate Frenchman was in New York at the time, who was supposed to be a Roman Catholic priest, and accused of meeting the negroes and inciting them to rebellion.

Matches, Batches, and Despatches

Those that were discovered at secret meetings at this time were, says Mr. Dunlop, in his history of New York, the slaves of well-known townspeople. One of them was owned by Mr. Phillipse, and was called "Cuff Phillipse;" another belonged to a painter in the "Fly" named Cornelius Roosevelt; another to a tallow chandler named Slidell, and these men, with many others, were thrown into prison.

The common council met in April, with John Cruger, mayor, in the chair. The aldermen were Gerardus Stuyvesant, William Romaine, Simon Jonson, John Moore, Christopher Bancker, John Pintard, John Marshall; assistants, Henry Bogart, Isaac Stoutenburgh, Philip Minthorne, George Brinckerhoff, Robert Benson, and Samuel Lawrence. These names are well worth recording, as they or their children were foremost in the subsequent fight for American liberty, and the names of their descendants are prominent in the annals of the city of New York to-day.

One of the most badly frightened men was the recorder, Daniel Horsmanden, and it is to his pen that the chief incidents of the reign of terror are due; and contemporary authorities point out that he painted all the details of the affairs of the day in the blackest light, in order to shield himself from the charges of cruelty that were heaped on the officials of the city after the alleged culprits had been hanged, and the fright of the citizens had had time to subside, and they began to think and talk over matters reasonably. But the fright, while it lasted, was real, and contagious, and many people left town, carrying with them all their furniture and valuables. As a consequence the abandoned houses were entered and robbed by the thieves who abounded, while gangs of roughs insulted quiet citizens or fought with each other.

The "Fly-boys," who lived near the old "Vlye Market," and the "Longbridge gang" had frequent battles on the neutral grounds of the "Common," now City Hall Park, and on April 13th each alderman and constable was ordered to search his ward for strangers and suspicious characters, and the militia were turned out to assist them. No one was detected in wrong-doing, but some negroes were arrested on suspicion, and at the meeting of the Supreme Court, on April 21, 1741, a most notable group of the merchants of New York were called to compose the grand jury. Frederick Phillipse was chief-justice, Daniel Horsmanden, second judge. The names of the grand jury are worth recording, as they and their descendants formed the woof of the web that made the banner of the "Stars and Stripes."

They were seventeen in number, with Robert Watts, foreman. He was the husband of Mary Nicoll, daughter of William Nicoll and Miss Van Rensselaer. Next came Jeremie La Touche, who lived in King Street, "next to Mr. Bourdet." Both of these were prominent members of the Huguenot Church in New York. Mr. La Touche was the son of Isaac, the emigrant, and had married Jeanne Soumain, daughter of Simon Soumain and Jeanne Piau. These were no unimportant people in the town, as they were identified with the best interests of the Church in which they were so prominent, and also highly esteemed citizens. Mr. La Touche was the ancestor of some of the Cruger, Bunner, and Duer families.

Another member of the jury was Joseph Reade, for whom the street of that name was called. (His daughter had married James Abraham de Peyster.)

Anthony Rutger is next in order. He had a large piece of property near the Collect, and is the ancestor of the Lispenards, Barclays, and Gouverneurs. It was his niece who had then lately married Mrs. Alexander's son, John Provoost.

John McEver's name follows, from whom Livingstons, Saunders, and Cunards claim descent.

John Cruger, Jr., nicknamed the "Old Speaker," a bachelor, comes next on the list, and then Adoniah Schuyler, the husband of Gertrude Van Rensselaer, who afterward married one of the numerous Robert Livingstons. It is related of Mr. Schuyler that his own slaves were so fond of him that they refused their freedom when he offered to present them with it. From this kind-hearted man is descended one of our most distinguished naval officers, Captain Arent Schuyler Crowninshield.

Another member of this notable group was "old Isaac de Peyster," the uncle of Mrs. Alexander, and also Abraham Kettletas, the ancestor of the well-known family whose sons were noted for their bravery during the war, and the female members of which family are to this day distinguished for their remarkable beauty.

David Provoost, dock-ward chamberlain and city treasurer, and a very aged man, was another juryman, as was René Hett, one of the French colony, and a prominent member of the Huguenot Church. From this gentleman is descended many of the Jauncey, Bancker, and Clarkson families.

Henry Beekman comes next on the list. His second wife was Miss Gertrude Van Cortlandt, the young lady who had been inveigled to Lady Cornbury's court to play at being maid of honor, and who left such a vivacious account of the ceremonies of the mock court.

A prominent juror was David Van Horne. He was the husband of Anna French, from whom are descended Clarksons, Livingstons, Ludlows, Trumbulls, Edgars, and the Reeds of South Carolina. His sister, Anna Maria Van Horne, had (as has been mentioned) married Governor Burnet, and he was step-cousin to Mrs. Alexander.

George Spenser, Thomas Duncan, and Winant Van Zandt, all of them worthy merchants, who have descendants living in this city to-day, completed the list. No more patriotic citizens could be found. They were men of probity and worth, of mixed nationality, but bound together by a common cause, and not likely to be led astray by the tumult of popular opinion; but even they were hurried, by popular opinion and their own alarms, into condemning to death the unfortunates that were brought before them.

Mr. Phillipse charged the jury, and told them "that the people had been put to many frights and terrors respecting the repeated fires, burglaries, and conspiracies," and charged the grand jury to summon before them the arch-disturber of the peace, Mary Burton, who was frightened, cajoled, and bribed into making a deposition against three of the negroes, her former master, the innkeeper Hughson, and the unfortunate outcast (who was implicated as much by her bad character as anything that was proved against her), Peggy Carey.

All these persons were, therefore, summoned to appear before the grand jury, and Messrs. Murray, Alexander, Smith, Chambers, and others, were called on to act as counsel. The testimony against the negroes proved their dishonesty, but no conspiracy against the lives and property of the public. It was merely petty larceny, done individually, and without collusion with each other, and therefore not menacing to the public at large, and well within the province of the city watch. The charge of conspiracy to fire the island was accepted by the court on what was afterward acknowledged to be very insufficient evidence, but on it two negroes were condemned to be hanged on Monday, May 11, 1741. These were Prince, who had, as it was proved, led such a disorderly life that the community were well rid of him, and Cæsar. The latter was hanged on the gibbet, "on the Island near the Powder house," in the "Collect pond," which is now covered by the pretty little park called "Paradise," at the junction of Centre, Chatham, and Pearl Streets. The body hung in chains, swinging and creaking dismally, over the lovely little sheet of water, to the terror of all the urchins of the town for many a long year.

The whole summer of 1741 was spent in trials and prosecutions, and thirteen blacks were burnt at the stake, eighteen hanged, and seventy transported. The tavern-keeper Hughson, his wife and maid were proved to have received stolen goods, and to have kept a thieves' meeting-place, and they, as well as the Frenchman Ury, whose chief sin seems to have been his inability to speak English, were hanged. The latter was, indeed, accused of conspiracy, and of officiating as a priest, and was sentenced under an old law, that had been passed under Lord Bellomont's rule, about 1700, at a time when prejudices against the Roman Catholics were very strong. The more sober-minded of the citizens regretted the execution of the priest, but the mass of the inhabitants were mad with terror. Every man suspected a foe in his own household, and fancied that his negro servants were being suborned and bribed by this priest to enter into a plot for a general uprising against the whites.

The excitement was only allayed by passing severe laws against negro meetings, etc., which were recommended to the assembly by the grand jury, for which they received the thanks of the "House" for their zeal and courage and vigor in the detection of a conspiracy to burn the town and murder the inhabitants. It has been the custom in latter days to condemn the action of the government, and to declare that the soberminded citizens of New York allowed their fears to run away with them, and that no alarm need have been felt, either of an uprising of the blacks or an invasion of the Indians on the borders, incited to war by the priests of Canada. Safe in the protection of our civilization, we are in no position to judge of the state of alarm that the citizens of the day were constantly in from both these sources of danger, undoubtedly great at the time.

It is certain that the inhabitants of New York had for years dreaded outbreaks from both quarters, and had taken steps to protect themselves, and that many alarming incidents occurred at one and the same time, any one of which was grave enough to call for prompt action on the part of the authorities. That the citizens were unduly influenced by the mock confessions of a worthless girl, has been proved by the search-light of modern research, but at that time the stories of the miserable creature received full credence, and seem to have been supported by a certain amount of truth, and much sympathy should be felt for the citizens, who were being robbed daily and in broad daylight, by burly negroes, who, whether they belonged to an organized band or not, were certainly in the habit of meeting frequently and at unlawful hours at the house of Hughson, in whose pos session the stolen goods were found; and if there was no organized conspiracy to burn the town, that matters certainly pointed that way and looked very suspicious; so the good citizens had plenty of cause for alarm, even if it was not quite as bad as it was represented to be at the time.

The rigorous laws passed under these exciting circumstances soon fell into abeyance; and within ten years the negroes were admitted to the rights and privileges of free subjects. The citizens were more cautious about the class of negroes that were imported to the city, and those who had used their slaves with harshness, had had a fright that they did not soon forget, as they saw that the respectable citizens, who had been kind to their slaves, had been well protected by them during all the terrible time, while those who had been cruel were constantly being threatened with fire, robbery, and other alarms.

Public opinion was aroused on the side of the slave, and any ill-treatment of one that might, in the opinion of the citizens, arouse the hatred of the blacks against the whites, and so cause a general uprising, met with stern disapproval, both from individuals and also from the courts, who were no longer entirely on the side of the masters. Indeed, the kind-hearted Dutch now came to the front and insisted that the negroes should be treated uniformly, as they had always been by those of their own descent, and the result was a happy one. The status of the negro remained that of a trusted and happy menial, until he was finally freed by the freemen who had thrown off their own yoke, and who had no desire to see anyone a slave in this free and independent country.

The excitements and trials of the past months had come home to Mrs. Alexander more than once, and it had taken all her common-sense and courage to face the situation calmly. The first culprit had been owned by her neighbor, Mr. Hogg, and he had proved to be one of the worst of the offenders, and when Cæsar was hanged in chains on "the island" that had always been associated with the happy hours of Mrs. Alexander's childhood, and the creature was proved to be deeply dyed in guilt, the good dame felt as badly about the whole occurrence as if it had happened to one of her own household, and could hardly be convinced that the fellow that was accustomed to salute her pleasantly day after day, could have been employed over night in plotting against the lives of all who had been so kind to him, and she exerted all her influence, although in vain, to prevent the sentence of death being carried out.

The old house in Broad Street had also been in great danger of being burnt when the buildings in the fort were demolished. One of the worst fires in the city was directly behind Mrs. Alexander's home. This was in the storehouse of Mr. Phillipse, and one of his negroes was detected in having set fire to it. What was worse, one of Mrs. Alexander's own slaves was accused of assisting him, and finally was detected breaking into and stealing from her own storehouse, which it was supposed he intended to set on fire after he had plundered it, as had been done in so many instances.

When this last calamity happened, Mrs. Alexander felt as if, indeed, there must be some truth in all the rumors of an organized negro plot, as these repeated robberies and fires, coming so near her own home, had completely demoralized her. "Cuffie Alexander," as he was called, was sentenced to death for his crimes, and his unhappy mistress in vain tried to save him from his horrible fate, but the day was set for the execution and all her efforts were unavailing, when, to her amazement and pleasure, the life of the worthless slave was saved in a most unforeseen way. According to the New York "Post-Boy," of January 28, 1744, "the executor died suddenly the night before the sentence was to be carried into effect," and then Mrs. Alexander was rewarded for her exertions, and by her influence she had his sentence changed to transportation to one of the West India Islands, where she had the satisfaction of believing that the friends to whose care she sent the poor creature would be able to get him to lead a better life. This was the only one of all the negroes who were accused at this time who escaped punishment, and it was owing entirely to the humanity and moderation of Mrs. Alexander, who, unlike others, did not allow herself to be entirely carried away by her terror.

XXI

New York "in the Forties"

The Gout and its Remedies—Bishop Berkeley—The Wilden Visit the Town—Their Wares, their Manners, and Pursuits—The Kindness of Mrs. Alexander—Different Methods of Spinning—Evening Amusements—Newspaper Advertisements—The Jersey Boundaries—Iron Furnaces—Earthquakes—Death of Dr. William Alexander—Marriages of William, Betsey, and Kitty Alexander—Troubles with Army and Navy—Lady Carteret—Her Granddaughter—Captain Digby Fires on Colonel Ricketts's Yacht—Marriage of "the Widow Parker"—Sir Danvers Osborne—His Reception and Suicide.

COUNCILLOR ALEXANDER had suffered for many years with what his wife (who spoke Dutch as often as she did English) called "de pynen van de jicht," and the accumulated anxieties and excitements of the past sessions of council and legislature culminated in a very serious attack of gout, which all the old remedies failed to relieve him of. It was the fashion then to tie what were called "bootikins" on the hands and feet every night, the strings of which were drawn so tightly as to impede the circulation, and when this remedy did not avail in stopping the pain, the patient was forced to swallow before every meal large doses of "snail water." But this medicine had lately fallen into disrepute, as it had failed to save the life of the dramatist William Congreve, who had extolled its virtues; and doctors and patients had lately hailed with pleasure a new remedy that was now being tried by all gouty patients both in England and her colonies. Its herald was the famous Bishop Berkeley, who wrote what Horace Walpole calls "his mad book on tar water, which has made everybody as mad as himself." The medicine was, however, believed to be a sure cure, and was widely recommended. In a letter dated April 27, 1749, Mr. John Swift, of Philadelphia, wrote to "Governor Bedford, Esq., General Excise Office, London:"

"DEAR SIR,

"Your writing to me when in so painful a condition, is an unquestionable proof of your good nature. I am very sorry to hear of your being so often visited by that vile, troublesome gout. Drinking 'Tar Water' is found in this part of the world to be a remedy against it. I have heard of several that have kept it off by that means, particularly Mr. Alexander, of New York, who used to have it every year violently, and since he has used tar water has had but very slight fits and not so often as before."

There was a very good epigram written about this time on Bishop Berkeley and his remedy, which was sent by Mr. Walpole to his friend Sir Horace Mann. It was:

> "Who dare deride what pious Cloyne has done?
> The Church shall rise and venerate her son;
> She tells us all her Bishops shepherds are—
> And shepherds heal their rotten sheep with tar."

New York "in the Forties"

Bishop Berkeley's visit to this country is still commemorated in Rhode Island by various localities that have been named after him, particularly at Newport, where a huge rock, on which he was accustomed to sit and gaze at the ocean, is still called "Bishop Berkeley's Chair." He was a powerful talker, and on one occasion, it is related in his biography, he visited Paris and called on an eminent savant, whom he engaged in a spirited discussion. A few moments after he had taken his departure the savant fell from his chair, dead, completely exhausted by the controversy. Dr. Berkeley was a friend of Dean Swift, who introduced him to "the celebrated Vanessa," but the lady received Dr. Berkeley coldly, and after a few visits he moved to another part of the country, and never saw her again. Great was his surprise when, on her death, several years afterward, it was discovered that all her money and letters were bequeathed to him.

Dr. Berkeley and his newly wedded wife arrived in Newport during the summer of 1724, and he wrote to his friends at home a graphic description of the place, which he says is "the largest and most important town in America." During this visit the philosopher became acquainted with the virtues of "tar water," and after returning to England and being presented with the bishopric of Cloyne, he printed many sermons, essays, and treatises on different subjects—among others one called "Siris," published in 1744, containing strenuous advocacy of the virtues of tar water, which he recommended as a sure cure for consumption, small-pox, gout, ulcers, dysentery, and many other diseases.

The receipt for concocting this remedy was "one gallon of water to one quart of tar, stirred with a flat stick six minutes, and then covered closely and allowed to remain unmoved three days and nights, then skimmed and the water poured off and put in a tightly stoppered bottle." Half a pint of this decoction was to be drunk morning and evening, on an empty stomach, and the bishop declared that in 1741 he had cured twenty fevers with tar water, which he considered infinitely "superior to the *soapy* medicines then in use." He mentions in his book "that tar water moderately inspissates with its balsamic virtue, and renders mild the thin and sharp part of the blood, and that the virtue flowed, like the Nile, from a secret and occult cause into innumerable channels, conveying health and relief wherever applied," and therefore he calls his treatise "Siris, an ancient name for the Nile, which signifies 'chain.'"

Those were the days when great experiments were being bravely made by the English people, who were willing to try new and strange remedies, and kindly adopted inoculation when introduced by a woman to her fellow-countrymen, and the remedy of Bishop Berkeley, which he likens to a "chain" that winds through the system, cleansing every part of it, was as heartily adopted as was inoculation.

At any rate, the American cure, which was originally an Indian remedy, proved efficacious in the case of Mr.

New York "in the Forties"

Alexander, and his wife had the satisfaction of seeing him once more actively busied about his numerous avocations. About this time Mrs. Alexander had another grandchild added to her flock. This was Catharine Livingston, or Kitty, as she was called. The child was named after the mother of Van Brugh Livingston.

New York "in the forties" was little more than a village in size. Its houses were all clustered together below Wall Street, and the most fashionable quarter was close to the fort, or overlooking the Bowling Green. The Broadway struggled up the hill to pass in front of Trinity Church, and a few of the new houses were being built on either side of the street. Beyond the church, "in the fields," where St. Paul's Chapel now stands, there was a large wheat-field, and this was considered the outskirts of the town. On the east side of Broadway there was a thick wood, in which the boys went nutting, and in it the "Bob Whites" whistled to their mates. Pretty country houses were dotted over the rest of the island, and the villages of Greenwich, Chelsea, and Haarlem were in the outlying districts. The ancient Dutch windmill still waved its old sail-arms and ground the grist for its miller on the high hill that still retains the Indian name of "Catiemuts."

The tribes of the Rockaways from Sewan-ha-ka, and the Hoboken-Hackinagh from Wiehawken, were permitted to visit Mana-ha-ta once a year, and were allowed to land in their canoes in the great basin near Long Bridge, at the foot of Broad Street. The Wilden from the sea-side brought for sale dried clams strung on sea-grass, salt, dried fish, shells, and sand. The latter was always in demand, as housekeepers used it to strew their floors with every morning, and prided themselves on the patterns that they would sweep over their rooms by the dexterous turns of their brooms. The wild men also brought wax, that they had boiled down from the bay-berries that grew so plentifully on the Long Island coast, and this was prized by the "buis-vrouw," as from it they made their very best wax candles. The Wilden from "the Jarsies" brought cat-tails from the mosquito-infested salt marshes, and also willow withes, and oak knots, and from these the squaws would make baskets, brooms, chair-seats, mats, etc. The tobacco and the clay or copper pipes, made by the Wilden, were particularly esteemed. The former was prepared by being rubbed through the hands, and as the savages never washed even that part of themselves, the tobacco cured by them had, no doubt, as high a flavor as that which is now prepared by Spaniards, Italians, and Hebrews for the consumption of the present generation.

The advent of the Wilden was always eagerly hailed by all the children of the place. They came together in their large canoes, and proceeded in procession to the open space provided for them behind Mr. Phillipse's house, which had been kindly set apart for their use by that gentleman, when the ancient camping-ground on the Strand, by Dr. Kierstede's house, had been required by the builder. The march of the Wilden through the town was always preceded by the stately "Boo," or constable, and they were followed by crowds of eager children, who were particularly anxious for their arrival, as it was by the squaws that the baskets were made which served as badges for the different "companies." Each set selected a shape, size, and distinctive color, and these important points were always matters of long and serious debates, and when the matter was once settled and the choice made, each "company" made it a point of honor to consider their own selection as the handsomest, and were wont to deride and decry those of their rivals.

The rear of Mrs. Alexander's house overlooked the Wilden's encampment, and her garden opened on it. She was accustomed to visit her neighbors daily and exerted herself to civilize them, and as she could talk easily to them in their own language, which she had learned from them when playing with them in childhood, she was in consequence held in high esteem by the Wilden, who, as an especial mark of their favor, offered to adopt her into their tribe, and they gave her an Indian name by which she was always known among them.

As a leader of a "company" in girlhood, Mrs. Alexander had been one of the originators of the "Basket Badge," and she had hereditary rights as to selection. The peculiarly shaped basket that had been hers was now adopted by her eldest children as their uniform,

and the squaws were very proud of being allowed to work for her. As a child, Polly Spratt had been encouraged by her grandmother to make clothes for the poor savages, and to spend her pocket money in buying for them small articles of luxury, such as scissors, thimbles, needles, etc., which the squaws would not have been permitted by their men to purchase for themselves, as they preferred to spend all the cash that their wives brought in by their industry, in rum and tobacco. Mrs. Alexander was always ready to instruct and employ the young girls, and had them taught by her own maids to spin in the German fashion on a wheel, instead of rolling the flax up and down on the bare thigh, as was the custom among the aborigines of the Northern tribes. It is noteworthy that this method of spinning was peculiar to the Iroquois; those to the South, and more particularly in Mexico and Central America, use an upright distaff when spinning, which they stand before them balanced on a saucer, and steady it with a whorl of obsidian, precisely like the whorls of the same stone that were found by Dr. Schliemann among the remains at Mycenæ.

Mrs. Alexander's various deeds of kindness to the poor Indians, who were being rapidly driven away from the towns and exiled from their native homes, were often gratefully remembered, and she was called upon to take part in one of their numerous ceremonies and receive from them gifts of pottery, embroidered moccasins, wampum belts, and dried fruits. Each gift was handed to her with a sort of rustic bow, and the words "Yo-Hay" (Do you hear?), upon which all the members of the tribe would grunt in chorus, "Ugh!" This ceremony was similar to that performed at the large government councils, and the Indians would have considered that their gifts were not received in the proper spirit if the ceremony had been neglected or omitted, even when giving a simple present to an individual.

Among other wares for which the Indians were noted, were the crates, or baskets, that were indispensable for carrying potatoes, oysters, fish, etc., and also certain bags or nets, that the Wilden called "Notas," a word that in their language signified *belly*, and they gave this name to anything that was hollow, and that could be carried about and used as a receptacle. Mrs. Alexander was also highly esteemed by her wild friends as a great "medicine woman," and her salve for burns, which her grandmother had been taught to prepare by the great Dr. Kierstede, and which is to-day sold under his name, was much sought after, as was also her herb tea and other simple remedies. Many a sick person was brought to her door who never left it empty-handed, and her quiet sympathy and generosity probably did as much to effect a cure among the simple folks as did the contents of her herb-closet.

The "Wilde Manchen" were not all as peaceably inclined and devoted to industrial avocations as were those of the tribes that lived near Mana-ha-ta. Some of those who lived on the northern frontier, went on the war-path, and they now came down the Hudson River, to display the results of their battles to the governor and hold a conference with him. This was an unusual spectacle for the townfolk, as the Indian councils were usually held at Beverswyck, or some of the interior towns. It was, however, deemed important to show the savages the power and wealth of New York, and its reserved strength; therefore a large number of braves arrived in the town and landed at the old "Canoe place," now Canal Street, encamping on the beach at Hudson Street. They then marched in single file down the road to the Broadway, and through it to Fort George, each one hideously painted red, in stripes, with the juice of the blood-root, and with all their trophies displayed on long poles, that they carried over their shoulders, almost every one of them carrying the scalps of the unfortunate Frenchmen that they had lately murdered.

In September, 1746, Mrs. Alexander lost her little daughter Anne, a girl of fourteen. This child had been a delicate one from birth, and required constant attention and loving care. It was she who was always nestling to her mother's side, and when tempted to play with the other children, she would soon come running to the open arms of her mother, to be welcomed with a caress and the old Dutch greeting, "Bock agen?" The loss of this dear child was a bitter sorrow to both parents, and one from which they were long in recovering, but a great effort had to be made for the sake of the other daughters, who were then charming young women, surrounded by all the beaux of the town.

The tea-table of the councillor and his wife was now filled with the gay young people of the place, instead of the wise and troubled politicians who had so often congregated about Mrs. Alexander and her husband. The young ones would gather in the evenings in the large parlor, where they would sing and dance, or play at Basset, Pope Joan, or Brag, while their parents would sit in Mrs. Alexander's own room, and enjoy a quiet game of whist. A rubber was made up every evening for the grave councillor, and he and his wife loved nothing so well as their game, at which Judge Smith, Philip Livingston, and perhaps the governor himself, would take a hand. The tables were set with four great silver candlesticks, under which the servants had placed the counters. These were coins from various nations, Carolus, Louis d'Or, Doubloons, etc. "The children" used for their games ivory "fish," which in those days each family prided themselves upon having manufactured for them in China. They were always carved and engraved with the initials of the owner, and were kept in gold-lacquered boxes of quaint design and shape. At the elbow of each whist-player was placed a large gold snuff-box, which contained a mixture of green tea and tobacco, for which Mrs. Alexander was famous, her receipt being known to no one but herself, and always compounded under her own eye.

The advertisements in the papers of the day were

quaint and peculiar; one tradesman states that he has for sale "Orange butter good for slicking gentlemens hair and combing it up." All sorts of window-glass is to be sold "By Daniel Ebberts living in Marketfield Street, alias Petticoat Lane, opposite Mr. Alexander's." And again, "Just imported in ship Anne and Elizabeth Captain Peter Crawford a considerable number of *German passengers* chiefly young People unmarry'd. Their Times to be disposed of by *Philip Livingston* or said Master. The said ship will sail for Amsterdam in three weeks and will take freight and passengers." And a few years later, "James Murray apothecary has received orders to send fifty pounds weight of old linnen for the use of the wounded men. He hopes those who have any old linnen to dispose of will bring it to his shop opposite the Veal Market where they shall receive the full value for the same."

In the "New York Gazette," revived in the "Weekly Post Boy," July 11, 1748, is this odd effusion: "Nothing but a gilded introduction could atone for printing the following lines:

'Mr. Parker,
    'Please insert the following genuine Copy of Verses sent to a young lady by her ingenious Lover: I don't doubt that it will be very acceptable and diverting to some of your Readers; and you will very much oblige,
            'Your constant Reader And humble Servant, &c.

'To Miss ——,
        'Of all the Bauthy that e'er craud the land,
        Or ever was in Long Island;

New York "in the Forties"

Whar to begin, or what part first to prase
Is as impossible as the Dedd to rase
Without Enjustise don to the Rest, in a loer Frase.
But as the Hedd is the Nobler Part,
Thare I must begin, and at her Foots depart,
Such lovely Hare, in Lox hangs in her Neck,
As does my verry Hart to ayck.
Neglekted hangs the Lox from each oder part
More bauthyful styll, then if compel'd by Art;
And Hydes a Neck farr whiter than the Snow,
Such Fetres added appropo.
A noble Forred, with a pare of Eys
So black : with any Jett tha vys.
A grateful Look and not too bold,
As woomen used to practice of old.
Her lofely Cheecks, mixed with a lifely redd,
Adds a new Grace to the nobler Part.
Her Skin so white, so bauthful and fare,
With any anabaster may compare ;
Dimple rising in her Cheeks so sweate,
That when I'm in her Presence I sitt mute.
Hur mout so bauthyfuly, not large nor yet too small ;
Hur Chyn proporshoned, compleats it all.
A charming Waste, anoff alone to move
A Hart of Adamant, to what he call Lofe :
Her lovely Carriage, and so genteel an Are,
Getts me a Rivles anoff I fear :
One alreddy I am assured off ;
But him I'll turn away with Scorn and Scoff.' "

This is supposed to have been addressed to Miss Alexander, who was accused by many people of being a haughty damsel, and the peculiar spelling was indicative of the low origin of one of her admirers, whose attentions she had refused to receive. Some persons have attributed the verses to the pen of William Livingston, brother of Van Brugh Livingston, and afterward governor of New Jersey, who was said to have been refused by Miss Alexander.

Mr. Alexander had not been a member of the governor's council of New York for two or three years, although he had continued to serve in New Jersey. Lieutenant-Governor Clarke's reign came to an end when, on September 22, 1743, a new English governor arrived in the colony. This was Admiral George Clinton, a well-meaning, bluff sailor, who had nothing of the pirate in his composition, as so many of his predecessors had. Admiral Clinton was the son of the last Earl of Lincoln, and uncle to the one then living, and he proved to be a gentleman of charming manners, somewhat convivial in his habits, and well-disposed toward his subjects. But the colonists dreaded their foreign rulers, and had learned to evade their decrees, and as the local assemblies had discovered their prerogatives by experience, the wisest measures of the good-intentioned governor met with the most exasperating opposition. Governor Clinton soon selected friends from the gentlemen who received him on his arrival, and one of his first letters to the Lords of Trade was dated December 9, 1746, in which he prays that James Alexander may be restored to his place in his majesty's council, and further states, "I know of no man in this Province of greater abilities or longer experience in public affairs," and goes on to write, " It will contribute to His Majesty's service if he shall be pleased to appoint Cadwalader Colden Lieutenant-Governor of this Province."

Mr. Alexander was suffering from repeated attacks of gout, that not even the highly vaunted tar water could check or alleviate. But, notwithstanding, he continued to attend court and council-chamber with the regularity and attention to business for which he was noted. Governor Clinton favored him with many confidences, and insisted on being allowed to make one of the regular evening visitors at Mrs. Alexander's whist-table. This was an innovation that the dame hardly liked, as she had considered her evenings were always to be devoted to the politics of the province, when not fully occupied with cards. She did not care for the presence of the chief official, with whom she fancied that all her friends would soon quarrel, and she feared that they would then find some other rallying-place, and that, in the words of her intimates, "Petticoat Lane would no longer lead to the Fort." But Governor Clinton was not to be withstood, as he had quarrelled, "in his cups," with Chief-Justice de Lancey, and had dismissed his first friend, Dr. Colden, who, aiming at being president of the council, as its eldest member, would not advocate some of Governor Clinton's schemes, fearing they would endanger his promotion and the good feeling of his fellow-councillors. But Mr. Alexander was willing to be on good terms with the governor, as both of them were interested in the settlement of the New Jersey boundary lines. This had been a matter of dispute between New York and the New Jersey colonies for a number of years. Mr. Alexander had been one of a commission to determine the proper line by survey, and now Colonel Morris, Governor Clinton, and Mr. Alexander resolved to bring the question to a speedy determination. To do this, they held many secret and anxious consultations, and finally, at the particular request of Governor Clinton, Colonel Morris, who was a large land-owner in New Jersey, and had much at stake, sailed once more for England, in hopes that he would be able to lay the state of affairs in such a way before the Lords of Trade as to bring it to a conclusion.

At this time there were only two iron furnaces in this part of America. One of them was at Stirling, New Jersey, about twelve miles from Morristown. It was owned by Messrs. Alexander and Smith, and had been named by them after the House of Stirling, to which Mr. Alexander belonged, while the town and county of Morris were called after Colonel Morris, who for many years was the sole owner of that large tract of land. The other furnace was at Ancram, in the Province of New York, and it was owned by Mr. Livingston, who had called the place after one of the estates of the Livingston family in Scotland. It now became important for these infant industries of the colony to be protected by the laws, and the owners were also anixous to be permitted to export their iron, and will it be credited that this they were not allowed to do under existing English regulations, which always aimed at the suppression of any growth in the colonies? It was therefore determined to enact if possible such laws and regulations as would permit of exporting iron, and also allow the manufacturers to dispose of it in the colonies to advantage.

There was a slight earthquake on Mana-ha-ta in 1747, which shook up the little place and greatly frightened its inhabitants. The lower classes fancied it was a visitation of Providence, owing to the treatment the negroes had received. Mrs. Alexander's son William wrote to his brother-in-law Van Brugh Livingston: "I was very glad yesterday to find that Mama and none of the family had heard of the earthquake that we had about four o'clock in the morning. I felt it, and it seemed to be a violent shock, but lasted a very short time." The ladies in New York did not go to the extremes that their sisters in London did at about the same time, when that place was also visited by earthquakes, which seem to have been no more violent than those on Mana-ha-ta. The English women (according to Horace Walpole's letters to his friend) prepared for the worse as they thought they were to be swallowed alive, and therefore had "grave-clothes" made for themselves, or what they called "earthquake-gowns," which they studied to make as becoming as possible, and which they donned every evening after ten o'clock in order to be ready for emergencies. A certain day was appointed by popular opinion when the most terrible quake was to occur, and some ladies retired to the country, believing that they would be safer there than in London, while others stayed in town, preferring company in the anticipated peril. It is unfortunate that Mr. Walpole did not give a description of the evening that was prepared for with so much dread, and it passed off without any disturbance.

Another scourge of fever prevailed during the summer of 1747. Mr. Alexander had the sorrow of losing by it his promising young nephew, Dr. William Alexander, the heir to the title of "Stirling," and the death of the young man revived in the councillor's mind the question of claiming the title which was still in abeyance, and to which, on the death of his nephew, he himself was now heir. The letters from Scotland had confirmed his right to the title, and had proved his descent from John of Gogar, and shown that he was "eldest male heir holding the name and title of Alexander." It now became a question of returning to Scotland to press the claims, and Mr. Alexander determined to do so, as soon as he could dispose of the weighty public and private affairs that pressed on him.

Just at this time the only son of Mr. Alexander acquainted his parents "with his affection for Miss Sarah Livingston," the sister of Van Brugh Livingston, and the daughter of Philip, Lord of the Manor of Livingston, and the young man requested his father to ask

New York "in the Forties"

Mr. Livingston for permission to pay his addresses in form. Mr. Livingston's town house was within a stone's-throw of Mr. Alexander's, and the gentlemen met at the card-table nearly every evening, but the councillor deemed it best to write a formal letter on such an important occasion, and he therefore sent a communication (of which the careful gentleman kept a copy, that is still in the possession of one of his descendants) in which he asked Mr. and Mrs. Livingston to allow his son to become the husband of Miss Sarah Livingston.

The father of the young lady seems to have been well prepared for the demand, for he replied without loss of time that his "daughter was an obedient, pious, virtuous young woman," and that he and his wife "know of no young gentleman to whom they should prefer before Mr. William Alexander to give their daughter to." These negotiations took place at the end of February, 1746, while Mr. Alexander was suffering from one of the most severe attacks of gout that he had ever had, which incapacitated him for a long time from attending to business, and it was a year before the settlements for the marriage could be drawn up and all the arrangements completed. William Alexander took out his license February 29, 1748, and the marriage was performed with great ceremony on March 1st. The wedding of "Brother Bill and Sallie Livingston" was hardly over, and the bride and groom returned from the Livingston Manor House, where they passed the honeymoon, before a double wedding took place in Mrs.

The Goede Vrouw of Mana-ha-ta

Alexander's family, and at one blow she lost two of her daughters. Betsey, the eldest, who was just twenty, married John Stevens, a gentleman of fortune, who was the grandson of Lord Niel Campbell, son of the Duke of Argyle; and Kitty, a year younger, was married to Elisha Parker, the son of a gentleman whose country place adjoined that of Mr. Alexander at Perth Amboy. The groom had studied in Mr. Alexander's office and was then a practising lawyer. He was thirteen years older than his bride, but the father was extremely fond of his former pupil and was pleased to see his daughter so happily married. She was a charming girl, with bright, vivacious manners, and an especial favorite with all the young people. The double ceremony was performed by the rector of Trinity Church, and the parlors of the old house were crowded with all the good people of the town. Suky Alexander was now the only child left at home with her parents.

Mrs. Alexander was greatly distressed at losing her only brother, in the spring of 1749. John Spratt had never married, but had led a gay bachelor life in New York, where he held the by no means onerous post of captain in a military company. He was a man of ample means, inherited from his father, John Spratt, and also from his grandmother, Mme. de Peyster, and he concerned himself but little with commercial or political affairs. His most intimate friend was Richard Ashfield, who married Miss Isabella Morris, and to the three youngest children of his friends Mr. Spratt left in his will "all rights in the estates of Mme. de Peyster," his grandmother. We have no means of knowing why this money was diverted from the children of his sister, Mrs. Alexander; but it is more than probable that he had given them large sums of money when each one married, and the kind old bachelor desired to place the children of his friends in an independent position, as they were by no means wealthy.

Grandchildren were now plentiful in the family of Mrs. Alexander, but she was none the less pleased when a daughter was born to her son William. The birth of this child was alluded to in the following playful words by Robert Livingston, who wrote to his brother-in-law, William Alexander, from Kingston, May 28, 1749, on the arrival of his eldest daughter, Mary Alexander, named after her father's mother: "I congratulate you on the increase of your family, and hope in the future my sister will beget a more masculine kind, and not spoil the family with such Lilliputians as your daughter."

The English officials in America never lost an opportunity of asserting their superiority to the colonists and displaying their power over them, from the governor down to the lowest person who held a commission from the English government. None were more arrogant than the army and navy officers. The former expected free quarters, and to be served with every luxury wherever they went, and the colonists were now smarting from the treatment that they had lately received from the English general in command of the forces in New York, who had demanded that the troops under his command should receive all their rations from the New York colony, although the army had been sent to America at the entreaty of the New England colonies, to protect their interests against encroachments from Canada and the Indian tribes, incited to war by the inhabitants of the French colony. The citizens of New York believed that the expenses should be distributed through all the colonies that shared equally in the protection to be afforded by the English troops, and that they ought not to fall entirely on one locality. The general pressed the subject at the point of the sword, and quartered his soldiers where he pleased, treating the inhabitants as if they were in a state of rebellion instead of being peace-loving subjects of the same king as himself. The matter caused an open rupture between the assembly, that wished to protect the interests of the plantation, and the governor, who sided with the general in oppressing the colonists.

The officers of his majesty's navy were no less aggressive and domineering. If by chance they were short of men, they would send a boatload of sailors on shore and seize the first strong, lusty young fellow they came across and impress him into his majesty's service. They also demanded that great respect should be paid to them on sea and shore, and as each commander who entered the harbor made new and vexatious rules, the colonists were daily aggravated by petty insults and troublesome, useless demands, and they became hourly more exasperated against the English government, that did nothing to protect its colonists, and expected them to contribute largely to her own expensive government, turned the riff-raff of their own adherents into officials to govern the colonies, and upheld these men in their most unconstitutional and dishonest actions. This was not only the case in the New York colony. There were several others in America that were groaning under oppression and the maladministration of the English governors. Connecticut and Pennsylvania had their own charters and an independent government, and were thriving in a way that made all the other colonies discontented with the existing state of affairs.

New Jersey was at the time governed by Colonel Morris, who, being a large landed proprietor and having great interests at stake, was doing everything in his power to advance the growth of the plantation. One of his predecessors had been Lord Carteret, the son of the gentleman in the naval board of which Samuel Pepys was secretary, and about whom the diarist had much to say. Governor Carteret had come to the country a widower, but he soon married a buxom widow with five children, who was considered "a fortune." The lady who became his wife was Mrs. William Lawrence, one of the Smith family of Long Island, and by reason of her family connections and those of her first husband, she was a person of considerable importance. She was a woman of strong character and great determination,

and was appointed "Regent of the Province of New Jersey" during some of Lord Carteret's frequent absences on official business, and many of the documents of that time are signed by her as regent. This is a noteworthy instance of the only woman who ever ruled over an American colony.

The granddaughter of this lady was Mary Emott, who married Colonel William Ricketts, an officer in his majesty's service, who were living in a pretty house at Perth Amboy. Colonel Ricketts and his family passed the winter of 1755 in New York, where they attended the assemblies, and were favorites at all the tea-tables of the good ladies who led the fashions in the town. Mrs. Ricketts was an intimate friend of Mrs. Van Brugh Livingston, and she and her husband were among the group of friends who went to bid the colonel and his wife farewell at the Whitehall steps when they started with their little family to return to their home at Amboy one bright spring morning, intending to sail in their own yacht across the bay. The "birdgee" flag of the owner flew from the masthead, and the boat was skimming over the water; Mrs. Ricketts was seated beneath the awning busily plying her knitting-needles, her children, under the charge of their nurse, were close beside her, chatting to the steersman, and her husband was stretched on the cushions lazily reading his letters and papers, when suddenly a shot whizzed through the rigging, and all started to their feet in consternation. Colonel Ricketts tried to reassure his wife and children by declaring that it must be an accident, and that the sailors of the English frigate Greyhound, which they saw in the distance, must be practising at a mark, and that it could not occur again. As the colonel was speaking, a second shot passed through the mainsail and struck the nurse, who was holding an infant in her arms, in the head, and the woman fell dead at the feet of her horrified mistress. The boat was at once put about and ran up to the Greyhound, and Colonel Ricketts asked the officers on board for aid, supposing the occurrence to have been accidental. To the surprise and indignation of the English officer, he was answered with curses, and told that he should have shown his respect to his majesty's ship by lowering his flag when passing it.

This altered the state of affairs, and the yacht was immediately put about and returned to New York, where the high-handed action of Captain Digby was reported to the governor. An inquest was held on the body of the young woman, and a verdict of wilful murder was brought in. The fight was not quite the usual one, and only between a colonist who had been wantonly injured and an English official, but it was also between two branches of the English service, and promised to be a stormy one. The colonists took the part of the poor young creature who had been murdered in such a wanton manner. For some unaccountable reason, the governor took the part of Captain Digby, and extended his protection to the naval officers, which roused the officers of the army to take sides against the governor.

The Goede Vrouw of Mana-ha-ta

The people of New York, who were smarting under the repeated outrages committed by the naval officers, from which there seemed to be no escape nor redress, now broke out into open rebellion. Mobs filled the streets, and attacked every sailor who ventured to show himself. The funeral of the unfortunate girl was attended by crowds of people of all classes of society. The governor was hooted at whenever he appeared, and it was with difficulty that the tumult was repressed. From the members of the council to the poorest citizen, all felt that they had been humiliated, and were considered as inferiors by the English officers, as they were called upon to acknowledge the superiority of the latter by making a signal of deference to them, on sea and on land. Another "stripe" was being added to the banner of freedom, although the haughty Englishmen were too blind or indifferent to see it.

Governor Clinton, writing to the Duke of Bedford (Lords of Trade), June 12, 1750, deftly slurs over Captain Digby's outrageous conduct, and excuses himself for not taking action in the matter, as he "conceives that his commission is not clearly expressed as to his authority over the ships of war sent to the colony." It was pointed out to the governor at the time that his jurisdiction extended over the harbor of New York, and that it was quite within his province to make the rules governing the shipping, and that no government regulation had ever been issued regarding the salutes to be offered to war-vessels; that no com-

New York "in the Forties"

mander of any vessel, be he English or colonial, had any right to sail into the harbor of the town, and promulgate a series of rules and regulations for the guidance of its inhabitants, and take their lives if due respect to these arbitrary and unconstitutional acts was not paid. It was proved at the inquest that the yacht was not close enough to the ship-of-war to be prepared to signal, that the owner's "birdgee" was flying according to law, although the English commander had pleaded in extenuation that it was not, and Captain Digby could only allege in his defence that an act of discourtesy had been shown to him, as the flag of the yacht had not been lowered when passing his vessel. It was proved in answer to this statement that, in fact, the yacht was not passing the man-of-war, but was far on the other side of the harbor, that the private signal showing her to be a yacht was flying in plain sight, and that all matters of etiquette had been fulfilled. In spite of the English captain having been proved entirely in the wrong, not only by wantonly attacking innocent travellers, but by appearing in court and openly stating things that were proved on the testimony of many witnesses to be false, the governor upheld him, and a precedent was created for firing on a private vessel in the home harbor at a time of peace. There was already much ill-will between the army and navy, and this insult to Colonel Ricketts was deeply resented by his fellow-officers. The disrespect to Mrs. Ricketts was keenly felt by the New York officials, owing to her close connection with the ruling powers, and the death of an innocent girl was deplored by all parties. There was no doubt in the minds of anyone that the outrage had been committed with deliberation, as it was proved that the flag of the owner had been recognized by those on board of the war-vessel, who determined to have "some fun" at the expense of the colonel. This lamentable incident, which could have been smoothed over by Captain Digby, if he had chosen to apologize, instead of resorting to falsehood to defend himself, injured the aggressors in the opinions of all parties, except that of the governor, and of the home government, who seemed pleased at every insult that was shown to the colonists.

Births and deaths now followed each other with startling rapidity in Mrs. Alexander's family, as in March of 1751, Elisha Parker died suddenly, leaving a pretty, young, childless widow, who returned to her father's house, where she was warmly welcomed by her old friends. Among the young people who were attracted to Mrs. Alexander's house was an English officer, a major in the Royal American Regiment, who arrived in New York in 1756, and immediately fell in love with the captivating young widow.

It was not long before Walter Rutherfurd and "the widow Parker" resolved to make a match, and they were married in Mrs. Alexander's parlor, December 21, 1758. The match was a happy one, the groom was a sweet, lovable fellow, and they were a most devoted couple. Their home was on Broadway, on the corner of Vesey Street. It was a large, handsome house, and one of the first to be built "up town."

Government affairs were, as usual, in a turmoil; things were going from bad to worse, the governor and the legislature always at odds. Mr. Alexander, as a member of the council, tried to keep peace, but the effort was too much for him and brought on constant attacks of gout, while the governor became exasperated with the contumacy of his subjects, and wrote to the Lords of Trade begging to be recalled. In the meantime he went to Flushing, a pretty town on Long Island, to spend the summer, and Mrs. Alexander carried her family to Perth Amboy, hoping that the quiet and salubrious air would restore her husband's health.

According to Governor Clinton's request, a new governor was appointed for New York, who arrived in the colony on October 7, 1753. This was Sir Danvers Osborne, brother-in-law to the Earl of Halifax. His wife had just died, and as seems to have been the custom in appointing governors to the Province, this gentleman was sent to America to console him for being a widower. He was in a most melancholy state of mind, and arrived in the colony in no fit condition to take up arduous and uncongenial duties. The ex-governor and the colonists at once began to pour complaints into the ears of Sir Danvers, and the contradictory reports worried him to desperation, and caused him to receive the acclamations of the populace who escorted him to the State-house to take the oaths of office with a serious air. During the long ceremonies of the installation, the new governor turned to his predecessor and expressed his sympathy for the bad treatment he had received from the colonists, although the ex-governor would have found it hard to discover what it had been, further than that the colonists would not allow themselves to be imposed upon past a certain limit. Sir Danvers also was heard to say to Admiral Clinton, "It will be my turn soon to receive unjust criticism."

At the great dinner of welcome given to the new governor, he sat listless, to the surprise of his hosts, hardly returned the greetings and toasts that were extended to him on all sides, and retired from the scene as early as possible. His conduct was ascribed to the English hauteur from which the colonists had already suffered so greatly, and the gentlemen who witnessed his behavior were most unpleasantly impressed with their new ruler's manners and deportment. Mr. Alexander on his return from the dinner related all these occurrences to his wife, and expressed his regrets that such an uncongenial ruler should have been again sent by the English government to preside over the affairs of the colony, that required so much judgment and prudence to control. No one was prepared for the tragedy that followed. Mr. Alexander and Mr. Smith were roused very early on the morning of Friday, October 12th, by the doorkeeper of the council with a summons to attend at Mr. Murray's house, at which place Sir Danvers Osborne had taken up his abode on his arrival. All the councillors were hurriedly assembled, and then conducted to the garden, where the body of the unfortunate governor was found hanging from a picket of the fence, suspended by his own silk handkerchief.

The valet of the unfortunate gentleman testified that his master had been melancholy for some time, and that he had become worse during the voyage. Before leaving England he had attempted to cut his throat with a razor, and his friends had insisted on his trying a change of scene in hopes of diverting his mind. But the turmoil in which he foresaw that he would be engaged as the governor of a contentious body of colonists, drove him to despair, with the sad result that he took his own life as speedily as possible.

Mr. Alexander was appointed one of a committee to take the depositions attending the facts of his death, and he and his associates succeeded by their exertions in having the coroner's jury bring in a verdict of "Non compos mentis." If it had not been for this verdict the body would have been refused Christian burial. The next step of the councillors was to approach Dr. Barclay, the rector of Trinity Church, and request him to conduct the services over the remains of the late governor. Dr. Barclay attended a meeting of the council, and respectfully but firmly refused to perform the ceremony, or allow the interment to take place in Trinity

Churchyard, alleging that the rubrics of the Church would not permit him to read the burial service over a suicide. Mr. Smith, one of the council, thereupon remarked "that a person who died in a high fever was often not in their right mind, and they were not refused the Christian rights," and as Mr. Smith was a Presbyterian, this unexpected remark of his had more weight, coming as it did from one of a different creed, than if it had proceeded from a member of the Church of England, and Dr. Barclay, who was only desirous of keeping within the letter of the law of the rubric, was satisfied to change his opinion, and perform the ceremony. The late governor was buried with great pomp and solemnity on the following Sunday, within a week after landing in the Province.

The colony of New York had been treated to a variety of rulers since the English had taken possession of the Dutch Colony. They had had men of dissolute character, men who were palpably dishonest, weak and incompetent, and had nearly run the gamut of governors endowed with every vice known. They were fortunately spared the dominion of a madman, who succeeded a dipsomaniac in the chief office of the Province.

Governor Clinton sailed for England in November, and Mr. Smith, who was one of the council, records his impressions of him in the following terms: "In a Province given to hospitality, he (Governor Clinton) erred by immuring himself in the fort or retiring to a grotto in the country, where his time was spent with his bottle and a little trifling circle, who played billiards with his lady and lived on his bounty. He sometimes took money for offices, and even sold the reversions of those that were merely ministerial. He became afterward governor of Greenwich Hospital."

XXII

The Last of the Dutch Matrons

Chief-Justice de Lancey as Governor—Social Evening Amusements—Society Library—King's College—Braddock's Expedition—Governor Shirley—William Alexander Appointed Major and Private Secretary to the Governor—The Acadians—The Young Partners—Sir Charles Hardy—The Earthquake—Death of Mrs. Livingston—Death of James Alexander—Major Alexander Sails for England—Lord Stirling—Death of Mrs. Alexander, the Last of the Dutch Matrons.

THE death of Sir Danvers Osborne left a vacancy that had to be filled by a member of the council until such time as a new appointment could be made in England. There had been considerable rivalry in that body as to which of its members should be its president, as that official was the next in rank to the chief, and succeeded him in emergencies like the present. It is not necessary now to enter into the divers disputes of the councillors, who were divided into factions. The larger number were opposed to Chief-Justice de Lancey, as the position that he had taken during the rule of Cosby was hardly to be forgiven by the men who had been injured by the abuse of the power that he then had shown. And when Cosby's government came to an abrupt end, and right reasserted itself under his successor, and the combatants met as colleagues in the council-chamber, it was not to be supposed that harmony would reign among them. Chief-Justice de Lancey, as presiding officer, now became acting governor, and although of American birth, was as much at variance with his countrymen as any of the English governors had ever been. Dr. Colden, who was next in seniority, and who had hoped to have the position, retired in disgust to his country seat and tried to forget the vexatious state of political affairs by writing his famous history of the Indian nations, and Governor de Lancey, finding his most outspoken opponent had left the field, set himself to govern the colony to the best of his ability.

During this time of political inaction, the more educated people of the colony set themselves to social enjoyments, and began to turn their attention to literary affairs. There were one or two societies that met biweekly and exchanged essays, poems, etc., and distributed them among their own members, and Mrs. Alexander's daughters had for some years held a species of "salon," at which it was the custom to play at making rhymes and amusing verses that related to passing events among the young people. One of their principal amusements was making conundrums. The parents did not disdain to contribute when occasion offered, and the rhyming letters of the grave councillor often added much to the evening's amusement, as he had the gift of relating a story in an entertaining way, and could put it into verse that detracted nothing from its wit or point.

The need of a good library was greatly felt, as the books sent to the colony by the Society for the Propagation of the Gospel had not been followed by any other contributions, nor had any provision been made by that society or the authorities in New York for distributing the books or adding to their number. The library that the colonists had at first hailed with such delight had been placed in a room, it is true, but no librarian had been provided, and the conveniences for distribution were so inadequate that the public ceased even to try to get at the books, which finally became scattered and lost, or were stored in inaccessible places and were hardly worth searching for, as they were only on controversial, doctrinal subjects that were now obsolete.

One evening Mrs. Alexander had a large gathering of her old friends seated around her tea-table. Among them was Mr. William Smith, and with him she discussed the difficulty that she experienced in getting good books to read, and proposed that a circulating library should be started, the subscribers to collect sufficient money to send to England for all the newest and best books, which should be arranged in such a way that the members could take them from the library at their own convenience. The idea was eagerly hailed by all present, and the gentlemen occupied themselves during the rest of the evening in drawing up rules for the library, and making out lists to be distributed the following morning, in hopes of getting a large subscription. Messrs. William Smith, Philip, William, and Robert Livingston, John Morin Scott, and William Alexander headed the list, with a liberal subscription from each one toward buying the books. The subject was more thoroughly discussed evening after evening in Mrs. Alexander's parlors, and was gradually laid before the public.

It was so favorably received by the friends of the original members, that subscription books were opened and carried (as a matter of courtesy), first to Lieutenant-Governor de Lancey, then to the members of the council, and, with their official seal set upon the undertaking, there was no necessity for persons to be entreated to subscribe, for many of the inhabitants of New York now implored to be allowed to contribute, and a considerable sum was raised.

An institution was now formally organized, and each person after being elected a member was called upon for a yearly subscription of ten shillings. The books donated by the S. P. G. were used as a nucleus for the library, which in later years received a royal charter from Governor Tryon. During the War of Independence the books became scattered; but when peace was restored they were collected, and the association was reorganized, and is now known by the name of the Society Library. Many of the original shares are still held by the descendants of the first subscribers. The first trustees were James Alexander, his son William Alexander, Lieutenant-Governor de Lancey, John Chambers, John Watts, William Walton, Benjamin Nicoll, William Smith, Rev. Henry Barclay, and William Livingston.

For a number of years the citizens of New York had exerted themselves to found a college for the better education of the youth of the colony. The matter had taken time to arrange, as it gave rise to bitter religious and political disputes. There were not above a dozen graduates outside of the medical and clerical professions in the colony, and those had received their diplomas in England. Philip Livingston (who is now known as "the signer," from having signed his name to the Declaration of Independence) had been entered by his father at the Temple, and he and his brothers, Robert, Van Brugh, and William, all graduates of English colleges, were foremost in promoting the American university. Unfortunately for the enterprise, this family were stanch Presbyterians, and the chief support of the college was promised by the government and by the wardens and vestry of Trinity Church, who had come forward in 1752 and offered part of the estate of their opulent corporation for the erection of a college and toward its maintenance. "This would naturally give," says Mr. Smith, in his relation of the affair, "an Episcopal bias to the views of the college, which was abhorent to the Livingston family." The subject was disputed for many months, and was finally compromised by the election of Dr. Johnson, an Episcopal minister, as first president, and Mr. Whittlesey, a Presbyterian minister, as his assistant, and a large building, to be devoted to educational purposes and called "King's College," was finally erected on a high bank overlooking the Hudson River, close to Trinity Church.

The French had been encroaching on the English settlements in Ohio, and in 1754 the government determined to send an expedition against them, under General Braddock. New York and Massachusetts were also threatened, and a council was called, at which the governor of Massachusetts was appointed major-general, and, on February 2d, opened the northern campaign by proceeding to Oswego. Troops were sent to the colony from England, and many of the young men of the different plantations hastened to enroll themselves in the native militia, that was being rapidly organized, or else bought commissions in the English regiments. General Shirley arrived in New York from Boston, about the middle of April, and was received with unwonted hospitality, as he had taken the trouble to provide himself with letters of introduction to many of the principal families, a thing that was generally omitted by the British officers, who trusted to their own fascinations to make them acceptable and welcome to the colonists.

There was a considerable amount of friction and jealousy over the campaign that was just opening, and some discussion as to whom the command of the expedition should devolve upon. The Eastern colonies wished to have entire control, while they desired that New York should bear the burden of paying for it. General Shirley assumed command under these disadvantageous circumstances, and at once appointed Mrs. Alexander's son William his private secretary, signing his commission, December 7, 1755, and the young man took leave of his wife and mother, and accompanied the general on his tour up the Hudson River to Albany, where the troops were being gathered as rapidly as possible, so that they might be pushed on to the frontier.

Mrs. Alexander had not been well for some months, and her husband and children were anxious about her health. She had exerted herself to receive and entertain General Shirley during his stay in New York, but the old hospitality for which she had been famous was no longer spontaneous, and the effort had left her listless and weak, and so depressed in spirits that Mrs. Livingston persuaded her to sail up to the Livingston Manor, with her daughter-in-law Sallie and the children, and spend the summer there.

Van Brugh Livingston wrote to his brother-in-law, July 9th, saying: "Your mother is very unwell; she hurt herself the day before yesterday in falling down. Your wife has still a pain in her face. Mrs. Livingston has a young son." The letter alarmed Major Alexander, but his professional duties kept him in Albany, and he was obliged to content himself by sending a messenger down the river, who was ordered to bring him an immediate account of his mother's condition. Van Brugh Livingston was able in reply to send a better account the next day, and say, "Your mother is better to-day, but not able to come down stairs. She has no fever. I hope she will soon be well, as she is on the recovery. Mr. Alexander is at Amboy, where the Assembly is sitting." The news of his mother's illness worried her son, who was devotedly attached to her, and it was aggravated by the thought that his father was necessarily absent on his official business. It was feared that the fall was caused by a slight attack of apoplexy, and although he knew that she was receiving the best of care, not only from his own wife but also from his sister, Mrs. Van Brugh Livingston, who was also at the Manor, his anxiety was not fully allayed until he was able to rejoin his family, when to his great relief he found his mother better than he had expected, and he persuaded her to return to town with him, and place herself under the care of Dr. Farquhar, the family physician, after which the major followed his commander-in-chief to Boston.

That town was full of English regiments, who were being sent from England to take part in the campaign. The governor's daughter, Miss Ann Shirley, wrote to Mrs. Rutherford: "The young ladies are beginning to hold down their heads and look melancholy; and indeed I do not wonder, for by Friday night we sha'n't have a beau left. Poor Boston! What a falling off! But New York will fare no better, for the handsome fellows must all march to the war. Last Sunday I attended Miss Shirley (that was) to church, and according to custom there were a great many people to look at the bride. Her dress was a yellow lute string, trimmed with silver, with one flounce at the bottom, which was esteemed by everybody to be very genteel, and I was not a little pleased with it, as it was in a great measure my taste."

Major Alexander was forced by his duties to travel to Virginia, and while on this expedition he made the acquaintance of Captain George Washington, and began a friendship with that great man that only ended with life. During the winter of 1755 the inhabitants of New York were racked with news of war, rapine, and murder from every quarter. On the Virginia border the Indians and French were only held in check by the impossibility of carrying on a campaign through the deep snows of the mountain-passes. Murders and outrages were the rule on the northern boundaries of New York, and there were disturbances at the Livingston Manor. James Alexander wrote to his son-in-law, Van Brugh Livingston, in December: "The manner of beginning this war must have surprised the nations of Europe, as it has the American colonies, but the way in which it has been carried on is still more surprising. General Braddock was sent over as commander-in-chief, and how the ministry came to intrust full powers to such a man has perplexed us all — a man of no knowledge, civil or military, who by all accounts has spent his life

The Last of the Dutch Matrons

in the most profligate manner, made no pretensions to morals, and the loose indecency of his conversation showed what company he had been accustomed to frequent. From such an officer nothing could have been expected but disgrace to the British arms."

The intelligence of the defeat and death of General Braddock, on July 9th, paralyzed the energies of the Northern campaign, which was at the best times in a chaotic condition. An expedition had been sent to Nova Scotia, where two forts were captured by the English fleet. This might have reassured the colonists had it not been accompanied by the most brutal outrage on the inhabitants—who were a pastoral people, in nowise interested in a war that had been planned in the French cabinet, and of which they were the unfortunate victims. In order to paralyze the inhabitants of Acadia, the English commanders ordered that they should be seized on September 10, 1755, when the men were marched on board of the men-of-war, under a strong guard, while almost all the women and children were left on shore, homeless, friendless, penniless, to follow their natural protectors to unknown ports as well as they could. For months after this, the papers of Boston, New York, Philadelphia, and other places were filled with agonized advertisements from husbands seeking wives, mothers their children, and helpless people begging for sympathy and aid. English writers have sought to palliate and excuse this piece of needless brutality and cruelty, on the plea of "military necessity," without pointing out the proof of such "necessity," and the episode adds another blood-stain to the English flag.

William Alexander had for some years taken an active part in his mother's business, and their firm had supplied the commissariat of the expedition to the North. This had been done with such promptness and despatch that it was now determined to undertake to supply the troops of the Southern campaign, and to do this the more thoroughly a business partnership was entered into, January 14, 1756, between William Alexander, Van Brugh Livingston, John Erving, Jr., and Lewis Morris, Jr., and the first orders received by the firm were for supplying the expedition against Niagara. This order was given to the new firm much against the wishes of Lieutenant-Governor de Lancey, who hoped that his brother, Oliver de Lancey, would receive it, and be appointed agent. Accordingly, he bitterly opposed giving the commission to the young firm, but his wishes were overruled by General Shirley, who wisely foresaw that the success of the expedition largely depended upon the promptness with which it received its supplies, and there was no one in the colony who was able to do this better than Mrs. Alexander and her partners, who had great experience and facilities in the business.

The correspondence of the young partners is full of the details of this great work, and contemporaries point out how well and how thoroughly it was carried out. At the same time Richard Peters, of Philadelphia, was the agent for the Southern department, and through him all supplies were forwarded to Virginia. Mrs. Alexander took an active interest in all these preparations, and supplied the money to carry them out.

Mr. de Lancey was succeeded as governor of the New York Colony on September 2, 1755, but he continued to take an active part in the government, as Sir Charles Hardy, the new governor, was a man of weak character, who has been called " an unlettered admiral." He was indolent and of convivial habits, and he wished to draw his salary and do no work. He was glad to allow others to govern in his stead, if by so doing they saved him trouble, and his only wish was to be permitted to enjoy the pleasures of the table undisturbed by contending factions.

The next shock experienced by the citizens of New York came from Mother Earth. They were shaken from their beds at four o'clock on the morning of November 18, 1755. The moon was full and the sky clear and bright, and it was perfectly calm, which seemed to add to the fright of the startled people, who rushed half-clad from their houses. Windows rattled, chimneys fell, and great fissures were made in the walls of many of the houses. China was cracked and rattled, women screeched and fell on their knees, praying and calling on Heaven for help. Everyone ran without knowing where to go, and several fires broke out in different parts of the town to add to the fright and confusion. The houses were of two, or at the utmost three, stories in height, built of wood, and usually at a distance of several feet from each other, and therefore no very great damage was done to the city. The steeples of the churches tottered and were thrown out of line, and some of them had subsequently to be torn down; but the place was soon put in repair, and only the terror and the fright remained impressed on the minds of the inhabitants to recall to them their disagreeable experiences.

Mrs. Alexander had a great sorrow in the death of her life-long friend and companion, Mrs. Livingston (Katharine Van Brugh), a lady, like herself, of Dutch descent, and imbued with all the doctrines of the pioneer women of Mana-ha-ta. Both ladies despised the new customs and innovations that had been introduced by the English rulers; both of them had married Scotchmen of ancient lineage, who were averse to the Hanoverian dynasty. Their children had twice intermarried, to the great satisfaction of the mothers, and Mrs. Alexander mourned for her friend with heartfelt sorrow. Her husband wrote to his son-in-law, Van Brugh Livingston, February 11, 1756, a letter in which he speaks tenderly of the recent loss of his "good mother," and continues: "Her very sudden death must have surprised you all, as it did me. I heartily sympathize with you. She was a good woman and a very kind mother. Few women that I have ever been acquainted with equalled her in sweetness of temper and good sense. Whatever changes her death may occasion in the family, I hope it will not lessen the union and harmony. Let me recommend you to see each other often, and cultivate intimacy, for, believe me, the credit, the power, and interests of families depend chiefly on this. Interest often connects people who are entire strangers, and sometimes separates those who have the strongest natural ties. Whatever matters of property are to be settled, the sooner it is done the better, and I hope will be satisfactory to all concerned."

It was with a heavy heart that Mrs. Alexander saw her husband leave the house morning after morning to attend to his professional duties, or the meetings of the council. The governor was constantly swayed back and forth in his opinions, according to the views of the last person who had had his ear. Grave matters were before the council, upon the decision of which the lives and property of many of the colonists, to say nothing of the army in the field, depended, and yet the governor could hardly be induced to remain sober long enough to give a coherent opinion on any subject. Sir Charles Hardy would waver and vacillate, and after giving his assent to a measure one day, he would rescind it on the next.

The debates in the council were warm and vexatious, and after them Mr. Alexander would return to his home thoroughly exhausted. These agitating scenes culminated in a prostrating fit of the gout, which alarmed his wife, as she thought the symptoms were more severe than usual. She contrived to keep him in the house for several days, but a summons came from the government house to attend a meeting of the council on a subject that was of more than usual importance, and Mr. Alexander insisted on going to the meeting, while suffering severely. The result was that he caught a cold, from which he died within a few days, on April 2, 1756. The papers of the day record his death in the following words:

"NEW YORK MERCURY, Monday, April 5, 1756.

"To the unspeakable loss of his family and to the public, on Friday evening last, died the Honorable James Alexander, Esq., in the sixty-fourth year of his age. A gentleman in his disposition, generous, courteous, and humane, delicate in his sense of humor, steadfast in friendship, of strict probity, temperate in his diet, and in business indefatigable. The relations of husband, father and master, he sustained with the highest reputation. In these parts of the world, few men surpassed him either in the natural sagacity and strength of his intellectual powers, or in his literary acquirements. In the mathematical sciences his researches were very great. He was also eminent in his profession of the law, and equally distinguished by his superior knowledge and long experience in public affairs. He had the honor to serve the King in several important offices, and was a wise and faithful Councillor to his Majesty for the Provinces of New York and New Jersey. Always true to the interests of his country, well knowing that the rights of the crown are the bulwark of the liberties of the people; that the liberties of the people are the safety and honor of the crown, and that a just temperament of both in the administration of government, constitutes the health of the political body. His zeal for the defence of the public cause against the common enemy led him to council, when he was not sufficiently recovered from the gout. From

The Last of the Dutch Matrons

thence he brought those mortal symptoms that closed his days within about a week. His remains are to be interred this evening in his family vault in Trinity Church Yard."

James Alexander had lived for forty-one years in the land of his adoption, revered and esteemed by his fellow-citizens. From the time that he came to the Province until his death, he had held high official positions, and by his steady application to business, had become a large land-owner in the plantation of New Jersey, although his life was spent on the Island of Mana-ha-ta, where he was identified with all the best interests of the place. It was well known that Mr. Alexander was a champion for the rights of the citizens, as his influence had been exerted again and again in their behalf, when the various governors sent to this country by the English ministers tried to enrich themselves and their masters at the expense of the colonists.

The home-life of Mr. Alexander was happy in the extreme. He was a devoted husband and father, and his keen wit met with a ready response in the bright repartee for which his wife was famous, and which made their household celebrated for clever sayings, that were the theme of island chit-chat, and were always being repeated at the tea-tables of those who admired while they were not able to emulate.

Mr. Alexander's last wishes had been that his son William should proceed to Scotland and establish his claim to the earldom of Stirling, and as General Shirley

had received his recall to England, he entreated both the wife and mother of his friend to take advantage of this opportunity, and allow Major Alexander to cross the ocean with him. The major was unwilling to leave his family when they were in such grief, but it seemed his wisest plan as, by accepting Governor Shirley's invitation, he would be introduced, under the most agreeable auspices, to the powerful friends that he would need in the English Parliament, when the time came to present his claims to the earldom. The governor was also under some obligations to his willing secretary, as charges of malfeasance in office had been brought against him, that he was to answer to on his arrival in England, and it was most desirable that Major Alexander should be present at the trial, in order to testify in behalf of his old chief.

It was accordingly arranged that Major Alexander should sail for England with Governor Shirley, and he took leave of his family with great reluctance. It proved fortunate for the ex-governor that he had been able to carry his young friend to England with him, as his testimony, given with the frankness and fervor inherited from his father, entirely cleared Governor Shirley from the charges of incompetency and mismanagement that had been brought against him, and made him the lifelong friend of Major Alexander.

As soon as this important affair had been disposed of, Major Alexander proceeded to press his claims to the earldom of Stirling, which were presented in Scotland to the proper authorities, and duly acknowledged by them as authentic. The original grant had been, "To the eldest male heir bearing the name and arms of Alexander," and as Major Alexander was able to secure the attendance of several old retainers, who had lived on his grandfather's estates, and who testified to the descent of John of Gogar, and his relation to the first Earl of Stirling, and established beyond a peradventure that the eldest male heir of the house of Alexander was the young American, he therefore triumphantly took his place in the Scotch house and voted there with the full approbation and consent of its members. After this public acknowledgment and ratification of his claims, Major Alexander assumed the title of sixth Earl of Stirling, Viscount Canada, etc., and was always afterward addressed by his proper title, not only by his fellow-peers, but also by all his Scotch relations, who cordially invited him to their homes, and received and acknowledged him as the head of their house.

On the return of Lord Stirling to London he sat to Sir Joshua Reynolds for his portrait (which is now in New York in the possession of his great-grandson), intending the picture as a present for his mother on his return to America. But he was never destined to see her alive again. Four years after the death of her husband, Mrs. Alexander had a sharp attack of pleurisy, and although attended by the best physicians, she died, April 18, 1760, in her old home in Broad Street, surrounded by her daughters and grandchildren.

The Goede Vrouw of Mana-ha-ta

The funeral services at Trinity Church were attended by crowds of all classes of people, and both the governors of New York and New Jersey did honor to the widow of the councillor by signifying their desire to be allowed to act as her pall-bearers, and Mrs. Alexander was laid to rest beside her husband and children in the vault in the yard, close to the chancel of Trinity Church.

The last of the Dutch matrons passed away on the death of Mrs. Alexander. She had been stanch and true to the traditions taught her by her grandmother, who had been one of the pioneers of Mana-ha-ta. The rule of the Dutchmen had, it is true, ended with the retirement of Governor Stuyvesant to his Bowerie, but their dames had not so easily relaxed their grasp on the reins of social power as their husbands had on the political supremacy that they had wielded, and the ladies themselves, and the descendants of Cornelia Lubbetse, Margaret Hardenbroeck, Annekje Jans, Annekje Lockermans, and Catarina de Boorgh held sway, and they persisted in upholding the cherished Dutch customs, until after the death of Mrs. Alexander, when the intermarriages of the young people of the colony with persons of other nationalities infused a new flavor into the ethics of the social life of Mana-ha-ta.

Index

A

Aanspreecker, 63, 64
Abantzeeme, 91
Addison, 241
Adventure, the, 322
Advertisements, newspaper, 357-359
Albany, 4, 23, 111, footnote, 148, 186, 231, 311, 386; marriage records at, 66; county of, 91
Albertsen, Nicolas, 77
Alexander, Anne, 269, 327, 356
—— Catharine, 269, 327, 366. See Parker, Mrs. Elisha
—— Catherine, 249
—— Christina, 249
—— "Cuffie," 346
—— David, 324
—— Elizabeth, 249
—— Elizabeth, 269, 327, 366
—— Henry. See Stirling, the third Earl of
—— James, 291, 292, 312, 321, 325, 326, 328, 334, 348, 351, 357, 387, 389, 392, 393; family of, 247; settled in America, 248-251; his mathematical instruments, 249; made deputy clerk in the council, 250; studied law, 250; founded the American Philosophical Society, 250; his many offices, 250; friendship with Governor Burnet, 254, 256; advanced in office, 254; friendship with Mrs. Provoost, 260; marriage of, 261; his letter to his brother, 262; his extensive law practice, 264; joined the English Church, 272; his growing prominence, 276; made Freeman of the City, 277; conference of, with Colonel Morris, 280; his support of Van Dam, 281, 283; communicated with Morris, 287, 288; incendiary letter to, 294; contended against convicting Harison, 296; accused by Harrison, 297; thought to be the author of articles in the "Weekly Journal," 299; his connection with the Zenger trial, 301-305; contemptuously treated by Chief-Justice De Lancey, 302; denounced the Governor's latest proceeding, 313, 314; his removal with his family to Perth Amboy, 314; reinstated at the bar, 316, 317; his bills in the assembly, 318; his succession to the title of Stirling, 323, 324; his letter to David Provoost, 333; the negro troubles, 341; his gout, 347; enjoyed the confidence of Governor Clinton, 360, 361; sailed again to England, 362; determined to press his claim to the title of Stirling, 364; a trustee of the first library, 384; meeting with George Washington, 388; his death, 394, 395; his character, 395

Alexander, Mrs. James (born Polly Spratt), 239, 272, 276, 279, 280, 284-287, 293, 300, 308, 316, 321, 325-330, 333-335, 339, 340, 345, 346, 351, 357, 361, 363, 366, 367, 374, 381, 390-393; childhood of, 228-232; second marriage of, 261; birth of her daughter, 262; a social leader, 263; her influence, 264; her hospitality, 265; her biscuits, 266; her supper-parties, 267; the death of her grandparents, 268; her children, 269; a New Year's reception, 292; her advice to her husband not to leave New York, 302, 303; secret interview with Andrew Hamilton, 304, 305; her balls, 309; her home at Perth Amboy, 322; letter to her son David, 333; her efforts to instruct the Indians, 353-355; bereaved of her child, 356; her plan

Index

for a library, 382, 383; ill-health, 386; her gift of bright repartee, 395; her death, 397; funeral services, 398. See Provoost, Mrs. Samuel

Alexander, James, son of James, birth of, 267; death of, 269
—— Janet, 249
—— John, 247
—— Kitty, 262
—— Mary (Polly), 262, 325, 326, 327, 359, 360. See Livingston, Mrs. Peter Van Brugh
—— Mary, 367
—— Susanna, 269, 327, 366
—— Sir William, accomplishments of, 122; his friendship with James VI. of Scotland, 122, 123; the King's gift of land and his colonization, 124; made Earl of Stirling, 126. See Stirling, the first Earl of
—— William, 249, 262, 324
—— Mrs. William (born Elizabeth Lumsden), 249
—— Major William, sixth Earl of Stirling, 326, 327, 328, 360, 363, 364, 366, 383, 384, 387, 388; birth of, 269; marriage of, 365; appointed private secretary to General Shirley, 386; undertook to supply the troops in the southern campaign, 390; desired by his father to go to Scotland, 395; pressed his claims to the earldom of Stirling in Scotland, 396; made sixth Earl, 397; his portrait, 397
—— Mrs. William. See Livingston, Sarah
—— Dr. William, 262, 324, 325, 364
Algonquin language, 7, 22, 74
American Philosophical Society, 250
Ancram, 362
Andros, Sir Edmund, retook New York, 139; the rumor of his removal, 166; his arrest, 167
Anne, Queen, 220, 223, 224, 241, 243, 246, 282
Appamapagh, 147
Archangel, the ship, 190
Argyle, the Duke of, 246, 366
Ashfield, Richard, 366
—— Mrs. Richard (born Isabella Morris), 366
Assemblies, 140, 215, 260
Avery, John, 277

B

Bacchus, feast of, 132
Backgammon, 81
Backus, Jan, tavern of, 81
Balfour, Sir James, 126
Bancker, Anna, 151
—— Christopher, 337
—— Maria, 151
—— family, the, 340
Barclay, Dr., 377, 378, 384
—— family of, 339
Basket Badge, the, 353
Bastiens, Hachin, 206
Battery Park, 6
Baxter Street, 44
Bayard, Balthazar, 27
—— Mrs. Balthazar (born Maryje Lockermans), marriage of, 27; a relative of Judith Varleth, 148
—— Judith, 239
—— Colonel Nicholas, chosen to the council, 138; marriage of, 148; member of the King's council, 168; his beautiful country home, 171; his arrest at Leisler's command, 172, 173; released from prison, 191
—— Mrs. Nicholas (born Judith Varleth), 17; married, 148; imprisoned as a witch, 171; released, 172; insulted by Leisler's men, 172 et seq.
—— Peter, 80
—— Mrs. Peter. See Kierstede, Blandina
—— Samuel, 103
—— Mrs. Samuel (born Anna Stuyvesant), emigrated to America with her brother, 103, 104, 172; her accomplishments, 104; interfered in behalf of a Quaker, 110; present at New Year's festivals, 131, 132
—— family, the, 140, 256, 260
Beaver Street, 153
Bedford, the Duke of, 372
—— Governor, 348
Bedlow, Mr., his arrival in New York, 226; purchase of "Bedlow's Island," 227
Bedsteads, 30, 31, 75
Beekman, Cornelia (Mrs. Guysbert Livingston), 186
—— Cornelia (Mrs. Richard Van Dam), 239

Index

Beekman, Colonel Henry, second marriage of, 223; on a grand jury, 340
—— Mrs. Henry (born Gertrude Van Cortlandt), 223, 340
—— Jacobus, marriage of, 229
—— Mrs. Jacobus (born Elizabeth de Peyster), 229
—— William, 37, 38, 106, 138
—— Mrs. William. See Van de Bourgh, Catarina
—— family, the, 261, 274
—— Street, 38, 39
Belleville, 102
Bellevue Hospital, 194
Bellomont, the Earl of, 342; made Governor, 201; his jealousy of his wife, 202; shut off his wife from social intercourse, 202; a "reformer," 202; his attempt to raise a navy and its bad results, 203 *et seq.*; abandoned Captain Kidd to his fate, 209; death of, 212; coffin-plate of, 212
Bellomont, Lady, 201, 202
Benson, Robert, 337
Berkeley, Bishop, his cure for gout, 348; arrival of, in Newport, 349; his treatise called Siris, 349, 350
Bestevaars Killitje, 32, 322
Betty, "Topknot," 82
Beverly, 256
Beverwyck, 23, 90, 109, 111, 158, 350; church at, 95; settlement of the Schuylers at, 97; settlement of Mrs. Bogartus at, 148
Birth, customs attending, 54 *et seq.*
Black Horse Tavern, 310
Bleecker, family of, 261
Bleeker, John R., 93
Blockhouse, Peter Minuit's, site of, 6
Bogart, Henry, 337
Bogart's biscuits, 266
Bogartus, Rev. Everardus, minister in the Dutch Church, married Annekje Jans, after the death of her first husband, 20; personality and home, 21; his death by drowning, 103
—— Mrs. Everardus. See Jans, Annekje
Bogartus Farm, 20
"Boo," the, 353
Bootikins, 347
Boston, 166, 167, 209, 210, 211, 218, 285, 287, 289

Boston Highway, 43, 286
Boudinot, Mr., 338
Bound Brook, 102
Bourdet, Mr., 338
Bouwerie, 23, 119, 132; of Governor Stuyvesant, 286, 398
Bowerie, Bossen, 322
Bowery, the, 219
Bowling club, the, 80
—— Green, 6, 351
—— green, the, 80
Braddock, General, 385, 388, 389
Bradford, Governor William, 105
Bradly, Samuel, 203
—— Sarah, married to Captain Kidd, 203
"Brant," 83
Bread, 108
Breakfasts, 73
Bridge over the Graft, 49
—— Street, 6, 147
"Brief Relation of New York, A," 7
Brinckerhoff, Abram, 101
—— Dirck, 101
—— George, 337
Broad Street, 29, 37, 46, 49, 51, 146, 152, 153, 263, 330, 345, 351, 397
Broadway, 104, 224, 286, 351, 356, 375
Brockholst, Captain Anthony, his marriage to a Schrick, 149
Bronck, Jonas, the widow of, 94
Brower Street, 29, 35
Brown, Charles, 108
Browne, William, 256
—— Mrs. William (born Mary Burnet), 256
Bunker Hill, 40
Bunner family, the, 339
Burgoyne, General, 83
Burnet, Bishop, 252, 253
—— Mary, 256
—— Thomas, 256
—— Governor William, 321, 325, 340; reception of, 252; courtly manners of, 253; weekly tea-parties of, 254; marriage of, 255; reasons for his many friends, 256; Godfather of Mary Alexander, 262; became Governor of Massachusetts, 270; his death, 270
—— Mrs. William (born Mary Van Horne), 255, 256, 262, 270, 340
Burton, Mary, 330, 331, 332, 341, 342
Bushwyck, 77; new settlers of, 90
Buttermilk Channel, 101

Index

C

Camm, Mrs. Thomas (born Christina Alexander), 249
Campbell, Lord Neal, 366
Canada, 169, 243, 336, 343, 368; county of, 126; title of Viscount Canada, 162 et seq., 397
Canal Street, 40, 356
Candlemas, 131
Canoe Place, 32, 40, 356; tide-mill at, 43; old tavern and bowling green at, 80
Capsey Rocks, 6, 52, 104, 200
Cardinal, 265
Cards, 81, 82
Carey, Peggy, 332, 341
Carpsey, Gabriel, 50, 51
Carteret, Governor, marriage of, 369, 370
—— Mrs., 369, 370
Catiemuts, 39, 42; windmill on, 43, 351; building of the New York Life Insurance Company now on, 44
Catskills, 93, 181
Cattle, care of, 50, 51
Caudle, 56
—— parties, 55
Centre Street, 342
"Chair, Bishop Berkeley's," 349
Chambers, John, 384; founder of bowling club, 80
—— Mr., 341
—— Street, the "tea-water" pump near, 52
Champlain, Lake, 95
Charles II., 11, 120 et seq., 178, 180, 183; in Holland, 97 et seq.; his Dutch friends, 98
Charles, voyage of the, 34
Chatelaines, 28, 70
Chatham Street, 342
Chelsea, 351
Cherry-tree Harbor, 210
Children of the first settlers, 76. See Companies
Christ Church, Jamaica, 238
Christening, 54
Christian names, 19
Christy, Alice, 257
Churches, 272 et seq.
Churchill, John, 113
City Hall, 194, 252, 276
City Hall Park, 51, 80, 338. See Common

Clarke, Lieutenant-Governor, 313, 314, 315, 316, 332, 360
Clarkson, Matthew, 230
—— Mrs. Matthew (born Cornelia de Peyster), 229
—— family of, 261, 340
Claver Waytie, de, 46
Claverack, 159
Clermont, Robert of. See Livingston, "Robert Second"
Clinton, Admiral George, 375, 376, 378; made Governor, 360; his confidence in Alexander, 361; took the part of Captain Digby, 371; letter to the Lords of Trade, 373; return to England, 378
Clopper, Cornelius, 50, 193
Cloyne, 348, 349
Club, the bowling, 80
Cod, Cape, 106, 126
Colden, Dr. Cadwalader, 248, 253, 381; his friendship with Governor Burnet, 254, 256; his studies, 257; his children, 258; Rutherfurd's description, 259; made Lieutenant-Governor, 361; opposed Clinton, 361
—— Mrs. Cadwalader (born Alice Christy), 257
—— Jane, 258. See Farquhar, Mrs. William
—— family, the, 261
Coldenham, 258, 259
Collect, the, 42, 171, 230, 286, 339, 342; windmill at, 43; filled in by municipal authorities, 42; site of, 44
College of XIX., formation of, 4; decrees and aims of, 5; sent Oloff Stephenzen to Mana-ha-ta, 29; grant of lands to the Patroon Van Rensselaer, 91; influence of the Patroon with, 100
Collinson, Peter, 258
Columbia College, 263
—— County, 91
Colve, Admiral, made Governor, 137; resigned office, 139
Common, the, 50, 51, 80, 338. See City Hall Park
Companies, children's, 230, 266, 326, 327, 353
Coney Island, 162
Congreve, William, 348
Coninck Davit, 28
Connecticut, 108, 152, 171, 205, 369

402

Index

Connecticut River, 160; fort at the mouth of, 206
Coote, Richard. See Bellomont, Earl of
Corlear, Jacob, 38
—— Hoeck, 38
Cornbury, Lord, 319; sent as Governor to New York, 220; dissolute character of, 220; stories concerning, 223 *et seq.*; his undignified exploit, 224; reduced to extreme poverty, 225; collected money due Bedlow, 226; his flight from the yellow fever to Jamaica, Long Island, 237; secured Presbyterian manse and chapel for the Church of England, 238; his way of securing money for his wife's funeral, 239; recall of, 240; imprisoned, 241
—— Lady, 232, 239, 340; beautiful ear of, 220; extravagance of, 220; scheme of, for securing free service, 221 *et seq.*; isolation of, 225; thievery of, 225, 226; her death, 226
Cortlandt Street, 45
Cosby, Elinor, 286, 287
—— William, 314, 316, 380; appointed Governor, 278; insolent treatment of Chief-Justice Morris, 279; his dishonesty, 281; elected to the "Humdrum Club," 281; ball of, 282; discredited by Morris, 283; abused his councillors to the home government, 284; eluded by Colonel Morris, 285–289; his plot to intimidate the council, 294; retreat of, to Perth Amboy, 297, 298; plan to prosecute Peter Zenger, 298 *et seq.*; demanded attendance of council at cremation of a paper, 301; outwitted by Mrs. Alexander, 306, 308; death of, 311; last council of, 312; his deposition of Governor Van Dam, 313
—— Mrs. William, 281, 282, 297, 313
Council, the, 76, 77, 254, 256, 276, 281, 285, 291, 294, 300, 301, 313, 314; provision made for orphans by, 83; composition of, 108; abused by Governor Cosby, 283, 284; plot to intimidate the, 294 *et seq.*; terrified by the conspiracy to fire the island, 337

Cowfoot Hill, 40
Cox, William, 211
Crawford, Captain Peter, 358
Cribblebush Swamp, 38
Crimes, punishment of, 77
Crol, Sebastian Jansen, 8
Crowninshield, Captain Arent Schuyler, 339
Cruger, John, 337
—— John, Jr., 339
—— family, the, 339
Cunard family, the, 339
Curacoa, 103, 161, 209
Cuyler, Sara, marriage of, 23; daughter of, 184; father of, 184

D

Daly, Chief-Justice, quoted, 317
De Boorgh, Catarina. See Van de Bourgh, Catarina
De Bruyn, Francis, marriage of, 149
—— Mrs. Francis (born Catherine Varleth), 149
De Forest, Isaac, first brewer of New York, 196, 239
—— Mrs. Isaac, 239
De Key, Tunis, 23
De la Court, Jan, 88
—— Mrs. Jan (born Susanna Van Rensselaer), 88
Delafield, Mrs. Joseph, 179, 186, 224, 225
De Lancey, Chief-Justice James, 277, 361, 383, 384, 390, 391; member of Governor Cosby's party, 301; his contemptuous treatment of James Alexander and William Smith, 302; the trial of Zenger, 306; his objections to Cosby's actions, 311; acting Governor of New York, 380, 381; his jealousy of James Alexander's business enterprise, 390
—— Oliver, 390
—— family, the, 256, 260, 291
De la Noy, A., 269
Delaware River, 38, 105, 126
Denton, Daniel, his history of New York, 7; account of him, 141; quoted, 141, 142
De Peyster, Abraham, 215, 216, 217, 230, 268, 269, 327; prominence of,

Index

37, 150; marriage of, 151; captained a company raised by himself, 169; made Mayor of New York, 193; gifts of land to the city, 193; his beneficence, 195; resigned as treasurer of the province, 264

De Peyster, Mrs. Abraham (born Margaret Van Cortlandt), 264
—— Abraham "de Jonge," 264
—— Catilina, funeral of, 65, 66
—— Cornelia, 37, 151, 214, 269
—— Cornelia. See Clarkson, Mrs. Matthew
—— Cornelius, 269
—— Elizabeth, daughter of Abraham, 262
—— Elizabeth, daughter of Johannes, 229
—— Isaac, brother of Johannes, 151
—— Isaac, son of Johannes, 151, 269, 276, 339
—— Mrs. Isaac (born Maria Van Balen), 151
—— James Abraham, 339
—— Mrs. James Abraham (born Sarah Reade), 339
—— Johannes, 214, 229; emigrated from Holland, 36; his marriage to Cornelia Lubbetse, 36; connection with the government, 37; member of the council, 108; chosen to the new council, 138; residence of, 150
—— Mrs. Johannes (born Cornelia Lubbetse), 18, 213, 228, 266, 292, 366, 367; emigrated from Holland, 36; wedding of, 36; children of, 37; her receipt for making caudle, 56; residence of, 150; children of, 150 et seq.; her suggestion regarding salt, 161; will of, 268; death of, 268
—— Johannes "de Jonge," marriage of, 229; heir to his mother's estate, 269
—— Mrs. Johannes (born Anna Schuyler), 229
—— Maria, 37, 269; betrothal of, to Paulus Schrick, 151; her first marriage, 152; her house, 153; her marriage to John Spratt, 154; the house in Prince's Graft, 156; her opposition to Jacob Leisler, 170 et seq.; wisdom of, 189; her interest in the welfare of the colony, 192; domesticity and influence of, 197; her courage in adversity, 213; her marriage to David Provoost, 214, 215; her weekly receptions, 215; her death, 216; allowance for her children from her late husband's estate, 216, 217

De Peyster family, 140, 261, 274
De Riener, Margaretta, 147
De Trico, Catelina, 6
De Vries, Eva, marriage of, to Jacob Van Cortlandt, 33; voyage to the New World, 34; her daughter, 80, footnote
—— Peter Rudolphus, 33
—— Mrs. Peter Rudolphus. See Hardenbroeck, Margaret
Digby, Captain, 371, 372, 373, 374
Dircksen, Jan, 93
Director, "der Groot," 95 et seq.
Dobb's Ferry, 328
Dock, the, 49
Dominies' Hoeck, 23
Dongan, Governor, 146, 181
Dornick, Marcus, 154
Doughnuts, 55
Drake, Rodman, 160
Dress, 69 et seq.; of Dr. Kierstede, 24; of a bride, 68; of officials, 69; of women, 69, 70; richness of, 71
"Drum, Major," 333
Drummond, Mrs. David (born Elizabeth Alexander), 249
Duane Street, 44
Duer, William Alexander, 262
—— family, the, 339
Duncan, Thomas, 340
Dunlop, Mr., 337
Dutch Church, the, 194, 240, 272, 273, 338, 339; the first church, 194
—— East India Company, 2, 3, 4, 85, 108
—— language, superseded by the English, 163
Duval, John, marriage of, 146
—— Mrs. John (born Caty Van Cortlandt). See Phillipse, Mrs. Frederick
Dyeing, 70, 73

E

Earthenware, 43
Earthquakes in New York, 364, 365, 391
East Hampton, 141

Index

East River, 8, 24, 38, 39, 44, 48, 194, 200
Ebberts, Daniel, 358
Edgar family, the, 340
Elizabeth, Queen, 11, 98
Ellis, John, 258
Elm Street, 441
Emott, Mary, 370. See Ricketts, Mrs. William
England, Church of, 272, 274
English, visits of, to the Dutch colonies, 15; their usurpation of Dutch territory, 90; their attitude toward the Dutch, 92, 105 et seq., 115; their expedition against the Dutch, 120 et seq.; New York acquired, 129; New York surrendered, 137; retaking of New York, 139; intercourse with them avoided by the Dutch in New York, 271 et seq.
—— church-yard, the, 226
Erving, John, Jr., 390
Esopus, 118; marriage records at, 66
Exchange, the, 48, 49, 50
—— Place, 49, 51, 153, 194

F

Fairfield, 72
Farquhar, Dr. William, 259, 387
—— Mrs. William (born Jane Colden), 258, 259
Feast-days, 131
Fifth Avenue, 195
Filipse. See Phillipse
Finger-plays, 61 et seq.
Fire, precautions against, 83 et seq.
Fireside pastimes, 60 et seq.
Fish, 158 et seq.
Fitzroy, Hon. Augustus, 286, 287
"Flatbush, History of," 58, 70
Flattenbarack Hill, 50, 229
Flax, 46
Fleming, Mary, 179
Flushing, 152, 204, 375
Fly-boys, 338
Fly Market, 193, 337, 338. See Vlye-Market
Forrester, Major, 127, 205
Fort on Mana-ha-ta, 6, 8, 104, 116, 332-334, 361
—— the Indians', on Catiemuts, 39, 44

Fort Orange, 4, 111, 148; first voyagers to, 6; new settlers at, 90
Forty-eighth Street, 195
France, flag of, planted at headwaters of the Hudson, 3
French, the, in America, 92, 107 et passim
French Anna, 340
—— Philip, marriage of, 35
Fromer, Hans, lawsuit of, 16
Funeral customs, 63 et seq.
Fuyck, the, 111

G

Gables, 31
Gallows-field, the, 286
Games, 81
Gardiner, Captain Lion, his purchase of land from Indians, 205; his bravery, 206; arrival of, in America, 206; further purchases from Indians, 207; his grandson, 208 et seq.
—— Mrs. Lion, 206
—— manor, 207
Gardiner's Bay, 205
—— Island, 45, 127, 205
"Gazette, the New York," 282, 358
George I., King, 246, 298
—— Fort, 356
Geues, Madame, the napkins of, 109
Goede vrouw, the, 14, 25, 34, 52, 74, 79, 139, 196; dress of, 70
Goede Vrouw, the ship, 89
Goelet, Peter, 58
Gogar, John of, 247, 323, 324, 364, 397
Gold, sought by the Dutch in America, 102, 103
Golf, 81
Gout, 347 et seq.
Gouverneur, Nicholas, marriage of, 192
—— Mrs. Nicholas, 192. See Leisler, Mary
—— family, the, 339
Governor's Island, 101
—— mansion, the, 35, 48, 49
Graft, the Prince's, 49, 152, 153, 156, 213, 216
Grafton, the Duke of, 286, 287
Grant, Mrs., 231, 327
Gravesend, 109
Greenwich, 322, 323, 350

Index

Greenwich Hospital, 379
Grevenerat, Andrew, marriage of, to Anna Van Brugh, 23
Greyhound, the, 371
Groen, Claes, shepherd, 51
Guelderland, family estate of the Van Rensselaers in, 87

H

Hackensack River, 2, 26, 47
Hague, royal archives in the, 91
Halifax, the Earl of, 281, 375
Hall of Records, the, 40
Halle, der, 46, 48, 50
Hals, Franz, portrait of Rev. John Livingston by, 177
Halve Maen, 2, 7
Hamilton, Andrew, 304, 305; appearance at the trial of Zenger, 306; applauded in New York, 307; tendered a dinner, 308
—— Colonel John, 230, 262, 295
—— Mrs. John (born Elizabeth de Peyster), 262
Hanover Square, 129, 150, 199
Hardenbroeck, Margaret, 110, 150, 161, 198, 396; pioneer, 18; married, 33; account of, 34; her death, 35
Hardy, Sir Charles, Governor of New York, 391, 393
Harison, Francis, 276, 295, 297, 301; sympathy of, with the "court," 291; suspected of authorship of a letter to James Alexander, 296
Harlem, 286, 351
—— River, 285
Hartford, 152, 171, 175, 176
Hell Gate, 288
Hempstead, 237
Henry II., of France, 177
Hett, René, 340
"Historic Tales of Olden Times," 179
Hoboken, 118, 171
—— Hackingach, 41, 351
Hoekies, 43
Hogg, Robert, 330, 345
Holland, laws of, in the colonies of the New World, 4, 5; intelligence and refinement in, 11; care of the sick and aged in, 82; religious tolerance in, 111; cultivation of vegetables in, 157

Hominy, 72
Hoogh Straat, 22
Horse-mill, site of the first, 8
Horsmanden, Daniel, 337, 338
Hospital, New York, founded, 82
Houses of the settlers, 14, 31, 32, 75
Hudson, Hendrick, 2
—— River, 1, 2, 8, 14, 20, 26, 39, 40, 41, 44, 47, 91, 100, 106, 111, 114, 116, 118, 139, 158, 159, 160, 164, 171, 181, 183, 200, 203, 256, 271, 275, 328, 330, 334, 356, 385, 386; claimed to have been discovered by Verrazzano, 3; site of the Bogartus farm near, 20; site of Mrs. Van Brugh's farm on, 23; Mrs. Van Cortlandt's farm on, 32; settlement at the head-waters of, 85 *et seq.*
—— Street, 356
Hughson, the inn-keeper, 330, 331, 341–343
—— Mary, 331
Humdrum Club, the, 281, 287
Hunter, Governor Robert, 217; successor to Lord Lovelace, 241; his visit to the manor of Rensselaerswyck, 241, 243; visit to the Livingston manor, 244; purchase of land on Raritan Bay, 244, 245; death of his wife, 251; his return to England, 251
—— Mrs. Robert, 251
Huybert, Goody, 109
Huybertsen, Maeyken, 16
Huyck, Jan, 8
Hyde, Anne, 220
—— Edward. See Cornbury, Lord

I

Indian villages, 91
Indians. See Wilde Menschen
Iphetonga, 48
Irish settlers in Massachusetts, 158
Iroquois, 354
Izer-cookies, 57 *et seq.*, 266

J

Jackson, William, 269
Jaimeson, William, 277
Jamaica, 237, 238, 262, 270, 324. See Sewan-ha-ka

Index

James I., 246
—— II., 246
Jans, Annekje, 129, 199, 398; pioneer, 18; marriage of, 19; second marriage, 20; her farm, 20; her home, 21; descendants of, 21; daughters of, 22, 23; position of, 26, 32; sons of, 27; a leader of social festivities, 148
—— Ariantje, 28
—— Maryje (mother of Annekje Jans), first midwife, 8; pioneer, 18, 19
—— Maryje (sister of Annekje Jans), 27, 150, 174
Jansen, Elsie, 27, 168
—— Sara. See Kierstede, Mrs. Hans
—— Tryntje, 22, 199
—— Jansen, Tymen, 27
—— Tytje, 22, 33
Jauncey family, the, 340
Jay, Peter, 80
Jersey, West, 250
Jerseys, the, 311, 352. See New Jersey
Jesuits, the, 243, 336, 343
Jew's Alley, 263, 330
Johnson, Rev. Dr., 385
Jonas. See Jans
Jonson, Simon, 337

K

Kanaomeek, 91
Kearney, Peter, 322
Kennebequi, 126
Kermiss, 78 *et seq.*
Kettletas, Abraham, 340
—— family, the, 340
Kidd, Captain William, marriage of, 203; vessels of, 203; appointed privateersman, 203; supposed hiding-places of treasure of, 204; boarded the Quidder Merchant and secured cargo, 205; visit to grandson of Captain Gardiner, 208; detained in Boston Harbor, 209; his letter to the Governor, 209; discovery of his treasure, 210; hanging of, 211
—— Kidd, Mrs. William (born Sarah Bradly), 203, 211
Kidd's Hollow, 210
Kieft, Governor William, 102, 103

Kierstede, Blandina, marriage of, to Peter Bayard, 80, footnote; a relative of Judith Varleth, 148
—— Dr. Hans, 352, 355; marriage of, 24; daughter of, 80, footnote; market near the house of, 25, 79; entry in Trouw Boeck, 24, 29; kermiss held near house, 79; chief in authority in first hospital, 82
—— Mrs. Hans (born Sara Jansen), 22, 23, 24, 26
—— Dr. Hans "de Jonge," 27
—— Mrs. Hans "de Jonge" (born Jennetje Lockermans), 27
King, Rufus, the fire-bucket of, 84
—— Street, 66, 338
King's College, 329; founding of, 384, 385. See Columbia College
"King's House," the, 332, 333
Kip, Jacobus, 108
—— Samuel, 276
—— family, the, 140
Kitch-a-wan, 146
Kloch, the, 32, 39, 40, 43, 45; filled in by the municipal authorities, 42; site of, 44
Kloch-Hoeck, 42
Knickerbocker, Diedrich, 8, 73
"Knight, Madame," 218, 219
Koseka, Meta, 110
Kottomack, 91
Kranck-besoeckers, 8, 20
Kromme Gouw, 205

L

Laap-haw-ach-king, 3, 90
Labbadist missionaries, 34, 159
Landed gentry, provision for, in the New World, 5
La Noy, P. D., 269
La Touche, Isaac, 338
—— Jeremie, 338, 339
—— Mrs. Jeremie (born Jeanne Soumain), 339
Lawrence, Samuel, 337
—— Mrs. William, 369. See Carteret, Mrs.
—— family, the, 140
"Laws, the Duke's," 201
Lee, William Philips, 323
Leevens, Annekje, 69
Lefferts, 70
—— family, the, 70

Index

Leisler, Jacob, 197, 198; marriage of, 27; in command of a company against the French, 168; announced himself Governor, 169; cast Colonel Bayard into prison, 170; detestable character of, 173; his dispute with Robert Livingston, 187 *et seq.*; self-assumed patent as Governor not confirmed by King William, 188; commanded the marriage of his daughter, 190; death by hanging, 191; his deeds not defensible, 192; the family estates restored, 192
—— Mrs. Jacob (born Elsie Jansen), 27, 168
—— Mary, enforced marriage of, 190; second marriage of, 192
Lenox Library, 28
Leonard Street, 44
Liberty, the statue of, 227
—— Street, 45
Library, the first public, 271; its development, 382–384
Lierescou, Pieter, 51
Lights in the streets, 84
Lincoln, the Earl of, 360
Lindsey-woolsey, 15, 70, 160
Linnæus, 258
Lispenard family, the, 339
Livingston, Mrs. See Van Rensselaer, Gertrude
—— Alexander, 177
—— Barbara, 177
—— Gilbert. See Guysbert
—— Guysbert (or Gilbert), 186
—— Mrs. Guysbert (born Cornelia Beekman), 186
—— Katharine, 185, 351
—— Rev. John, portrait of, 177; his retreat to Holland, 178; marriage of, 179; death of, 180
—— Mrs. John, 179
—— Mary, 177
—— Peter Van Brugh, 351, 363, 364, 370, 384, 388, 392; engagement of, 326; wedding of, 327; member of the "Committee of One Hundred," 328; his anxiety about Mrs. Alexander, 386, 387; his business enterprise, 390
—— Mrs. Peter Van Brugh (born Mary Alexander), 325, 328, 370, 386, 387
—— Philip, second lord of the manor, 326, 357, 358, 362, 364, 365; marriage of, 184; prominence of his family, 186
Livingston Mrs. Philip (born Katharine Van Brugh), 351, 365, 386; marriage of, 184; handsome dower of, 185; education of, 185; marriage-chest of, 185; children of, 186; death of, 392
—— Philip ("the Signer"), son of the second lord, 383, 384
—— Philip ("Gentleman Phil"), grandson of the second lord, 328
—— Robert, first lord of the manor, 248; ancestors of, 176 *et seq.*; sailed to New Netherlands, 180; obtained patent of the manor of Livingston, 181; piety of, 181; capabilities of, 182; marriage of, 183; gave his son a portion of his estate, 187; his dispute with Leisler, 187; his voluntary exile, 188; reception to Governor Hunter, 244; friend of Governor Burnet, 256
—— Mrs. Robert (born Alida Schuyler), second marriage of, 183; her children by this marriage, 184. See Van Rensselaer, Mrs. Nicolaus
—— "Robert Second," son of the first lord, education of, 186; the "Lower Manor," 187
—— "Robert, Jr.," a cousin of "Robert Second," 186
—— Robert, third lord of the manor, marriage of, 240; a letter, 367: a subscriber to the first library, 383; one of the first trustees of the library, 384
—— Mrs. Robert (born Mary Long), 240
—— Sarah, 364, 365, 386
—— William, 383, 384
—— family, the, 274, 291, 339, 340, 384
—— Manor, 71, 181, 183, 244, 255, 365, 386, 387, 388
Lockermans, Annekje, 398; pioneer, 18; betrothal and marriage of, 29; death of, 144. See Van Cortlandt, Mrs. Oloff Stephenzen
—— Govert, 23, 150, 199, 214; marriage to Maryje Jans, 27; home in William Street and family history of, 27; first marriage, 28; member of the Council, 108

Index

Lockermans, Mrs. Govert (born Ariantie Jans), 28
—— Mrs. Govert. See Jans, Maryje.
—— Jacob, 27
—— Jennetje, 27
—— Maryje, married to Balthazar Bayard, 27; entry of her birth in a Bible, 28; a sister-in-law of Mrs. Nicholas Bayard, 148
—— family, the, 140
Lombardy poplars, 15
Londonderry, 158
Long Bridge, 351
"Longbridge gang," the, 338
Long Island, 48, 101, 109, 121, 126, 141, 193, 204, 205, 207, 237, 262, 324, 352, 358, 375; ferry to, 50
Long Island Sound, 204, 288
Lovelace, Colonel Francis, 241; successor to Governor Nicolls, 135; entertained at Rensselaerswyck, 136
Lubbetse, Cornelia, 18, 398; marriage of, to Johannes de Peyster, 36; death of, 268. See de Peyster, Mrs. Johannes
Ludlow family, the, 340
Lullabies, 59, 63
Lumsden, Elizabeth, 249
Lurting, Robert, 276, 295, 300, 301
Lutheran Church, the, 194

M

Maadge Paatje, 46
Machicana, 118
Maiden Lane, origin of the name of, 46
Mana-ha-ta, colony of, 100, 103, 105, 119, 121, 139, 392; Denton's history of, 7, 141; houses of the colonists, 31, 32, 74; manners and customs of the early settlers, 54, 72 et seq.; marriage records in, 66; the first kermiss, 78; named New Amsterdam, 115; the expedition of the English against, 120 et seq.; taken by the English, 129; recaptured by the Dutch, 137; retaken by the English, 139; food of the colonists, 156 et seq.
—— island of, 1, 2, 45, 50, 95, 98, 101, 102, 104, 107, 109, 111, 118, 130, 140, 147, 150, 152, 156, 158, 162, 164, 181, 192, 196, 200, 214, 232, 242, 255, 268, 285, 322, 351, 355, 363, 395, 398; settlement of, 3, 6, 8, 89, 161; selected for a plantation by the College of XIX, 3; signification of the name of, 6, 8; pioneers of, 13, 39; house of Margaret Hardenbroeck on, 35; wild animals on, 44; importation of cattle, 51; contention between the governors of, and the directors of Rensselaerswyck, over ownership of territory, 90
Mana-ha-ta tribe, 6; home and industries of, 40, 41; village of, 42; disappearance of, 43. See Wilde Menschen
Manchannock, 207
Manitou, 43
Mann, Sir Horace, 319, 348
"Mannados, the Towne of," 114
Manor, the Lower, 187
—— Phillipse, the, 35, 45
Manors offered for sale, 6
Mar, the Earl of, 246
Marck Velt, 79, 80
Maria, Queen Henrietta, 157
Marketfield Street, 263, 358
Markets, order for, issued by the Council of New Netherlands, 25; site of the first, 48; the bridge over the Graft, 49
Marlborough, Duke of, 112
Marriage customs, 66 et seq.; dress of the bride, 68
Marshall, John, 337
Maryland, 27
Masquaas, 118
Massachusetts, settlers of, 105 et seq., 164, 206; state of, 256, 270, 385
Mather, Dr. Increase, 165
Matowack, 126
Maurice, Prince, entry into Amsterdam, 86
May, Captain, 6
Mayflower, the, 106
May-poles, 66
McClish, Mrs. John (born Janet Alexander), 249. See Petticoat Lane
McEver, John, 339
Meanagh, 147
Medici, Catherine de, 177
Medicines of the Wilden, 74
"Mercury," the New York, 394
Meyut, Madame, 148

Index

Micella, Dominie, 68
Midwife, first, 8
Milborne, Jacob, 190; hanged, 191
—— Mrs. Jacob. See Leisler, Mary
Mill Street, 263
Minetta Water, 32, 322
Minorca, 278, 282, 284
Minthorne, Philip, 337
Minuit, Peter, purchase of Mana-ha-ta from the Indians by, 6; first Governor of Mana-ha-ta, 20; successor of, 100
Moeneminues, 91
Mohawk reservation, the, 311
Mohicanehuck River, 2
Money Pond, 204
Montauk, 204
Montgomery, Colonel John, Governor of New York, 270, 271, 276, 277, 297
—— County, 258
Moody, Lady, 109, 110
Moore, Governor Henry, 15
—— John, 276, 337
Morris, Euphemia, 285, 286, 287, 288, 310
—— Isabella, 366
—— Colonel Lewis, 280, 281, 291, 307, 311, 362, 369; a friend of Governor Hunter, 244; a friend of Governor Burnet, 254; episode with Governor Cosby, 279; delivered an "opinion" in favor of Governor Van Dam, 283; his secret departure for England, 284–289; author of articles in the "Weekly Journal," 300; fruitlessness of his appeal to the home government, 310, 314; made Governor of New Jersey, 315
—— Mrs. Lewis, 289
—— Lewis, Jr., 300, 317, 390
—— Robert Hunter, 244
Morrisania, 285, 288
Morristown, 362
Mount Pleasant, 40
Murray, Mr., 341, 377
—— James, 358

Negroes, 318; burying-ground of the, 43; convicted or suspected of crimes in the city, 330–346
New Amsterdam, the colony of Mana-ha-ta named, 115
Newanemit, 91
Newfoundland, 124
New Hampshire, 270
—— Jersey, 102, 121, 244, 245, 250, 253, 315, 360, 362, 369, 370, 394, 395, 398
—— London, 205
—— Netherlands, colony of, 9, 14, 25, 100 et seq.; flag of, 114
Newport, 349
Newtown patent, 238
New Year's, 131, 291, 292, 293
—— York, 184, 196, 197 et passim; birth of, 129; described by a Boston lady, 218 et seq.; its aspect "in the forties," 351. See Mana-ha-ta and New Amsterdam
—— York Historical Society, old fire-bucket in the possession of, 84
—— York State, 91, 121, 162, 193, 238, 258, 385
Niagara, 390
Nicholson, Lieutenant-Governor, 167
Nicoll, Benjamin, 384
—— Mary, 338
—— William, 338
—— Mrs. William (born Anna Van Rensselaer), 338
Nicolls, Colonel Richard, Governor of New York, 120, 129, 242; at the head of the English invasion, 130 et seq.; his anxiety about the savages, 134; demanded his recall from the home government, 135
Ninetieth Street, 288
Norris, Captain, 288, 289, 307, 308
—— Mrs., 308, 310. See Morris, Euphemia
North River. See Hudson River
Notas, 355
Nova Scotia, 125, 126, 389
Nutten Island, purchased, 101; battle with the Indians on, 118, 119

N

Narrows, the, 119, 190, 288
Nassau, or Long Island, 101, 109, 121. See Long Island
Negagonse, 91

O

Ohio, 385
Oorst, John, 203
—— Mrs. John (born Sarah Bradly), married to Captain Kidd, 203

Index

Orphans, 83
Osborne, Sir Danvers, 380; made Governor, 375; dinner of welcome to, 376; violent death of, 377
Oswego, 385

P

Paas, 131
Paatje, T'Maadge, 46
Palisadoes across the island of Manaha-ta, site of, 8
Pall-bearers, 64, 65
"Paradise," 342
Park, City Hall, 51, 80
—— Street, 44
Parker, Elisha, 366; death of, 374
—— Mrs. Elisha (born Catharine Alexander), 366, 374. See Alexander, Catharine, and Rutherfurd, Mrs. Walter
Passaic River, 2
Patroon, title of, 5, 96
—— Van Rensselaer. See Van Rensselaer, Kiliaen
Paupers, 83
Pavonia, 118
Pearl Street, 8, 23, 134, 146, 342
Pedlers, 52
Pemaquid, 126
Penn, William, 121
Pennsylvania, 302, 369
Pepys, Samuel, 121, 369
Perth Amboy, 245, 298, 305, 308, 314, 321, 323, 328, 366, 370, 375, 387
Petanock, 91
"Peter, Old," 292, 293, 300, 334
Peters, Richard, 390, 391
"Petes," significance of, 262
Petticoat Lane, 153, 263, 264, 360, 361. See Marketfield Street
Philadelphia, 236, 304, 305, 307, 308, 348, 389, 390
Phillipse, Annekje, marriage of, 35
—— "Cuff," 337
—— Frederick, second husband of Margaret Hardenbroeck, 33; voyage to New World, 34; married Mrs. John Duval, widowed daughter of Oloff Van Cortlandt, 35, 197; children of, 35; member of the king's council in New York, 166
—— Mrs. Frederick. See Hardenbroeck, Margaret
—— Mrs. Frederick (born Caty Van Cortlandt), her marriage, 146; relatives of, 197; her interest in the natives, 198; her endowment of a church, 198
Phillipse, Frederick, grandson of the above, 276, 337, 345; chief-justice at the trial of the negroes, 338; summoned some disreputable characters before the grand jury, 341; provided a camping-ground near his house for the Indians, 352
Phipps, Sir William, 165
Piau, Jeanne, 339
Pier, Rachel, 68
Pigeons, the great flight of, 74
Pilgrims, 105 et seq.
Pine Street, 35
Pintard, John, 337
Plaster, oyster-shell, 42
Ploeg, Albert Hendrickse, 68
Plymouth colony, the, 105
"Post-Boy," the, 346
Potatoes introduced by the Dutch, 158
Poughkeepsie, 186
Powder-house, 342; site of, 40
Presbyterian Church, 184, 240, 273, 274
Prince, hanging of, 341
—— Street, 328
Princess, the, 103
Produce Exchange on the site of Johannes de Peyster's house, 36
Provoost, David, 214
—— Colonel David (grandson of David), 232; marriage of, 214; made Mayor, 215; in debt to the Spratt estate, 216; put under custody of the sheriff, 217; his indebtedness adjusted, 218; death of, 267, 268; on a grand jury, 340
—— Mrs. David. See de Peyster, Maria
—— David, son of Colonel David, 233, 327, 329, 333
—— John, 233, 327, 329, 339
—— Mrs. John (born Eva Rutgers), 327, 329, 339
—— Maria, 255
—— Samuel, marriage of, 232; family of, 233; death of, 234, 261
—— Mrs. Samuel (born Polly Spratt), capabilities of, 233; children of, 233; assumed control of her husband's business, 234; her ingenious pavement, 235; fame of her shop,

411

Index

236; hospitality to James Alexander, 250; admitted Governor Burnet to her hospitality, 255; second marriage of, 261. See Alexander, Mrs. James
Provoost, Bishop Samuel, 329
—— family, the, 140
Public Library, the first, 271, 382–384
Pump, the "tea-water," 52

Q

Quakers, persecution of, by Governor Stuyvesant, 110
Queen Anne, 220, 223, 224, 241, 243, 246
—— Elizabeth, 11, 98
"Quidder," the. See Schuyler, Peter
Quidder Merchant, the, 205, 208, 209, 210

R

Raritan Bay, 244
Raritans, 41
Reade, Joseph, 339
—— Sarah, 339
Records, the Hall of, 40
Reddergoed, 87, 124
Reed, family of, 340
Regiment, the first, 100
"Relation, a Brief, of New York," 7
Rensselaer County, 91
Rensselaerswyck, colony of, 19, 89 *et seq.*, 100, 111, 118, 121, 127, 136, 167, 179, 181, 182, 183, 198, 241–245; first settlement of, 89; site of, 91; leases to tenants, 92; conditions to settlers, 93; churches and ministers, 93; rights of the directors settled, 112; the aid of the colony sought by Governor Stuyvesant, 116, 117. See *infra*
—— manor of, 6, 160, 185; the manor house, 71; disposition of the estate after the death of the Patroon Van Rensselaer, 94. See *supra*
—— in Holland, 87
Reynolds, Sir Joshua, 397
Rhode Island, 349
Richards, Stephen, 23

Richards, Mrs. Stephen (born Maria Van Brugh), 23
Ricketts, Colonel William, 370, 371, 373
—— Mrs. William (born Mary Emott), 370, 371, 373
"Road, the," 29
Rockaways, the tribe of, 351
Rocks, the Great, 2, 47
Rodenburg, Lucas, marriage of, 22
Romaine, William, 337
Rondel, the, 48
Roosevelt, Cornelius, 337
—— James, 276
Rosby, Christopher, 211
Russell, Andrew, 180
Rutger, Anthony, 339
Rutgers, Catharine, 327
—— Elsie, 327
—— Eva. See Provoost, Mrs. John
—— Hermanus, 327, 329
—— Mrs. Hermanus (born Catharine Meyers), 329
Rutherfurd, Mr. Livingston, 236
—— Walter, 259, 374
—— Mrs. Walter, 374, 387. See Alexander, Catharine, and Parker, Mrs. Elisha

S

Sachems, Indian, names of, 91
Sack posset, a, 67
Sagiskwa, 91
Saint Croix River, 124, 126
—— Lawrence River, 92, 124, 126
—— Margaret's, Westminster, 98
—— Mark's, 144
—— Paul's Chapel, 274, 275, 351
—— Thomas Island, 209
Salt, 161, 162
Samp, 72
Samp-Mortar Rock, 72
Sandilands, Robert, 249
Sandy Hook, 159
Sapocanichan, 33, 322
Sassafras wood, bedsteads of, 30
Saunders, family of, 339
Schaape Waytie, de, 51, 153
Schenectady, 20; settlement of, 94
Schliemann, Dr., 354
Schrick, der Heer Paulus, 149, 152
—— Mrs. Paulus (born Maria Varleth), 148, 149, 151
—— Paulus "de Jonge," 173; mar-

412

Index

riage of, 151; house of, 152; death of, 153
Schrick, Mrs. Paulus. See de Peyster, Maria
—— family, the, 140
Schuyler, Adoniah, 339
—— Mrs. Adoniah (born Gertrude Van Rensselaer), 339
—— Alida. See Van Rensselaer, Mrs. Nicolaus
—— Anna, 229
—— Brant, 146
—— Mrs. Brant (born Neltjie Van Cortlandt), 145, 146; death of, 196
—— Gertrude. See Van Cortlandt, Mrs. Stephanus
—— Peter, power of, with the Indians, 243; acting Governor, 251
—— Philip Pieterse, 182, 184; marriage of, 97; The Quidder Merchant, 205
—— Mrs. Philip Pieterse (born Margretta Van Schlectenhorst), 97, 182, 231
—— family, the, 261
Scott, John Morin, 383
Second Avenue, 288
—— River, 102
Selyns, Dominie, 152, 154, 190; lines of, on the picture of Nicolaus Van Rensselaer, 99; lines of, on Governor Stuyvesant, 144; epitaph for der Herr and Madame Van Cortlandt, 144; marriage of, to Mrs. Steenwyck, 147; his notice of the death of Paulus Schrick, 153
Semessarse, 91
Sempel, Lord, 177
Seneca oil, 75
Servants, 16, 17, 76, 318, 344, 345; the Wilden as, 75; position of, 293, 294. See Slaves
Settlers of Dutch colonies, first shipload of, 6
Sewan-ha-ka, 2, 41, 102, 237, 351. See Jamaica
Sewant, 41, 109
Shirley, Ann, letter of, 387, 388
—— General, 266, 387, 390, 395; arrival of, in New York, 385; expedition of, 386; cleared of charges of malfeasance, 396; returned to England, 396
Shrewsbury, 285
Singleton, Thomas, 34
Slaap-bauck, 30

Slagboone, Antonia, 94
Slaughter, Governor Henry, arrival of, 190; took oaths of office, 191; signed Leisler's death-warrant, 191; recalled, 201
Slaves in America, 318, 319, 320, 344, 345. See Negroes
Slidell, ——, 337
Slip, Coenties, 134
Sluys, 43, 49, 132, 219
Smith, Chief-Justice William, 248, 251, 277, 281, 282, 283, 285, 287, 291, 295, 311, 316, 341, 357, 362, 377, 378, 382, 383, 384; accused by Harison, 297; suspected of authorship of the articles in the "Weekly Journal," 299; connected with the Zenger trial, 301-305; contemptuously treated by Governor De Lancey, 302; a born orator, 317; reinstated at the bar, 317; a trustee of the first library, 384; his "History of New York," 285, 294, 295, 312, 315, 316; description of New York and of New York women in, 290, 291
—— Mrs. William, 316
Smits Vlye, de, 50
Society, the, for the Propagation of the Gospel, 271, 382
—— Library, the New York, 382-384
Solebay, the ship, 277
Sophia, Princess, 246, 253, 254
Soumain, Jeanne, 339
—— Simon, 339
—— Mrs. Simon (born Jeanne Piau), 339
South Carolina, 340
—— River, 38, 105
—— William Street, 8, 37
Spenser, George, 340
Spoons, 56, 65
Spratt, Catharine, 213
—— Cornelia ("Neltje"), 213, 217, 232, 239; birth of, 155; her disposition, 228; death of, 233, 234
—— John, 156, 215, 248, 366; marriage of, 154; member of Abraham de Peyster's company, 169; his support of Jacob Leisler, 170; speaker of the assembly, 173; his activity in public affairs, 197
—— Mrs. John. See de Peyster, Maria
—— John, son of John, 213, 217,

Index

229, 267; birth of, 155; his sister's Bible, 283; his death, 366
Spratt, Mary, 155, 213, 217
—— Polly. See Provoost, Mrs. Samuel, and Alexander, Mrs. James
Staat family, the, 261
Stadt-Huys, the, 49, 109, 134, 138, 191; fire-buckets hung beside, 84; succeeded by City Hall, 194
State Street, 6
Staten Island, 33, 110, 118, 190, 211
Steendam, ———, 163
Steenwyck, Cornelius, marriage of, 147; entertainments at the house of, 147
—— Mrs. Cornelius, 147
Steinwicks, 71
Stephen III., 97
Stephenzen, Oloff, marriage of, to Annejte Lockermans, 29. See Van Cortlandt, Oloff Stephenzen
Stevens, John, 366
—— Mrs. John. See Alexander, Elizabeth
Stirling, the first Earl of, 247, 249, 269, 323, 397. See Alexander, Sir William
—— the third Earl of, 121, 127, 128
—— the fifth Earl of, 205, 247, 323, 324
—— the sixth Earl of. See Alexander, Major William
—— New Jersey, 362
—— the county of, 177
—— the island of, 121, 126, 127. See Long Island
Stone Street, 29, 30, 35
Stoutenburgh, Isaac, 337
Strand, the, 24, 25, 48, 79, 194, 352
Stuyvesant, Anna. See Bayard, Mrs. Samuel
—— Gerardus, 276, 337
—— Governor Petrus, 170, 172, 242, 254, 286, 398; a friend of William Beekman, 37; legislation of, against hogs running in the streets, 52, 108; successor of Governor Kieft, 102; personality and family of, 103; gubernatorial mansion, 104; received a letter from Governor Bradford, 105; troubles as Governor, 107, 108; his kind treatment of Lady Moody, 110; his harshness to the Quakers, 110; quarrelled with Brant Van Schlechtenhorst, 111, 112; his provisions against invasion, 115, 116; begged money from Jeremiah Van Rensselaer, 116; his visit to Rensselaerswyck, 117; his absence when the Duke of York's expedition arrived, 119; his seizure of Major Forrester, 127; his return to New Amsterdam, 128; the surrender, 129; his death, 143; his epitaph, 144; interference of, in behalf of Judith Varleth, 171
Stuyvesant, Mrs. Petrus, persuaded her husband to protect Lady Moody, 110; her bravery, 119
—— family, the, 140
Sunday, observance of, 138
Surnames, 19
Swedes, the colony of, 38, 105, 107, 108
Swift, Dean, 241, 349
—— John, 348

T

Tar water as a cure for the gout, 348, 349, 350
Tartar, the, 288, 307
Teller, Andrew, marriage of, 146
—— Mrs. Andrew (born Sophie Van Cortlandt), 145, 146
Temple, Sir William, 136, 137
Thimble, the, of Mrs. Kiliaen Van Rensselaer, 88
Tide-mill, 43
Tinton, 285
Tong, Mary, 240
—— Walter, 239, 240
—— Mrs. Walter (born Calatyntie Van Dam), 239, 240
"Topknot Betty," 82
Trade, the Lords of, 203, 209, 277, 281, 360, 362, 372, 375; sent Lord Bellomont to New York, 201; made William Cosby Governor of New York, 278; the plan of the colonists to make their grievances known, 284, 288; the failure of the appeal, 310, 311, 314, 315
Tree, "der groot," 46, 48, 50
Trico, Catelina de, 6
Trinity Church, 20, 66, 226, 269, 272, 273, 274, 329, 351, 366, 377, 384, 385, 395, 398
Trouw-Boeck, 23, 29, 68, 152

Index

Trumbull, Sir William, 323
—— family, the, 340
Tryon, Governor, 383

U

United States Treasury, 193
Ury hanged as a conspirator, 342

V

Van Balen, Maria, 151
Van Benschoten, Nicholas, 88, 89
Van Brugge, Margaret Gillis, 214
Van Brugh, Anna, 23
—— Catharine, daughter of Johannes Pieterse, 23
—— Carel, 108
—— Helena, 23
—— Johannes Pieterse, created alderman, burgomaster, and schepen, 22; marriage and wedding-presents of, 22; house and bouwerie, 23; children of, 23; reception of, in honor of the English invaders, 129, 130; wealth of, 184; a witness in an interesting law case, 199
—— Mrs. Johannes Pieterse (born Tryntje Jansen), 129, 199; marriage of, 22; bouwerie of, 23; children of, 23; residence of, 27; chatelaine of, 28; farm of, 32
—— Johannes, son of Johannes Pieterse, 23, 184
—— Katharine, granddaughter of Johannes Pieterse, marriage of, 184. See Livingston, Mrs. Philip
—— Maria, 23
—— Peter, 23, 184
—— Mrs. Peter (born Sara Cuyler), 23
Van Bylant, Hillegonda, mother of Johannes Van Rensselaer, 87
Van Corlear, Arent, appointed to colonize America and to take charge of Kiliaen Van Rensselaer's affairs, 89; a representative of the Patroon, 94; marriage of, 94; death of, by drowning, 95
—— Mrs. Arent (born Antonia Slagboone), marriage of, 94; first husband of, 95

Van Cortlandt, Caty, first marriage of, 146; second marriage of, 196. See Phillipse, Mrs. Frederick
—— Gertrude, 223, 340
—— Jacobus, marriage of, 33; daughters of, 80, footnote
—— Mrs. Jacobus (born Eva de Vries), marriage of, 33; voyage to the New World, 34; daughters of, 80, footnote
—— Margaret, 264
—— Maria. See Van Rensselaer, Mrs. Jeremias
—— Neltjie. See Schuyler, Mrs. Brant
—— Oloff Stephenzen, 223, 322; betrothal and marriage of, 29; his house in Stone Street, 30, 31; purchase of a country place, 32; neighbor of Phillipse, 35; the daughter of, 96; chosen to the council, 138; death of, 144; children of, 145, 197
—— Mrs. Oloff Stephenzen (born Annekje Loockermans), 96, 223, 322, 398; pioneer, 18; betrothal and marriage of, 29; house of, 30; her house-warming, 31; farm of, 32; constancy of, 35; opposed to war, 117; death of, 144; her epitaph, 144
—— Philip, 230
—— Sophie, 145; marriage of, to Andrew Teller, 146
—— Stephanus, 197, 223; his purchase of land from the Indians, 146; marriage of, 146; a member of the king's council, 167; sheltered Robert Livingston, 176
—— Mrs. Stephanus (born Gertrude Schuyler), 182, 221; marriage of, 146, 147; insulted by Leisler, 174; death of her child, 174
—— family, the, 140, 260, 274
—— manor, 71, 146
Van Dam, Calatyntie. See Tong, Mrs. Walter
—— Richard, 239
—— Mrs. Richard (born Cornelia Beekman), 239
—— Rip, 239, 240, 298, 310; marriage of, 196; his appointment as Governor not ratified, 277; his refusal to meet demands of Governor Cosby, 280; law-suit of, 282, 283; author of letters in the "Weekly

Index

Journal," 300; presided at a brilliant ball, 310; deposed by Governor Cosby, 312, 313
Van Dam, Mrs. Rip, 239
Van de Bourgh, Catarina, 18, 87, 398
Van der Donck, Guysbert, 16
—— Mrs. Anna, 16
Van der Speigle, Laurens, 196
Van der Ween, Peter Cornelius, the widow of, 168
—— Walwyn, 268
"Vanessa," 349
Van Horne, Abraham, 255, 256
—— Mrs. Abraham (born Maria Provoost), 255
—— David, 340
—— Mrs. David (born Anna French), 340
—— Mary. See Burnet, Mrs. William
—— family, the, 260, 333
Van Iselstyn, Jan Willemsen, 77
Vanlooe, Mary, 127
—— Sir Peter, 127
Van Maesterlandt, Roelof Janse, bouwmeester, 19; daughters of, 22, 23; Van Schoendervelt his friend, 148
—— Mrs. Roelof Janse. See Jans, Annekje
Van Ravensleyn, Paulus, 28
Van Rensselaer, Anna, 338
—— Elenora, 88
—— Gertrude, 339
—— Hendrick, 23
—— Mrs. Hendrick (born Catharine Van Brugh), 23
—— Hillegonda, 88
—— Jan Baptist, marriage of, 88; director of the colony, 95
—— Mrs. Jan Baptist (born Susanna Van Weely), 88
—— Jeremias, "der Groot Director," 95, 96, 145, 242, 243; marriage of, 88; ordered to assume the directorship of Rensselaerswyck, 112; his aid asked by Governor Stuyvesant, 116
—— Mrs. Jeremias (born Maria Van Cortlandt), 88, 148; marriage of, 95, 146; portrait of, 96; wealth of, 117; her opposition to a war, 117
—— Johannes, 87, 95
—— Mrs. Johannes (born Elizabeth Van Twiller), 87
—— Kiliaen, first Patroon of the manor of Rensselaerswyck, became commissioner of the College of XIX., 4; created Patroon, 6; sent Van Maesterlandt to Rensselaerswyck, 19; the village of, 23; advised Johannes de Peyster to emigrate to America, 36; history of the family of, 85–87; marriage of, 87; children of, 88; sent colonists to America, 89; land investments of, 90, 91; will of, 94; death of, 94; influenced the College of XIX. to appoint his nephew Governor, 100; a friend of Rev. John Livingston, 179
Van Rensselaer, Mrs. Kiliaen (born Anna Van Weely), marriage of, 87; famous needle-work of, 88; the gold thimble of Nicolas Van Benschoten, 89; her sister, 198
—— Kiliaen, grandson of the Patroon, children of, 87, 88; succeeded to the directorship of Rensselaerswyck, 95; visited by Governor Hunter, 243
—— Mrs. Kiliaen (born Hillegonda Van Bylant), 87
—— Maria, sister of the first Patroon, 87
—— Maria, great-granddaughter of the first Patroon, 88
—— Rev. Nicolaus, marriage of, 88, 182; emigration of, to America, 97; intimacy of, with Charles II., 96; prophecy of, as to the King's future, 96, 182; made chaplain of St. Margaret's, Westminster, 98; owned first watch imported to America, 99; sudden death of, 183; settled on his father's American estates, 180
—— Mrs. Nicolaus (born Alida Schuyler), first marriage of, 88, 97, 182; married to Robert Livingston, 183; children of, 184
—— Patroon. See Van Rensselaer, Kiliaen
—— Rikert, 88
—— Stephen (third), the last Patroon, 97, 185
—— Mrs. Stephen (born Katharine Livingston), 185, 351
—— Susanna, 88
—— family, the, 260; in Holland, 85, 86; the family estates, 86, 88
Van Schaick, Annekje Leevens, 69

Index

Van Schaick, Goosen Gerritse, 69
—— Mrs. Goosen Gerritse (born Annekje Leevens), 69
—— family, the, 260
Van Schlechtenhorst, Brant Arentse, 95, 97, 111 *et seq.*, 116, 167, 183
—— Margretta, 97. See Schuyler, Mrs. Philip Pieterse
Van Schoendervelt, Rutger Jacobsen, 148
Van Teenhoven, ——, 106
Van Twiller, Elizabeth, 87
—— Rikert, 87
—— Mrs. Rikert (born Maria Van Rensselaer), children of, 87
—— Wouter, nephew of Kilisen Van Rensselaer, arrival of, 20; parents of, 87; appointed guardian of the Van Rensselaer minors, 94; Governor of colonies, 100; gave name to island, 101
Van Vlecq, Isaac, 269
Van Weely, Anna, 87. See Van Rensselaer, Mrs. Kilisen
—— Johannes, 87; administrator of the estate of the Patroon Van Rensselaer, 94
—— Susanna, 88
Van Wen, Peter Hartgers, marriage of, to Tytje Jans, 23
Van Wevereen, Cornelius, father and son of the same name, 27
Van Zandt, Winant, 341
Varick, Cæsar, 332, 341, 342, 345
—— John, 331, 332
Varleth, Catharine, 149
—— Mrs. Caspar, 148
—— Judith. See Bayard, Mrs. Nicholas
—— Maria, 148; second marriage of, 149
—— Nicholas, 173
—— family, the, 140
Varravanger, Dr. Jacob, first city physician, 82
Vegetables introduced into America by the Dutch, 157, 158
Velt, D'Marck, 79 *et seq.*
Verplanck, Guilian, chosen to the Council, 138
Verrazzano, Giovanni da, 3
Vesey, Dr., 66, 273
—— Street, 375
Virginia, 152, 166, 316, 388, 391
Vlacke, de, 51
Vlye, de Smits, 50, 193

Vlye-Market, 338, 358. See Fly-Market
Vosbocha, Mrs. Abraham, 69

W

Waffle-irons, 58
Wall Street, 46, 194, 252, 351
Walpole, Horace, 364; quoted, 319, 320, 348, 363
Walton, William, 384
Wampum, 41, 109
Warren, Peter, 277
—— Sir Peter, 323
Washington, George, 194, 388
—— William d'Hertborne, 252
Watch, the, of Nicolaus Van Rensselaer, 99
—— the Rattle, 83
"Watering Place," the, 190
Watts, John, 384
—— Robert, 338
—— Mrs. Robert (born Mary Nicoll), 338
Way, the Broad, 104. See Broadway
Waytie, de Claver, 46
—— de Schaape, 51, 153
Weather, predictions of the, 47
Webber, Annekje, 19
—— Wolfert, 19
Weddings, 66 *et seq.*
"Weekly Journal," the, 298 *et seq.*, 310
"Weekly Post-Bag," the, 358
Wendell, Evert Jansen, 148
Weselasen, Maria, 69
West India Company, 1, 4, 6, 8, 13, 15, 16, 20, 24, 33, 51, 85, 90, 91, 114, 138, 155, 242; store-house of the, 36
—— Indies, the, 346
—— Jersey, 250. See New Jersey
Westchester County, 95
White Hall, the, 35, 104, 115, 221, 222, 224, 252, 254, 260, 268, 281, 308, 310, 370
Whitehall Street, 6, 29, 36, 147, 191
White Street, 44
Whittlesey, Rev. Mr., 385
Wiebocken, 2, 47, 171, 351
Wight, Isle of. See Gardiner's Island
"Wilde Menschen," the, 2, 6, 22, 25, 26, 30, 33, 39, 48, 72, 90, 93, 114,

Index

134, 159, 161, 169, 194, 204, 205, 207, 231, 237, 243, 244, 245, 255, 257, 266, 322, 343, 350, 368; encampment of, 40; customs of, 73, 74; purchase of Governor's Island from, 101; their favorite brew, 101; attitude of, toward the settlers, 105; massacres of, 118; their teaching the Dutch the use of the products of the country, 157, 158; their annual coming to market, 351, 356; purchase of the lands of Rensselaerswyck from, 90, 91

William IX., Prince of Orange, 19, 161, 220, 252; his attitude toward the colonists, 166

—— Street, 23, 27, 35, 43, 150. See also South William Street

Williams, Roger, 109

Williamson, Dirck, 206

—— Mrs. Dirck (born Hachin Bastiens), 206

Winckel Street, 36

Windmills, 43, 45; use of the sails for signals, 45; the first windmill, 43, 351

Winthrop, Governor, 206

Wolley, Rev. Charles, quoted, 74

Women of the seventeenth century, 10; in Holland, 11; their domestic accomplishments, 12; women in the colonies, 14, 16, 17, 18 *et passim*

Y

Yellow fever in New York, 237, 239

Yonge, Miss Charlotte N., 202

Yonkers, 35

York, James, Duke of, 112, 120 *et seq.*, 164 *et seq.*, 248, 328

Z

Zenger, Peter, publisher of the "Weekly Journal," 298; his attacks on Governor Cosby, 299, 300; imprisonment of, 301; famous trial of, 299, 306; the verdict of not guilty, 306; importance of the verdict, 307

—— Mrs. Peter, 301

Zoutberg, the, 20, 100

www.ingramcontent.com/pod-product-compliance
Lightning Source LLC
Chambersburg PA
CBHW080049190426
43201CB00035B/2144